Field, Camp, Hospital and Prison in the Civil War, 1863-1865

Charles A. Humphreys, Chaplain, Second Massachusetts Cavalry Volunteers

Charles Alfred Humphreys

PANTIANOS
CLASSICS

Published by Pantianos Classics

ISBN-13: 978-1-78987-551-5

First published in 1918

Charles Alfred Humphreys, c. 1918

Contents

Foreword v

Field, Camp, Hospital and Prison in the Civil War, 1863-1865 6

    Notes 128

Tributes 163

    I - Oration 163

    II - Memorial Day, 1894 170

    III - Dedication of Flags 172

Appendix 176

Foreword

I make no apology for printing this tale of the last two years of the Civil War even though another and greater war is engrossing the attention of the whole world. This greater war will soon end, and, as God lives, will end in the triumph of the right, and the nations will then be ready to enforce peace if any one should attempt to disturb it. My story will be in line with that great consummation. I feel so strongly that when war is seen in its true colors, it will not only lose all its allurements, but will excite a keener appreciation of the blessings of peace, that I think I could do no better service in the cause of peace than to present, as I intend, an unvarnished tale of war's scenes and labors, its trials and exposures. I shall weave them, in a measure, about my own personal experiences, but only so far as is necessary to present the various phases of war in definite outline and living reality.

CHARLES A. HUMPHREYS.

Field, Camp, Hospital and Prison in the Civil War, 1863-1865

THE Civil War had already raged two tedious years before the Union cause seemed so desperate that I could no longer keep from enlisting in its defence. It was difficult from the beginning to follow the pursuits of peace while so many were giving themselves to hard and perilous service in the field. But it had been easy to keep the ranks full till the year 1863, when a succession of defeats or fruitless victories checked voluntary enlistments, and compelled the government to resort to drafting. It was a time of great depression at the North. The Emancipation Proclamation had been issued under great complaints of an unconstitutional use of the war-powers of the government, and as yet it had not begun to give any effective aid to our arms. The disastrous defeat at Chancellorsville, May 1st and 2d, had caused a great reaction of opinion at the North towards compounding a peace. We had little or no sympathy from other nations in our struggle; and England — from whom we had a right to expect the most encouragement, especially after the cause of the Union was openly identified with the cause of freedom for the slave — not only turned to us the cold shoulder, but became quite demonstrative in its sympathy with the South. A month after the issuing of the Proclamation of Emancipation, the London *Times* said: "We hold the opinion that the cause of the South gallantly fighting against the cruel and desolating invasion of the North, is the cause of freedom." Two months later a prominent member of Parliament said publicly: "We cannot help seeing that while Abraham Lincoln is an incapable pretender, Jefferson Davis is a bold statesman. We may well wish to see the American States peacefully separate, we may well wish to see bloodshed cease and peace restored, but I contend — and I know that the majority of thinking men in England agree with me — that the best method towards that end will be the establishment of the complete independence of the Confederate States." It was a time when every one who loved his country and believed in its free institutions must do what he could to sustain its armies in the field; and, feeling that I might be of some service in the line of my chosen profession, I accepted, while I was yet in the Divinity School at Cambridge, the offer of a Chaplain's commission from Governor Andrew, and as soon as I could be ordained **(Note 1)** joined the Second Massachusetts Cavalry, a regiment composed of two battalions recruited in Massachusetts, and one recruited in California chiefly of natives of Massachusetts. Our Colonel was Charles Russell Lowell of Cambridge, a graduate of Harvard in the Class of 1854. He was a nephew of the poet James Russell Lowell, and had already seen two years of service. As soon as he reached the

Camp of the Second Regiment, Massachusetts Cavalry Volunteers, at "Ayr Hill," Vienna, Fairfax County, VA., 1863-1864

field with his regiment of Massachusetts Cavalry, he was put in command of the brigade with which it was connected, leaving our men under the direct leadership of Lieut. Col. Caspar Crowninshield of Boston. When I joined the regiment in August, 1863, it was brigaded with the 13th and 16th New York Cavalry regiments, and was, with them, doing service as an outpost picket before Washington, guarding thirty or forty miles of its exposed front, and constantly harassed by guerrilla raids under the leadership of Col. John S. Mosby, who called his followers Partisan Rangers.

Our camp was at Vienna, about fifteen miles from Washington, and was surrounded with a heavy abatis of felled trees branching outwards to guard against sudden attacks of guerrillas. Here we spent the winter of '63 to '64, and made ourselves as comfortable as we could, with board floors in our wall-tents, and with brick fireplaces, and with chimneys made of mud and sticks **(Note 2)**. Our chimneys were of necessity so shallow that on windy days the smoke would be forced in gusts down the flue into our tents, and I have often been driven out into the storm for self-preservation — though doubtless if I had stayed in I would have been preserved, but only as a smoked and dried specimen of suffering humanity. Still we had a great deal of satisfaction in our fireplaces, and when the nights were cold and clear, and the logs blazed brightly, our tents often resounded with laughter and song, and all went merry as a marriage-bell **(Note 3)**.

A Chaplain's duty is not prescribed by army regulations, except so far as to require him to hold service on the Sabbath when convenient, and to bury the dead. But there are many ways in which a Chaplain can make himself useful in camp, and by alluding to some of them I shall give an insight into the alleviations as well as the trials of camp life.

I felt it a pleasure as well as a duty to visit the men in their tents and to encourage them to come freely to mine. By the kindness of friends at home I had an excellent library of two hundred volumes, gathered largely by Rev. Henry W. Foote, H. C. 1858, among the attendants at King's Chapel **(Note 4)**. These kept both officers and men in reading matter, and lightened the tedium of many a dull winter's day. Some lady friends — chief among whom was Mrs. John M. Forbes of Milton — knit several hundred cavalry mittens, especially adapted for holding the bridle rein, and I distributed them through the regiment, and they saved the men from many a bite of frost, and filled a want that the government did not supply. Mrs. Forbes, besides keeping her own fingers busy, kept six women knitting for the regiment. On January 12, 1864, I received from her forty pairs of cavalry mittens, and — without giving notice of their arrival — I gave them to any who came to my tent to inquire if I had "some of those warm mittens," and they were all gone before night. From the same bounty came knit caps to protect the head at night, and these I distributed to every officer in the regiment. And besides these gifts Mrs. Forbes' supplies of delicacies for the sick in our brigade hospital were unstinted.

"Ayr Hill," the Headquarters and part of the Regimental Camp, Second Massachusetts Cavalry, at Vienna, Fairfax County, VA., 1863-1864

Chaplain Charles Humphreys
His tent at Vienna, Va., Winter 1863-1864. His horse "Jaques" captured by Mosby's guerillas, July 7, 1864. The regimental mailbox is in front of the door of the tent. The other box on the platform is for firewood. The barrel at the top of the chimney is to facilitate the draft at the fireplace.

Besides being thus the almoner of the overflowing charities of friends at home, the Chaplain could often serve the men by acquainting these same friends with the needs of the soldiers' families. Thus a word to Rev. Edward Everett Hale used to send at once his most efficient lady visitors to the homes of any of my men whose families in Boston needed aid. I could draw at sight on that rich bank of sympathy and helpfulness. And so elsewhere, the need had only to be spoken and the help was at hand. As we were very near to Washington, I could also send money home for the soldiers, and after pay-day I have sometimes taken to the office of the Adams Express Company in that city more than fifteen hundred dollars to be scattered in small sums among the soldiers' families. And oftentimes, when pay-day was delayed, the men would freely come to the Chaplain, and the loan of a few dollars would frequently relieve distress and always make the men more contented with their lot. I used to have several hundred dollars thus floating round in the regiment, and, though much of it got water-logged and sunk never to return, I felt that it had done good service.

There were so many Californians in my regiment who had a great admiration for Rev. Thomas Starr King and attributed to his patriotic devotion and eloquent appeals the keeping of California in the Union, that I ordered from Black — the best Boston photographer in the sixties — several dozen copies from his negative of King, and distributed them through the companies from California.

A very important labor that usually fell to the Chaplain was to be postmaster, to receive and distribute the mails, and to frank letters for any who could not prepay them. I also furnished, freely, paper and envelopes to any who applied for them, thinking it the best service I could do to encourage the men to keep up a frequent correspondence with their homes.

The Chaplain's ear became naturally a convenient receptacle for all sorts of complaints, chief among which were those that grew out of the chafing under the severities of military discipline. It was so hard for a freeman nourished in independence to submit absolutely to the will of another — perhaps no wiser than he; to make himself part of a machine without questioning any of its adaptations or uses! The Chaplain could often by words of counsel or explanation allay such discontent — which frequently in the weariness of camp life festers into insubordination.

And again the Chaplain kept always a kind of confessional, at which men might unburden their anxieties and doubts, and pour the story of their lives into sympathetic ears. These stories were often more entertaining than books, and stranger than fiction. Some told of hairbreadth escapes in fights with Indians on the border; others, of adventures among the wild islanders of the South Seas. There were trappers from the Rocky Mountains, who had had bears for pets; tall lumbermen from Maine, who had dared the foaming rapids and the raging torrent; old sailors, who had played with the sea-lion and sported with the storm; rough-bearded miners, who knew all the tricks of the gambler, and were familiar with the code of the duellist. One young man revealed to me this strange experience: He was born in Massachusetts, but before he was fifteen he thought he would shift for himself, and ran away and settled in Columbia, S.C., working in a gun-factory and joining a volunteer battery. When the war broke out — looking upon it as a kind of holiday frolic, and loving adventure — he followed his battery to Charleston, where his services were very much in demand as there were few skilful gunners among the Charlestonians. When it was known that the "Star of the West" was coming to bring supplies to Fort Sumter, he was recalled from his own to take charge of the Cummings Point battery, and trained the gun that made the ship lower its flag. This was the first time that the United States flag had been lowered to a hostile shot since the War of 1812, and, though Edward Ruffin of Virginia had been granted the privilege of discharging the gun, strange to tell, it was charged and trained by a Massachusetts man. He afterwards joined the Second South Carolina Infantry, and was ordered to Virginia, and helped to drive the Fourth Ohio out of the very place where we were then encamped. But when it came to meeting Massachusetts regiments and perhaps his own brothers in the fight, he felt the stronger drawing of the old home ties, and deserted and came within our lines at Alexandria and was now fighting under the old flag.

The recounting of these and like experiences was not only intensely interesting, but offered many opportunities for the expression of helpful sympathy and timely counsel.

But the most important of the Chaplain's duties were in the hospital. It was a delight here also to be the almoner of friends at home, and of the Sanitary Commission, and to distribute delicacies among the patients to relieve the dreary monotony of the regular rations. Some ladies at home, among whom again Mrs. J. M. Forbes was chief, kept me supplied with hollow circular pillows, stuffed with the soft gossamer threads of the milkweed, to relieve wounds and bed-sores. I had also a great variety of games and puzzles which were a great attraction to the convalescents **(Note 5)**. My books were a constant delight to the patients, and in the severer cases of sickness I could often give comfort by reading myself. I was once reading Whittier's "Pipes at Lucknow" to a Scotchman named McFarland, a patient in the hospital, thinking to please him with a little of his native dialect, when he interrupted me with the exclamation, "I was there." Then he told me that he was one of Havelock's troops who carried relief to the besieged British garrison, and he had heard that "dearest of all music that the pipes at Lucknow played." Another patient wanted to read "Robinson Crusoe" because he himself had been on the island of Juan Fernandez, where the adventures of Alexander Selkirk are supposed to have furnished much of the material for the story of "Robinson Crusoe."

Of religious books, I furnished each patient with what he desired — thus distributing Catholic and Episcopal prayer-books and Methodist hymn-books, and supplying to Frenchmen, Italians, and Germans the New Testament in their native tongues. With the foreigners in the hospital I was greatly assisted by Mrs. Josephine Shaw Lowell, the wife of my Colonel, Charles Russell Lowell, the brigade commander, and sister of my classmate Robert Gould Shaw **(Note 6)**. Mrs. Lowell was spending the winter in camp and visited the patients very frequently, and she delighted the Frenchmen, Italians, and Germans by conversing with them in their own languages, that so vividly recalled their early homes. Her presence in camp had a refining influence upon officers and men, and in the hospital, by her tender sympathies and beautiful bearing and sweet simplicity, she was like an angel visitant. She often assisted in writing letters for the disabled soldiers; and, when I sought to give comfort to the dying, her presence soothed the pangs of parting with a restful consciousness of woman's faithful watching and a mother's tender love.

> "Whispered low the dying soldier, pressed her hand and faintly smiled:
> 'Was that pitying face his mother's? Did she watch beside her child?'
> Every voiceless word with meaning her woman's heart supplied,
> With her kiss upon his forehead, 'Mother!' murmured he and died."

At such times I have felt most vividly what a delightful trait in woman's character is this love of serving others. What a blessing and joy was woman's nursing to the sick and wounded soldiers!

"Not wholly lost, O Father, is this evil world of ours;
Upward through its blood and ashes spring afresh the Eden flowers;
From its smoking hell of battle Love and Pity send their prayer.
And still thy white-winged angels hover dimly in our air."

The chief of the specified duties of the Chaplain — to hold religious services — was the one it was hardest to fulfil, by reason of the difficulty of finding any convenient and comfortable place of meeting. I once succeeded in getting a hospital-tent for that purpose, and with the help of two of our men who had been carpenters I made some benches for the comfort of my audience, but before Sunday came the tent was moved away to be used for a court-martial, and I never recovered it. Once I took my colored servant and my little hatchet, and went out at nine o'clock Sunday morning, cleared away the underbrush from a small amphitheater in a neighboring wood, and at ten o'clock the chief bugler sounded the church call at the camp and then again at the place of meeting. Somehow it did not seem strange, but the most natural place in which to worship. "The groves were God's first temples." The service was as follows: I. I repeated the sentence "The Lord is in his holy temple; let all the earth keep silence before him." II. After a few moments of silent prayer I repeated the first stanza of Watt's hymn "From all that dwell below the skies," then led the singing of it to the tune "Old Hundred," in which all joined. III. Scripture reading — Matt. vii. 7-27. IV. Prayer. V. Address on three things that abide — Truth, Goodness, God. VI. Wesley's hymn "Love divine, all love excelling." VII. Benediction. The whole service took less than half an hour. The audience stood for the singing and benediction, but sat on the ground for the rest of the service. All uncovered during the prayer and benediction. This was my first and last service in that place. The weather was never again such that I could use it. Then I resorted to a barn near the camp, the auditors sitting on the beams and floor, the band accompanying the singing, and the cattle filling in the pauses with their lowing. But even with the shelter of the barn it was often too cold for the band to play, and we were as likely to be out on a raid Sunday as other days. Still, with all these inconveniences and interruptions, the simple presence of the Chaplain made Sunday a little different from other days, and frequently the bugle-call to worship revived memories of the church bells at home. My three services on Sunday in the three wards of the brigade hospital were seldom interrupted. As I finished each service it was very grateful to me to hear the "Thank you" gasped by the feeble patients on their various couches. It was a great joy to pour even one drop of comfort into the bitter cup that so many had to drain who threw In their lot with their country's peril. Sometimes besides the morning service in the barn and the three services in the hospital there was a regimental service at dress parade in the afternoon, and frequently a soldier's funeral added to the solemnity of the Sabbath hours. Union and Confederate were alike in their hospital treatment and their funeral honors, and I remember one mother of a Confederate coming to get some of the earth from his grave, vividly revealing that there were bleeding hearts and sacred devotions at the South as well as at the North. As to my work as a Chaplain, I find the fullest expression of it in a letter which I wrote from camp to Rev. Edward H. Hall, who had taken part In my ordination. This is the letter. It was returned to me after his death and more than fifty years after it was written, having been found among his cherished papers.

Cavalry Camp,
Vienna, Va., April 28, '64.

Rev. Edward H. Hall:

Dear Friend, — Your very kind letter of Feb. 4th was received, and would have been answered promptly but that the disaster to my regiment in the skirmish at Drainesville broke up all my plans and took me to Dorchester with Mrs. Reed, wife of the captain who was killed. I have not felt like answering it till now, because I have been diffident as to my ability to relate to you any experience of interest. I am now compelled by the necessity of the time to write to you at once however poor my letter may be. For the armies are beginning to move, and we must be ready to move at a moment's notice, and I may not have another chance to write for a long time. Burnside's army corps passed through here yesterday on its way to Leesburg and the gaps in the Blue Ridge, and everything looks like active campaigning. God speed the right.

You spoke in your letter very kindly of my Visitation part. It was the open expression of my deepest convictions; convictions which had been rather indefinite in my mind for years, and had been seeking expression. I knew that I should write on that subject more than a year before Visitation, and the thought of the whole year had been turned in that direction. I tell you this that you may know how inadequate the expression was to the thought in my soul. I am glad of your sympathy in these feelings. I think it is to be the work of the rising generation of liberal thinkers in some measure to free human thought from the bondage to the letter which now cripples it, and to turn it towards those inner revelations where God speaks directly to the soul; to unfetter human aspirations, to give dignity to human feelings and sanctity to human hopes; in a word, to find God in humanity rather than in the leaves of a book. How absurd to stop with the book when it is itself only an incomplete record of human struggles and aspirations towards God! I believe, however, that we should have nothing to complain of if the Bible was regarded in this light by every one; for thus interpreted it is an all-sufficient guide in the path of right, and an all-powerful incentive in the fulfilment of duty.

You enquire as to my method of labor. I have very little method, but from necessity more than from choice. If there is any single rule that runs through all my work it is this — to be kind to all. If this seems to be a low aim for one who was ordained to speak eternal truths, my only apology is my youth. Exhortation and counsel are more fitted for maturity and age. I think my work will be surer if I do not assume any premature dignity or unwarranted authority, but trust to the pervasive influence of charity and love. I would rather have men say of me: "I wonder what faith he belongs to. It must be pretty near the right one, he is such a nice fellow," than that they should say, "Well, our Chaplain made out a pretty strong case for his belief; you could hardly help believing that what he said was true." I prefer to work by my life than by my speech; I rely more on the little kindnesses, attentions, and words of cheer of every day than on Sunday preaching, or week-day advice and counsel, though I do not neglect the latter, nor consciously undervalue them. The work of some ministers is like the sunlight with healing in its beams and nourishment and strength for every plant and tender herb that comes within the scope of its influences. The work of others is like the burning fiery furnace seven times heated moulding everything to its own will. My aim is to be like the former. The routine of my labor is like this: I hold a service every Sunday morning in a barn floor near by, to which any one is free to come; there is no compulsion. I do not have a large audience, as I have never made it a special aim to increase it, I am so diffident of any ability in this line, or, I should say, so confident of my inability. I may say this — my services are very interesting to those who have any appreciation of religious duty and any taste for religious services. My aim in preaching is to elevate rather than to convert. I appeal to what is good and true in my auditors. If any are not already turned towards the good and the true, I suppose with them my preaching is vain, and I frankly acknowledge my weakness in this direction. I have the help of a good brass band in the service, and oftentimes the exercises have an unwonted solemnity with that help. I believe music may be made the handmaid of religion. I always speak without notes though never without full preparation, and never more than fifteen minutes. I use J. G. Forman's little hymn and service book for my introductory sentences and my hymns. We sing together one hymn always. The little interruptions (from the basement) of cows mooing, horses neighing, and dogs fighting, do not trouble us much. I have succeeded thus much at least — in making the men feel that there is a deep and solemn reality in religion whether they appreciate what it is or not. After the regimental service I go to the brigade hospital and hold a service in one or another of the wards, and visit all the wards, speaking to every patient. This is all the regular Sabbath work. The remainder of the day is like the rest of the week. The week-days are spent in visiting the hospital, caring for the mail, and receiving callers, the latter taking up the longest time. I do not make many calls on the men in their quarters; in military life it has too much the appearance of intrusion. The men do not expect it and are seldom prepared for it. But they call freely on me, bringing their complaints, or revealing their experiences, which are often intensely interesting. I have had an ample library all winter, and an unlimited number of games of various kinds. I have kept the men supplied with stamps even when they could not pay for them. I have sent to Washington daily by mail-carriers for little things that the men have wanted. The only general result that I have seen from my labor is that there is a little less open profanity and a great deal less complaining than when I first came. The results in individual cases of course I cannot measure. I do not believe in any adequate gage of moral influence like that which is flaunted before our eyes by evangelical sectarians in statistics of conversions and degrees of conversion. The results of my work if they could be chronicled would be — a little more kindness of heart in one, a little more elevation of purpose in another; a little more faith here, a little more charity there; here more reverence and there more truth. I trust that some such germs of good will grow and thrive in my daily path.

You ask about my relation to the officers. They are of the pleasantest kind. I have their respect and so far as I know their confidence. I have never asked anything of any of them that they have not readily granted. I am as a brother among them, not assuming any dignity from my profession except when I speak on Sundays. I am too young to rebuke them, too inexperienced to advise them unasked; but when on the Sabbath I speak in the name of my office, in the name of truth and of God, then I can do anything.

I am not much on tract-distributing; how was it with you? I half suspect that this is a failing in me; yet it goes against my feelings unless a very plain way is open for it. I have never held a prayer-meeting, partly because I had no place, partly because I saw little advantage to come of it. Of late I have been trying to serve the Lord on horseback, following the men into the field, lying at night under the tented sky, — which at this season, I assure you, is not so comfortable as canvas, — charging with them into the ranks of the enemy, and sharing all the dangers and exposure of active service. I carry no arms, but try by a cheerful courage to add a little to the effectiveness of those who do. Please let me hear from you.

C. A. Humphreys,
Chap. 2d Mass. Cav.

The hardest duty that ever fell to my lot as Chaplain was to prepare a deserter to die. He was one of our own regiment, and born in Massachusetts, but had early in life gone to California, where he led a wild and reckless career till he enlisted and came East. Now he had yielded to the fascinations of a Southern girl and been induced to desert, and was captured while fighting against us with a band of guerrillas. This offence was of course unpardonable in martial law; yet, as he chose me for his counsel at the trial by drum-head court-martial, I pleaded, in extenuation, his youth and the blandishments of the Southern beauty, but to no effect. Perhaps one reason why I did not win the case was that the opposing counsel was Lewis S. Dabney, whose legal acumen made him then Judge Advocate, and later made him one of the leaders of the Bar in Boston. Still I had to admit in my own mind that in the existing military situation the sentence of death must be pronounced. The poor victim chose to lean on my arm as he walked to execution behind his own coffin borne by his old messmates, while the band marched beside playing a funeral dirge. And he leaned still more closely on my faith that, though his country could not forgive him, beset as she was with enemies, God *would* forgive if he was truly penitent; and the thought appealed to the native nobleness of his nature, and awoke in him the desire even then to redeem himself and to serve the cause that he had betrayed. And the more he revolved this in his mind, the more he felt the inspiration of noble feeling, and, being permitted to speak a few last words to his fellow-soldiers who were drawn up on three sides of a hollow square to witness the execution, he said: "Comrades! I want to acknowledge that I am guilty and that my punishment is just. But I want also that you should know that I did not desert because I lost faith in our cause. I believe we are on the right side, and I think it will succeed. But take warning from my example, and whatever comes do not desert the old flag for which I am proud to die." Everything being now ready, I offered prayer with him and commended him to the mercy of God; then I bound the handkerchief over his eyes, and at his request asked the marksmen to aim steadily and at his heart. Then shaking hands with him in farewell, I said, "Now die like a man." He sat down upon the foot of his coffin in perfect composure, and said, "I am ready." Fronting him were six men in line, with carbines, five of which were loaded. Each man could persuade himself that his own carbine was the unloaded one, and so was relieved from the otherwise necessary conclusion that he had shot his fellow. The sergeant in command of the shooting squad gave the order — "Ready! Aim! Fire!" and the deserter in one moment was dead. The lesson of his punishment had never to be repeated in our brigade.

All this was Sunday morning. I did not feel like holding a service after it, and thought the ceremony of execution had preached more effectively than *I* could. One of the members of E Company, to which the deserter had belonged, said to me, "I wonder how you got enough influence over him to lead him to declare that he died believing our cause was just." I replied, "It was not *I* that did it but the awful presence of death." That made him see clearly the truth and his own terrible mistake. I doubt not that the intense self-examination and marvellous insight of his last hours influenced his character more than any other hours of his life, indeed more than whole years of thoughtless wandering and heedless sin. I was glad that I could induce him to keep up such good courage and die in so true a spirit, but hope I shall never have to witness such another scene.

Perhaps harder than this duty of attending the execution was the duty of writing of it to the deserter's mother. But I could speak so sincerely in praise of her son's brave ending after his full repentance that the hard duty was lightened, and I doubt not she cherished with a forgiving affection the little tokens of his remembrance which he asked me to send.

It was a great comfort while engaged in these difficult and oftentimes discouraging labors of a chaplain's life to get cheering letters from friends at home. Among these I prize most highly one from Rev. James Walker, ex-president of Harvard College, in which he wrote: —

You have often heard me say how little confidence I have in the usefulness of chaplains, taken as they rise. It is not enough that their heart is in the work; they must have a much larger share of practical sense than commonly falls to the lot of ministers, to be able to adjust themselves to their new and strange relations, or make much of their anomalous parish. Still I have never had any fear as to your success. I am sure you will leave untried no means of making officers and men feel that you can be serviceable to them in many ways. Ours, you know, is a profession which, unlike law or medicine, must first make men feel the want of what we can do before we can do it. Meanwhile you must not give up, or lose heart, if in stormy weather, or a dark night, or a hard chase to no purpose, you sometimes do hear a trooper swear. Believe that a quiet, persistent, tender fidelity always wins the day.

While you are serving the Lord on horseback I suppose you sometimes turn back your thoughts to those of us who are trying to serve him in our studies. I venture to send you three copies of my 'Address to the Alumni.' You can give the surplus to any Cambridge men who care to read them; or you may use them to kindle your camp-fires. They are not very inflammable, but they are very dry.

Thus far my poor lame fingers have been tolerably submissive in holding the pen; but they are beginning to be mutinous, and I must, therefore, conclude by assuring you that I am, with much regard.

Very truly and affectionately yours,

James Walker."

Now let us leave the camp and go out on a raid after guerrillas; for I wish to exhibit all sides of a soldier's life, and this was our frequent occupation for a whole year of our service. I will select one that we made only a few days before the grand movement of the Army of the Potomac across the Rapidan. It was doubtless a preparatory reconnaissance to make it certain that there was no especial danger to Washington in Grant's uncovering its front as he was about to do.

On the morning of April 18, 1864, while I was writing in my tent, I heard the bugle-call "Boots and Saddles," and learned that a large detachment of the brigade was just starting on a scout. Getting permission to go, I had two days' rations and three days' forage put up at once and was ready in about ten minutes, and by a short gallop caught up with the column and joined Colonel Lowell, who was riding at the head. With him was the noted traveller Herman Melville, who had charmed all lovers of the wild and picturesque by his accounts of his adventures among the savage islanders in the Pacific Seas in the books "Omoo" and "Typee," which I had in my camp library, and who shared with Richard H. Dana the honorable distinction of a pioneer in the work of lifting into popular literature the life of the merchant seaman. He was out now to learn something of the *soldier's* life and to see a little campaigning with his own eyes, preparatory to the writing of the book which appeared two years later, entitled "Battle Pieces and Aspects of War" **(Note 7).**

We rode till four o'clock, stopping every hour and a half to rest the horses a few minutes, and adjust the saddles to prevent galling. At four we stopped at Ball's Mill on Goose Creek to feed. A cavalryman always attends to his horse first; so I took the saddle from Jaques — whom my fellow-officer Lewis S. Dabney very disrespectfully called the "Parson's Old Cob" — and let him roll to refresh himself, and gave him a small feed of oats. Then I cooked some ham on the end of a stick over a fire of cornstalks, and sat down on a stone, and with dry bread made my dinner. At five we started again and crossed Goose Creek, which, though swollen so that a man could not stand in the current, was just fordable for cavalry. In attempting to keep my feet out of the water I carelessly struck my spurs into my horse, and for a few moments he plunged and dashed around in a way that threatened immediate and complete immersion to both horse and rider. But I got through safely, and at dusk we approached the city of Leesburg, the hot-bed of secessionism in those parts. It was about twenty-five miles from our camp at Vienna, and no Union troops had visited it that season. We expected that it would be full of Confederates; and surely enough, when the advanced guard approached they were fired upon, and word was sent back to us that the enemy was drawn up in line in the woods just before us. Colonel Lowell, without waiting to ascertain their numbers, at once ordered the charge, and the whole column immediately broke into a trot and then into a gallop. It was my first taste of the intoxication of battle. I had often felt the charm of *adventure* as we scouted frequently under the starry canopy of night or when the moon lit our way, and Bryant's "Song of Marion's Men" came to mind and we felt that the Revolutionary hero had a worthy successor in our Colonel Lowell: —

> "Well knows the fair and friendly moon
>   The band that Marion leads,
> The glitter of their carbines,
>   The scampering of their steeds.
> 'Tis life to guide the fiery barb
>   Across the moonlight plain,
> 'Tis life to feel the night-wind
>   That lifts his tossing mane."

Although I had no love of war and no arms with which to fight, yet as I rode along with the column I felt also something of the fascination of danger, and could partly appreciate the spirit of the old cavaliers as they sung: —

> "O for a steed of matchless speed,
>   And sword of metal keen!
> All else to noble hearts is dross,
>   All else on earth is mean.
> The neighing of the war-horse proud,
>   The rolling of the drum,
> The clangor of the trumpet loud
>   Are sounds from heaven that come.
> And oh! the thundering press of knights,
>   Whenas their war-cries swell,
> May tole from heaven an angel bright
>   Or rouse a fiend from hell.
>
> "Then mount, then mount, brave gallants all,
>   And don your helms amain,
> Death's couriers — Fame and Honor — call
>   Us to the field again.
> No 'woman's' tears shall fill our eyes
>   When the sword-hilt's in our hand,

> Heart-whole, we'll part, and nowhit sigh
>   For the fairest of the land.
> Let piping swain and craven wight
>   Thus weep and puling cry,
> *Our* business is like *men* to fight.
>   And hero-like to die."

It was very exciting to hear the commands — "Steady! Wait for orders! By platoons left, gallop, march! By fours, march!" — all shouted at the top of the voice, above the noise of the column, itself almost deafening with the clattering of the sabres and the thumping of the horses' hoofs upon the stony pike. At such times one is borne along in the rush and tumult of the onset, and can hardly think of fear.

> "When banners are waving
>   And sabres are glancing,
> When captains are shouting
>   And war-horses prancing,
> When cannon are roaring
>   And swift bullets flying.
> He that would honor win
>   Must not then fear dying.
>
> "Though shafts fly so thick
>   That it seems to be snowing,
> Though streamlets with blood.
>   More than water, are flowing,
> Though with sabre and bullet
>   The bravest are dying.
> We'll think of our homes, but
>   We'll ne'er think of flying."

The first squadron was dashing on with drawn sabres, the rest were holding their carbines in their hands ready to fire. Nothing could stand against the fury of the charge. The Confederates fired a few shots, then scattered through the woods like leaves before the wind, and we dashed on into Leesburg. But the first shot had given the alarm; and with all our searching we could not find a graycoat. We remained, that night, just outside the town, but did not dare to unsaddle nor to light fires, as we were in the heart of the enemy's country, and the frequent signal-rockets from the hilltops in front of us showed that the Confederates were gathering their clans. The night was very cold, too cold to sleep; and besides there were several attacks upon our pickets that brought us to our feet and made us stand to horse till the danger was past. It was about as easy to stand as to lie down that night. If we lay down, it was at our horses' feet with the bridal rein in our hands; and — not to speak of their uneasy stamping with their iron shoes upon the ground which was our bed, — if they got lonesome they would poke us with their noses, or if they got tired standing they would lie down at our side — either of which movements was, to say the least, not conducive to sleep. It seems a wonder that — crowded together as we were, the horses standing in column four-abreast in a narrow road — none of us were trampled under their feet. But the faithful animals seemed to appreciate the situation, and when they moved, paid due regard to their sleeping masters.

In the early morning, small scouting parties were sent out in various directions to scour the woods and pick up any of Mosby's men that might be hiding in the vicinity. In a short time they brought in one officer and ten men, all mounted — which was quite a catch, considering the wooded nature of the country and the open chances of escape. At ten o'clock we gave up all expectation of finding any more guerrillas in that region, and started back, re-crossed Goose Creek, and went into camp for rest and refreshment. While we were quietly dining at four o'clock, a friendly citizen brought in word that Mosby and one man had just passed through a field not two miles away from us. It seemed like searching for a needle in a haystack to chase Mosby in that hilly forest-country, yet Colonel Lowell made the attempt. "Boots and Saddles" was at once sounded, and, with abbreviated dinners, in a few minutes we were off. A lieutenant and ten men were sent to try to get on Mosby's trail, while the main column took a direct line across the country, if possible to head him off. Flankers were thrown out a distance of half a mile on either side of the advancing column, that we might sweep as wide an extent of country as possible. We struck for the pike that runs through Middleburg to Mosby's headquarters near Rectortown, but found, when we reached it, that Mosby had passed over it three-quarters of an hour before. That was aggravating enough; yet there was nothing to be done but to turn back to Ball's Mill and go into camp for the night. Now, for the first time since we started out, we had an opportunity to boil coffee and make ourselves comfortable with fires, and to unsaddle our horses and give them a refreshing rest. I made a luxurious bed of boards and dried leaves for Colonel Lowell and myself, and we lay down for the night, after the Colonel had sent a dismounted party towards Leesburg to take the city by surprise. He had learned by an intercepted letter that a Confederate soldier was to be married that evening in Leesburg, and that the beauty and chivalry of the country round might be expected; and, though he did not care to forbid the banns nor to start a frown on the face of beauty, he *did* wish, and it was his business, to gobble as many of the chivalry as possible. When this party got in sight of Leesburg, they could see the house brilliantly illuminated, and they hurried forward, but were too late, as the crowd was already dispersing and making a noisy demonstration in the street as if the apple-jack had flowed too freely; and as our men approached, they were fired into and two men killed and three wounded. Our men returned the fire, but to no effect, as the Confederates immediately scattered. The dead and wounded were left in the house where the marriage had been celebrated, and the rest returned to our night encampment at two o'clock with the sad news. At the earliest dawn we saddled up, and, taking an ambulance, crossed the ford and went once more to the city. I went with the surgeon to the house where the wounded men were lying, and helped bind up their wounds and put them into the ambulance. The landlord of the house was a gentleman with Southern hospitality and politeness, and kept a fine hotel adorned with elegant paintings. He had given every possible attention to the wounded, and proclaimed himself a Union man, and told us that if our party had been a half-hour earlier the previous night they might have bagged a good number of Pickett's and Mosby's men. I never heard again from this wedding till twenty-six years later, when on a visit to Fortress Monroe, I was introduced to a beautiful Southern girl who was visiting her brother, a lieutenant on duty at the Fort, and learned from them that they were from Leesburg and that their father had been a Confederate soldier, and, from the date and other circumstances of his marriage, I could have no doubt that it was his wedding that our forces came so near disturbing. It was a happy sign of a restored national Union that the children of that marriage were as warmly patriotic as any of us, and one of them was an officer enlisted in its defence. A quarter of a century had brought round this marvellous change.

After our sad experience in Leesburg there was nothing for us to do but to turn homeward, which we did at ten o'clock, stopping, as soon as we crossed Goose Creek and were safe from attack, to feed our horses and dine. After dinner a ride of twenty miles brought us to our camp at Vienna, where we were welcomed with patriotic music by the band, and were glad enough to get a good supper and rest. We had been out three days and two nights, and I had slept only two hours, and was so stiff from a cold caught the first night that it seemed as if I could count by its special ache each muscle in my body. But I had enjoyed very much the opportunities for seeing the country, and of talking with officers and men as we rode along. This was pastoral visiting under difficulties, but it was not to be neglected. Especially did I enjoy discussions with Colonel Lowell on metaphysics and mental philosophy — subjects in which he delighted and which now were the more fascinating as they were the farthest removed from the work which most employed our thoughts.

The experiences to which I have as yet alluded were connected with operations and movements that very slightly affected the main currents of the war, but which are worthy of note as giving interior views of the soldier's life in camp and hospital, and a glance at the difficulties and dangers of guerrilla warfare.

We will now pass in hasty review some of the grander and more decisive operations of armies, and follow the varying fortunes of the Union cause in Virginia through the closing year of the war from the Wilderness to Appomattox.

The spring of 1864 opened upon the armies of the Union and the Confederacy grimly watching each other from opposite sides of the Rapidan. Lee held the south bank of the river, his headquarters at Clark's Mountain, and his forces distributed along the railroad to Orange Court House and Gordonsville. Meade held the north bank, with his headquarters at Culpeper, and his forces distributed along the Orange and Alexandria railroad from the Rapidan back to the Rappahannock. There these two armies stretched their sinewy lengths like mighty wrestlers after many a fearful grapple lying prone upon the ground yet watching for the moment when they must join in a last decisive struggle, each aware of the other's strength, and both eager to improve every offered advantage. Up to this time fickle Success had alike encouraged and then discouraged the two champions as she led now one and now the other to delusive victories; and while the Union forces could boast a Malvern, an Antietam, and a Gettysburg, the Confederates took heart from the fields of Manassas, the heights of Fredericksburg, and the wilds of Chancellorsville. Still, though each army could thus boast its equal triumphs, the resources that were available for future successes were very unequally divided. The early enthusiasm of both sides had cooled, but it left to the North the energy of patience fed from a perennial fountain of moral renovation in the justice of their cause, while to the South was left only the energy of despair fed by the fictitious fear of losing everything they held dear, with the downfall of the Confederate Government. The latter energy is fitful, though it can, and did, inspire to the most intense devotion; the former is steady, but faithful to the end. No one could have more completely embodied the desperate determination of the South than General Lee, who now with unflinching resolution faced the fearful odds that must of necessity bring disaster and defeat to the cause he championed. And no one could have more completely embodied the Northern energy of patience than General Grant, who had just been raised to the supreme command of all the armies of the United States in order to bring them into mutual cooperation, and who now gave his personal supervision only to the Army of the Potomac. For to this was assigned the most momentous task of the campaign — to dislodge and if possible defeat the foremost army of the Confederacy under its foremost military chief, who still, after three years of terrible combat, covered Richmond, and thus held the prize for which the Army of the Potomac had so heroically fought. For three years, manoeuvres and pitched battles, each one of which was confidently expected to end the Confederacy at once, had left the Army of Northern Virginia as dangerous as at first. And now the Army of the Potomac was to advance again over fields which had been the scene of Hooker's disastrous failure at Chancellorsville, and Burnside's bloody repulse at Fredericksburg, and by a route made difficult by a heavily timbered country, broken by many streams running at right angles with the line of march, and easily held against a superior force. The North had now come to feel that war was no pastime but a terrible reality, and was ready for the new method of procedure which was proposed by General Grant, namely, "to hammer continuously against the armed force of the Confederacy until by mere attrition, if by nothing else, there should be nothing left capable of rebellion. No more ninety days' prophecies! No more nine months' enlistments! No more standing behind intrenchments and making tactical thrusts like a fencer behind his foils! No more sitting down at safe distances and watching the blaze and thunder of an artillery duel, and calling that fighting! War was seen to be what it really is — the most terrible of woes; and so, when on the third of May the command was given — "Forward," it meant no longer a holiday parade, but a fierce death-grapple, the air filled with groans and the earth choked with blood. The desolate region into which was now poured the living tide of one hundred thousand men is fittingly called "The Wilderness." It embraces a tract of country stretching southward many miles from the Rapidan, and westward beyond Mine Run, covered with forest and an almost impenetrable undergrowth of low-limbed scraggy pines, scrub oaks, and stiff-bristling chinquapins, or dwarf chestnuts. It is a tangled labyrinth of brambles and briers, a land of darkness and the very shadow of death. Into its horrid gloom when once the army entered, it was wholly lost to view. Within its trackless waste was enacted — all unseen but not unheard — the terrible drama of battle. There is a glory and a grandeur, a pride and a pomp in the marshalled ranks upon an open field; but you shudder to hear the desperate raging of musketry in the thick jungle where nothing is seen, only from out those gloomy depths soon comes a part of the ruin that has been wrought, in bleeding shapes borne in blankets or on stretchers, while a large part never returns — the silent, motionless shapes that lie in thick swathes along the front of battle, the ghastly harvest of death.

The advance into this horrible wilderness was led by General Sheridan, who had just been put in command of the Cavalry Corps of the Army of the Potomac; having been transferred from the Army of the Cumberland, where he had been leading an infantry division. But although he was an infantry officer, most of his earlier experience had been with the cavalry arm of the service, and everywhere he had shown those fighting qualities that Grant wanted now in this last great encounter. The first thing he did on assuming this new command was to persuade General Meade to relieve the cavalry from their excessive and unnecessary picket duty, guarding, as they had, a sixty-mile circle about the infantry and artillery — and scarcely one mounted Confederate confronting it at any point. The horses were worn and thin, and Sheridan did the best he could, in the two weeks before the campaign opened, to nurse them into a better condition. The next thing Sheridan did was to try to persuade Meade to make the cavalry more effective. General Meade thought cavalry fit for little more than guard and picket duty, but General Sheridan wanted to mass it and defeat the enemy's cavalry, and so give his men such confidence that they could march where they pleased for the purpose of breaking Lee's communications and destroying the resources from which his army was supplied. General Meade was not quite persuaded to let Sheridan have his way, at least not till after the battles of the Wilderness, when Grant intervened and gave the gallant cavalry leader free rein. But now Meade used the troopers in the old-fashioned way of protecting the advance of the infantry, while Sheridan felt that the infantry ought to be able to protect its own front.

The plan of operations was to cross the Rapidan and under cover of the dense woods to march by the left flank and if possible turn Lee's right and strike at his communications with Gordonsville. To this end, early on the the morning of the 4th of May General Sheridan crossed the river with about ten thousand troopers — Wilson's division crossing at Germania Ford and opening the way for Warren with the Fifth Corps, which reached Wilderness Tavern at noon and intrenched. Sedgwick with the Sixth Corps followed Warren and by nightfall had taken position on his right. Gregg with the second division of cavalry crossed the river, before daylight, at Ely's Ford, opening the way towards Chancellorsville for Hancock with the Second Corps, which encamped about six miles east of Warren. Behind the Second Corps, trailed along its almost interminable length the train of more than four thousand wagons covered and protected by Torbert's division of cavalry. This wagon-train in single line would stretch more than a hundred miles and yet it was all south of the river by the evening of the 5th. It carried ten days' rations for one hundred and fifty thousand men and three days' forage for I know not how many animals, and under the direction of Gen. Rufus Ingalls was very skilfully managed. Now all the army was across the river on the evening of the 4th except Burnside's corps, which had been ordered to remain about Rappahannock station to guard Grant's communications with Alexandria until he got word that the crossing had been safely accomplished. This he learned towards evening of the 4th, and by making a night march, although some of his troops had to walk forty miles to reach the river, he was crossing with the head of his column early on the morning of the 5th. Grant considered this movement across the river by his whole army in the face of the enemy's large, well-appointed and ably-commanded forces as a great success, and felt encouraged to think that he might turn Lee's right and force him to fight for his communications with Richmond. But Lee needed no forcing. That very morning, while Grant was crossing, he from his headquarters at Orange Court House had set his columns in motion by the Orange Turnpike and Plank Road, and by evening the advance of the two armies bivouacked unsuspectingly within a short distance of each other, and on the morning of the 5th, as Warren, in order to guard his right flank, sent out the division of Griffin on the turnpike and the division of Crawford on the Plank Road, the one encountered the advance of Ewell and the other the advance of Hill. But Generals Grant and Meade — who had now established their headquarters in the only open space the region afforded, near "Old Wilderness Tavern" — thought that this demonstration on the part of Lee was only a cover for a change of position towards the North Anna, and so, without changing the line of march of the main army, ordered an attack at once with such troops as happened to be near the threatened positions. In obedience to these orders, an impetuous charge was made by Warren at noon, and for a short time everything was swept before it. But soon, coming upon the main columns of the Confederate army, the advance was checked, and shortly driven back with great loss. Then General Grant, no longer in doubt that the enemy were present in full force, made his dispositions to accept the gage of battle, and immediately ordered Hancock, who was now with the advance of the Second Corps two miles beyond Todd's Tavern, to countermarch and as soon as possible support Getty, whose division of Sedgwick's corps was with difficulty holding its position on Warren's left. At a little past four o'clock the attack was opened by Hancock in repeated and desperate assaults upon Hill along the Plank Road, but the Confederates, under cover of the almost impenetrable thickets, met the advancing lines with such well-delivered and murderous volleys that our advance was every time checked and hurled back. The day was intensely hot, and in the close stifling ravines death held high carnival. Every advance was into an ambuscade, where our soldiers were mowed down by bullets from unseen lines of musketry. Yet Grant flinched not from his purpose, and showed his impregnable determination by giving orders that the bridge over which Burnside's corps had just crossed should be taken up. He thus cut off one opportunity of escape for stragglers, and said, "One bridge and the ford will be enough for all the men we have left if we have to fall back." I have told how the cavalry took the advance on the morning of the 4th, Gregg's division at Ely's Ford, and Wilson's, six miles above at Germania Ford. Before daylight they had driven the rebel pickets away, and had laid the pontoons for the crossing of the Infantry and artillery. Gregg had pushed on to Chancellorsville, where Sheridan fixed his headquarters. Wilson moved rapidly past Wilderness Tavern as far as Parker's Store on the Orange Plank Road. Here he received orders from Meade to leave one regiment to hold the position at the store and advance the rest of his force towards Craig's Meeting House. Here he encountered Rosser's brigade of cavalry and drove it flying for two miles. Then, hearing nothing of our infantry following to his support, and learning that the rebel Infantry was pressing past Parker's Store and so getting in his rear and between him and General Meade, Wilson determined to withdraw his cavalry to Todd's Tavern. But here again he encountered the Confederates and seemed to be caught in an ambuscade. He extricated himself, however, by making a detour and crossing the Po at Corbin's Bridge and then taking the direction of Todd's Tavern, where as he approached he was met by Gregg's division of cavalry, which had been sent to his relief by Sheridan, who, with that instinct which made him a great commander, suspected the direction that Wilson would take and so provided, at the right place and time, the necessary relief. Together they were able not only to check the Confederate pursuit but to drive back the rebel forces as far as Shady Grove Church. The First Massachusetts Cavalry did gallant work in this last charge.

Night now closed in and ended the struggle, which had been very severe without any marked advantage to either side except that Grant had crossed a formidable river in face of the enemy and had his whole army ready in one body for the action of the next day. This was indeed equivalent to a victory, but the losses had been great. In those few hours since twelve o'clock, five thousand on the Union side and at least three thousand on the Confederate side had either been killed, wounded, or taken prisoners. Yet these terrible losses did not make either side less determined to continue the fight, and early on the morning of the 6th, fifteen minutes before the time appointed by Grant for the general attack, a sudden outburst of musketry on his right flank announced that Lee was before him in offensive purposes. This would not have happened if Grant had not compromised with Meade's urgent desire to have the attack ordered at six and so deferred it a half-hour from the time he had first determined, which would have given him the advantage of Lee by fifteen minutes. This early attack by Ewell's corps on our right was planned by Lee chiefly as a cover for an intended heavier blow upon the Union left. But its meaning was suspected by Grant and was easily repulsed. Sedgwick with the Sixth Corps now held the right of our line of battle, and through the day made many gallant assaults upon the intrenched positions of the enemy, who, though he could not be dislodged, was thus prevented from withdrawing troops to the support of Hill on the Rebel right. On Sedgwick's left, two divisions of Warren's corps, which had suffered so terribly the day before, though engaged throughout the day in severe skirmishing, yet held chiefly a defensive attitude on the right and the left of the Orange Pike. On Warren's left, Burnside, who had by rapid and arduous marches brought up the Ninth Corps, occupied the space between the turnpike and the Plank Road, and, advancing through the forest in the morning, encountered the enemy on a wooded crest near the Plank Road, but, not deeming it wise to attempt to take the hill by assault, led his command farther to the left and became engaged with the enemy about noon, but with no decisive results. The brunt of the day's fighting was borne by Hancock, who had nearly half of the Army of the Potomac under him, being reinforced by General Wadsworth's division of the Fifth Corps, and General Stephenson's of the Ninth Corps. Hancock in person led the attack on the left of the Plank Road, and Wadsworth on the right, and the advance was made with such vigor that the Confederates under Hill were driven back in panic and utter confusion for a mile and a half; but here Longstreet, who had been making forced marches from Gordonsville, threw his veteran corps into the scale, and by desperate fighting regained all the ground which had been lost, and was making his dispositions to turn Hancock's left and thus strike a decisive blow, when a Confederate bullet — as had happened to Stonewall Jackson just a year before and near this place — disabled him and stayed the onset. This accident caused a delay of four hours, in which General Lee was making his dispositions and getting his troops in hand to carry out Longstreet's plan. On the left of Hancock, General Sheridan held the line of the Brock Road beyond the Catharpin Furnaces and thence around to Todd's Tavern and Piney Branch Church. General Stuart commanding the Rebel cavalry, with Wade Hampton and Fitzhugh Lee as his division commanders, tried to dislodge Sheridan from his position, but Custer's and Devin's brigades hurled back his attacks. This was in the morning; and now at four o'clock when Lee took personal command of the Rebel right, he ordered Stuart to attack once more while he himself threw Longstreet's and Hill's combined forces against Hancock's intrenched position. Stuart had no better success than in the morning. His assault was met gallantly, and severely repulsed by Generals Merritt and Gregg, leading the First and Second Divisions. General Torbert of the First had been taken ill and carried to the rear. In this cavalry fight Custer went in with his usual impetuosity, having his band playing patriotic airs near the front and himself charging at the head of his brigade while his artillery played hotly into the enemy. Lee's assaults upon Hancock were also unavailing, though for a little time the flags of Anderson's corps were planted on our intrenchments. "But Carroll of Gibbon's division moved at a double-quick with his brigade and drove back the enemy, inflicting great loss." Night again closed in on the terrible carnage, with the opposing lines in almost exactly the same position as in the morning. This day's battle added more than fifteen thousand to the frightful holocaust of the day before — the Union losses amounting to ten thousand and the Confederate exceeding five thousand. Grant thought that the Confederate losses must have been greater than his own. Possibly they were, in proportion to the whole force which Lee was able to bring into the field. But the admitted losses of both sides approached twenty-four thousand, and the two days together made the most destructive and the most hotly contested fields in the history of civilized nations up to that time.

The next morning both armies were too exhausted to renew the attack, though General Sheridan drove Stuart's cavalry from Catharpin Furnace almost to Spottsylvania Court House after very hard fighting, and so made it impossible for Lee to turn Grant's left or to threaten his communications. With the rest of the army the day was spent in caring for the wounded and burying the dead who lay within our lines. Grant had the one bridge transferred from Germania to Ely's Ford to facilitate the transportation of the wounded to Washington. But the debatable ground between the two lines of battle was still covered with its horrible harvest of death, the bodies lying in swathes where the dread reaper's sickle had ruthlessly swept the field. The ground fought over was more than five miles long and averaged three-quarters of a mile in width, and on the second day the fighting had continued with short intervals from five in the morning till dark. The killed and many of the severely wounded lay within this belt where it was impossible to reach them, piled up in ghastly heaps, gold-laced generals and ragged privates rolled in one indistinguishable medley of death. And as if this was not dreadful enough to appease the grim Moloch of War the fire-fiend added his hot fury, the woods were set on fire by the bursting shells, and "the wounded who had not strength to move themselves were either suffocated or burned to death." A month after the battle, I rode along this gloomy avenue between the intrenched positions, and there they still lay — some partially cremated, all unburied, "pleading in vain for a handful of earth," each in some position that told the tale of lengthened pain or momentary agony. Most had been stripped of caps and shoes and outer garments to cover the tattered and shoeless Rebel soldiers and camp-followers. You could hardly distinguish in some cases between the Union and the Confederate dead, unless you stooped to examine some token or written direction upon the person, telling of loved ones left behind, who should never get the tidings of how or where they fell. In some places the battle had raged so fiercely that trees a foot in diameter were mowed down with bullets. We could mark the fluctuating fortunes of the battle by the numbers and position of the dead. At one place there was evidently a terrible struggle before some strong Rebel earthworks where our dead lay in a long line; but we could see that the assault was at one time successful, for on the inside of the intrenchments was another line of Confederate dead mingled with our own, and further on the Rebels lay scattered where they fell before our advance. In one ravine it was plain to see by the bright uniforms — which the Rebels, not wishing to wear, had not stolen — that a whole regiment of Zouaves had been entrapped in an ambuscade of flame, and few could have escaped to tell the tale. Now with their tasselled caps and embroidered jackets and baggy breeches, so picturesque in life, so uncanny in death, they told the tale of the ghastly horrors of war. This was the 146th New York — the Irish Infantry (old Duryea's Zouaves, re-enlisted). They had charged here five times through the ravine and over the Rebel earthworks, singing, as they ran on the double-quick, the inspiring song "Rally Round the Flag, Boys!" Alas, that its echoes should have been the groans of the dying sinking away into the silence of the dead! But how glorious was this exhibition of the uniting of all nationalities in the North for the defence of freedom and union! The hot furnaces of war — seven times heated by civil strife — fused the diverse elements of our population into one homogeneous mass of patriotic devotion. On many a battlefield foreigners fought shoulder to shoulder with those who were native born, pressed on with patient persistence in a common partnership of peril, bowed to a common baptism of blood, and entered together the shadow of death.

We had entered that region of gloom to carry away any of our own wounded whom it might be possible to move. Word had reached Washington through some of our men, who had so far recovered as to be able to walk to our lines, that there were three hundred of our wounded men in a field hospital at Locust Grove in the Wilderness, and Colonel Lowell was ordered to take seven hundred men and fifty four-horse ambulances, and try to bring them away. We started from Vienna, June 8th, and crossed the Occoquan at Wolf Run Shoals, and the Rappahannock at United States Ford, wading both streams, passed through Chancellorsville, and took the Orange Plank Road to Parker's Store, where we found one small field hospital with thirteen of our men besides a number of Confederates. On examination, our surgeon decided that none of them could endure the journey to Washington. As I went from one patient to another, trying to comfort them, I came upon one of the Fifty-seventh Massachusetts Infantry, and, instead of speaking of himself and his own terrible doom, his first word was of affectionate solicitude for his Colonel — W. F. Bartlett of Pittsfield — and did I know whether he was badly wounded or not. When I told him that I had seen his gallant commander only a few days before, and that though severely wounded he was doing well, this poor dying soldier seemed perfectly happy and his eyes sparkled with delight. What a beautiful and pathetic tribute to General Bartlett! How we all delighted to honor him as one of the noblest of the young heroes of the war! He was just past twenty-one when he entered the army as Captain of the Twentieth Massachusetts Infantry, and he was only twenty-six when he was mustered out as Brevet Major General. He lost a leg in front of Yorktown, was wounded in the wrist and heel In the assault upon Port Hudson, was wounded in the head at the Battle of the Wilderness, and taken prisoner in the mine before Petersburg. On a bronze tablet under his bust in Memorial Hall in Cambridge is this motto in old English: "He was a very parfit gentil knight." He was indeed our modern "Bayard without fear and without reproach," and he showed a spirit of self-sacrifice finer than Sidney's. His was not a merely physical courage or the recklessness of a hot temperament. No one could have been more cool and calm than he, and no one so fond of peace. But he nerved himself to battle, by prayer, and by inward wrestlings whose outcome and end was always religious trust. After battle I have heard him laugh and joke about the wounds in his wooden leg; but to him, who never but once went into action without a bullet-scratch, fighting meant always close quarters with death, and he never blanched in that presence. After the war was over, and he had gone back quietly to the pursuits of peace, the same manly courage, moral force, and chivalrous daring made him stand up boldly against the vindictive passions of conquerors, and stand out conspicuously as the champion of the pitying sympathy of brothers. Without the art of the orator, his utter earnestness amounted to eloquence; and in the few years of peace spared to him he achieved even finer victories than in the war. His short speech at the Centennial of the Battle of Lexington, in which he sought "to heal the wounds his own valor had made," was perhaps the noblest fruit of that patriotic celebration. And yet we think of him chiefly as a *soldier*, our honored companion who loved his country and scorned death in her service. No wonder his men admired him, for he never asked them to go where he would not lead the way. I was delighted to be able to assure this one of Bartlett's brave followers, now wounded beyond cure and still lying on the field of the Wilderness, that his loved commander was doing well **(Note 8).** I took the names of all these patients, and such messages as they wished to send to their homes, and with unutterable regret that we could not transport them to Washington, we left them to the kindly though unskilled nursing that the place afforded.

While we were halting thus at Parker's Store, a detachment had pushed on six or eight miles further to Locust Grove, but found that most of the wounded had been removed to Orange Court House three days before. At this we were greatly disappointed, for we could easily have brought off two hundred. Still, as there were *some* left, Colonel Lowell took ten ambulances — sending the rest for safety back over the ford — and we found at Locust Grove forty-six of our men who, we thought, could safely be moved. Their wounds were all very bad, and the ride was to be very long — more than fifty miles, — yet they were all ready to take the risk and perfectly delighted at the prospect of getting among friends. There were two who were dying, and whom, of course, we would not move; yet even they longed to go, that at least they might close their eyes for the last time among friends. One of these, before he had been told that he could not go, although he was already so weak that he could not *turn* on his couch, asked me to take his haversack from under his pillow, that he might have some provision for the journey. But he had no need of food on the journey that his soul would speedily take, nor would he taste again the bread of earth till it was transformed into the bread of the immortal life. We hastily loaded the rest into the ambulances, all except three for whom there was no room. But their prayers to be taken along were so piteous that I begged Colonel Lowell to let me see that they were carried on stretchers to the ford where were the rest of the ambulances. He gave me a detail of forty-eight men, and I had twenty-four dismount at a time, the others leading the riderless horses, and I put eight at each stretcher, four to carry and four to rest alternately. In this way we carried them twelve miles between five and eleven o'clock. It was very hard work, as the road was exceedingly rough. I took hold myself a part of the time; and though I was very much exhausted, with lack of food and sleep, and with the peculiarly trying labors of the day, in the excitement of the occasion I felt very strong, and often carried alone one end of a stretcher with its precious but heavy load of suffering loyalty. To add to the difficulties of our weary tramp, towards evening it began to rain, and by nine o'clock it was so dark we could not see a yard before us, and we stumbled over every slightest obstacle. We reached the ford and the rest of the ambulances a little after eleven; but it was not safe to cross in the darkness, so we lay down on the wet ground till half-past three o'clock, when we fed horses and started again. This crossing of the Rappahannock was the hardest place in the whole journey for the wounded. All were now provided with room enough in the ambulances; but in descending the steep bank to the river, one ambulance was upset, throwing out three wounded men and breaking again the limbs which had first been broken by bullets. Like true soldiers these sufferers looked upon the bright side even of this calamity, and found some comfort in thinking that their limbs had been poorly set and would in any event have had to be broken again.

Then the crossing of the river was very rough. It seemed at times as if the large round stones in the bed of the river would upset the wagons into the water. In one of the ambulances a horse had given out, and we had supplied his place with a mule, but as the team entered the water the two animals — from incompatibility of temper — refused to pull together. The mule especially sulked, and seemed disposed to shift the burden upon his more aristocratic companion. So, procuring a long pole and putting a little pointed persuasion into the end of it, I managed by persistent punching, to induce the mule to draw at least his half, and at last we were out of the water. But in climbing the bank, the wheels got stuck in the mud, and then the *horse* refused to pull — showing how catching is depravity. In this complication I had ten men dismount, and what with pulling at the tongue and pushing at the back and tugging at the wheels and lashing the horse and punching the mule, the ambulance was finally drawn up the bank. But the sufferings of the wounded during these wrenchings and joltings of the wagon were simply indescribable.

We found a camping-ground about four miles from the river and halted for breakfast. We had concentrated beef-tea for the sick, and heated three large iron kettles full of it, and thickened it with soft bread. The patients had had nothing to eat for twenty-four hours, and it was a great refreshment to them.

I will not stop to give in detail the rest of the journey. Suffice it to say that only one of the wounded men succumbed to the dreadful fatigues. The rest reached Washington in safety. As we approached our camp late on the second night of our journey, I galloped ahead of the column, and waked up the band, and had them play a "welcome home" for the command as it came in. The joy of the wounded captives whom we had rescued may be imagined but cannot be described when they heard once more the inspiring strains of "The Star Spangled Banner" and "Hail, Columbia." For were they not also heroes who "fought and bled in freedom's cause," and did they not deserve the trumpet's "All Hail!" and do they not still deserve a nation's grateful remembrance?

Let us now follow again the movements of Grant and Lee, and watch them as they tear at each other like wild beasts of the jungle. As I have said, both armies were too exhausted after the two days' terrible combat in the Wilderness to renew the struggle. The Rebels had fought with great courage and tenacity, but they could no longer drive back the Army of the Potomac. It had at last found a leader worthy of its devotion. Lincoln said after the Wilderness battles, *'Any other commander would have fallen back." But this was altogether against the temper of Grant's mind. He knew no such word as "fail." He had just the quality that was needed at this stage of the struggle — the energy of patience. As soon as he found, by reconnoitring all along the line on the morning of May 7th, that the enemy would not attack him again in the open field, he gave the command — "Forward!" and that very night the columns were in motion towards Richmond, seeking to gain the next important strategic point, Spottsylvania Court House, fifteen miles distant, and thus Grant planned not only to put himself between Lee and Richmond, but also to keep Lee from detaching any force to oppose General Butler, who that very day had captured City Point and was threatening Richmond from the South. But Lee had divined Grant's plan, and instructed Anderson — now commanding Longstreet's corps — to break camp and bivouac so as to be ready to move to Spottsylvania in the morning. It was by the merest accident — one of those chances, however, that decides the fate of battles — that Anderson, not finding a good place to bivouac, began his march that night, and having fewer impedimenta than Warren, who led the advance of Grant's infantry, and having also a few hours the start, he reached Spottsylvania first, drove out the cavalry that Sheridan had sent ahead, and intrenched a little north of the Court House.

When on the morning of the 8th our advance — after driving before it the Rebel cavalry sent out to impede its march — came upon Longstreet's infantry thus securely intrenched, it made one furious onset, but was driven back by the steady fire from the Confederate lines, and began at once to throw up intrenchments for its own protection. Thus Lee blocked the second attempt of Grant to turn his right, and, gaining time on the 8th to throw up a strong line of defence on Spottsylvania Ridge, he was able for twelve days to hold the Army of the Potomac in check.

I have said that this seizure of the advantageous strategic position at Spottsylvania was the fruit of Anderson's accidental advance before it was ordered. Even thus he would not have succeeded but for an unfortunate overruling of Sheridan's plans by General Meade. Sheridan had on the 7th fought the Rebel cavalry at Todd's Tavern and routed them, thus opening the way for the infantry towards Spottsylvania. He had also on the morning of the 8th taken possession of Spottsylvania with Wilson's corps, and had given orders to Gregg and Merritt to join their divisions with Wilson's and hold Snell's Bridge over which Lee would have to cross to get to Spottsylvania. Our cavalry would thus have been able to check Anderson till Warren, who held our infantry advance, had intrenched himself at Spottsylvania. But Meade countermanded the orders to Gregg and Merritt and kept them from forming the junction with Wilson. Sheridan was so nettled by this interference that he told Meade that "such disjointed operations as he had been requiring of the cavalry in the last four days would render the corps useless before long." Meade, replying, suggested that "Stuart with the Confederate cavalry would do about as he pleased anyway." At this Sheridan retorted that he "could whip Stuart any day." Meade went at once to Grant and reported the conversation, and Grant answered: "Did he say he could whip Stuart? Well, he generally knows what he is talking about. Let him start right out and do it." Meade immediately gave orders to Sheridan to proceed against the enemy's cavalry, and Sheridan, though his men had been four days with very little food or sleep, yet at once issued instructions to his three cavalry divisions to concentrate at Aldrich's. So precipitate was the start that Sheridan did not wait to get extra rations, but doled out what he had on hand, — three days' rations for the men and half a day's rations for the horses, — and though he received the order for the expedition on the afternoon of May 8th, his column was in motion early on the morning of May 9th.

In order to deceive the enemy as to his intended movement — which the lines of dust made by his troopers might betray — he took up his march, first, straight away from them towards Fredericksburg. Then when he was well out of sight he turned sharply and marched around the right flank of Lee's army and took the telegraph road towards Richmond. His column was thirteen miles long, and the rear had passed Massaponax Church before Stuart suspected the movement. He immediately sent Fitzhugh Lee with Lomax's and Wickham's brigades to attack the rear of the column and try to hold it till he himself with the rest of his command should intercept Sheridan in front. Sheridan directed Davies' brigade at the rear of his column to hold one position after another just long enough to keep Fitzhugh Lee busy, but not to lose his connection with the main column, which kept straight on over the Ny, the Po, and the Ta Rivers, and at night reached the North Anna River, Merritt's division crossing at Anderson's Ford and camping on the south side of the stream, all except Custer's brigade, which kept on to Beaver Dam station to cut the Virginia Central Railroad and to secure a clear road to Richmond. Custer accomplished both ends in his usual swift and gallant way. Beaver Dam station was the goal and rallying-point chosen by Stuart; but Custer anticipated him, drove out a small force of the enemy, and recaptured four hundred prisoners who were being taken under guard to Richmond, and whose joy on seeing the flashing sabres of our cavalry can only be imagined. Custer also destroyed the station, two locomotives, three trains of cars, ninety wagons, ten miles of railroad, a million and a half of rations, and nearly all the medical stores of General Lee's army. These last had just been brought forward from Orange Court House for convenient use in Lee's retreat towards Richmond.

On the morning of the 10th, while Gregg and Wilson were crossing the North Anna, Stuart appeared, having crossed a few miles above on Davenport's bridge; but he was too late to throw any effective obstacle in Sheridan's path at that point; so he turned and started off once more, and urged his horses to the death to get ahead of Sheridan's column and interpose between him and Richmond. This left Sheridan's march almost unimpeded that day along the Negro-foot road, and his famished horses got well fed and rested, and he encamped for the night on the south side of the South Anna, congratulating himself that now he had drawn Stuart far enough away to fight him without fear of the intervention of Lee's infantry. At two o'clock on the morning of the 11th, Sheridan sent Davies' brigade to the Ashland station of the Richmond and Potomac Railroad, and, though it was guarded by a regiment of Virginians, he drove them out in a gallant charge led by the First Massachusetts Cavalry and then destroyed a locomotive and train of cars, and the track for a long distance, and got away before Fitzhugh Lee reached it — as he must in his march to join Stuart. This was one of numberless instances where Sheridan's sleepless vigilance and swift movements secured him great advantages over his enemies.

Stuart, by forced marches, reached Yellow Tavern, six miles from Richmond, on the Brook turnpike at ten o'clock on the morning of the 11th, and shortly afterwards Sheridan's advance under Merritt approached the place, and at once attacked and drove the enemy beyond the turnpike so that Wilson's division, immediately following with one of Gregg's brigades, was able to form an advantageous line of battle on the east of the pike. Here followed a very hot battle, which, however, was soon determined in Sheridan's favor by a brilliant mounted charge of Custer's brigade, supported by the whole of Wilson's division. This broke and turned the enemy's left, and then Gibbs' and Devin's brigades drove the enemy's centre and right from the field. At the same time Gregg charged upon and routed Gordon's brigade which had been hanging upon our rear; and thus the battle ended with Sheridan in complete control of the road to Richmond, with the enemy's cavalry broken up and badly beaten and Generals Stuart and Gordon killed.

Right here Sheridan — as he afterwards confessed to Senator Plumb — resisted the greatest temptation of his life. Richmond was right before him, drained of her usual defenders by Butler's demonstration on the south. Sheridan knew that he could dash in and burn and kill right and left, and knew also that the tidings of his being in Richmond would have set every bell in the North to ringing, and he would have been made the hero of the hour. But he knew also that it would cost the lives of many of his soldiers and for no permanent advantage; and as he thought not of glory but of results, he spurned the temptation as soon as it was suggested, and made his plans to extricate his command from the new combinations which the enemy would be sure to make. To this end he sent one party down the Brook turnpike towards Richmond, and they brushed away the guards and entered the outer defences of the city, and Sheridan — discovering a country road between the lines of earthworks — hoped by that route to reach Mechanicsville and thus save quite a distance in his march to Haxall's Landing. But not only was his path infested with torpedoes planted to obstruct his passage, but his advance under Wilson came upon General Bragg with three brigades of regular infantry — just called in from confronting Butler south of the James — and with four or five thousand irregular troops under the eye of Jefferson Davis. These advanced from behind their earthworks and attacked Wilson and at first drove him back. But when the Confederate advance came upon Gregg, he met them with such a hot fire, from his dismounted cavalrymen and from Robinson's batteries of horse artillery, that they began to waver, and then Wilson rallied his men and charged and turned the enemy's right flank, and compelled Bragg to withdraw his whole force within the second line of earthworks from which it had so confidently sallied forth.

Meanwhile Merritt had been sent with his division to secure Meadow Bridge for a crossing over the Chickahominy, but, finding it destroyed and the enemy's cavalry and a section of artillery guarding the opposite bank, it seemed hopeless to attempt to rebuild the bridge. But Sheridan sent word that it must be done at all hazards. So Merritt sent two of his regiments to ford the river above the bridge and try to drive away the enemy, but they failed and were driven back. Still his working parties kept on repairing the bridge though all the time exposed to a hot fire from the enemy, and soon Merritt was able to get his whole division over the bridge. He then dismounted them and charged and carried the enemy's line of entrenchments, and remounting pursued the fleeing Rebels as far as Gaines' Mills.

Thus Sheridan was both in front and rear master of the situation, and he was prepared for even more desperate straights. For while the battle with Bragg was going on he had sent out scouts who had discovered several fords over the Chickahominy by which he could have retreated, if necessary. It was this preparedness for all possible emergencies which made Sheridan the great General which all now admit him to have been. He remained on the field of his encounter with Bragg, undisturbed the rest of the day, and spent the time "collecting the wounded, burying the dead, grazing the hungry horses, resting his tired men, and himself reading the Richmond journals which an enterprising Southern boy had brought in."

The next day, Sheridan took up his march over Meadow Bridge and then turned southward and marched by way of Mechanicsville and Bottom's Bridge towards Haxall's Landing on the James, where it had been arranged that he should get supplies from General Butler.

Thus in four days the purpose of the expedition was accomplished. Lee's lines of railroad communication had been cut and for many miles destroyed, his supplies had been seriously depleted, his cavalry had been broken to pieces, and his favorite cavalry leader had been killed. Stuart up to this time had proved himself invincible. He was to the cavalry what Jackson had been to the infantry. His loss was an irreparable blow to the Confederacy, and Lee confessed to one of his staff that he could scarcely think of it without weeping. Sheridan had not only vindicated his boast that he could whip Stuart anywhere, but he had added wonderfully to the confidence of the cavalry corps both in him and in its own prowess. For now it felt that it could go anywhere and make itself a most efficient arm of the service.

After a few days' recruiting at Haxall's Landing, Sheridan crossed the Chickahominy at Jones' bridge and the Pamunkey at White House and on May 24th joined Grant at Chesterfield station on the Richmond & Potomac Railroad. Both Grant and Meade were warm in their praises of what Sheridan had accomplished, and admitted that he had aided materially in forcing Lee's retrograde march to the North Anna, and had made it easy to guard the immense train of Union wagons while changing to the new base of supplies at Aquia Creek. Up to this time Southern cavaliers had scoffed — and with some reason — at the Union cavalry. But henceforth under the inspiration of Sheridan's gallant leadership it became a very essential element in every successful movement of the Union armies in Virginia.

We left the Army of the Potomac on the 8th of May to follow Sheridan. Now let us return to the main column as it approaches Spottsylvania and finds the ridge strongly defended, and sets about intrenching itself.

On the 9th of May the army was all brought into line of battle, with Hancock on the right, then Warren, then Sedgwick, and Burnside holding the left. Aside from these movements to take up position and intrench, our forces were quiet during the day. The Confederate sharpshooters were however very active, and while Sedgwick was examining his line of defence he saw his men trying to dodge the stray bullets, and said: "Pooh, men, don't duck! They couldn't hit an elephant at that distance." As he spoke, a bullet pierced his brain, and he fell dead. He was a fine soldier; brevetted a Major for gallantry in the Mexican War, he had risen to be Major General in the Army of the Potomac and was the beloved chief of the Sixth Corps. Grant said he was worth more than a whole division.

On the following day. May 10, at 9.30 a.m.. Grant wrote this despatch to the Secretary of War: "The enemy hold our front in very strong force, and evince a strong determination to interpose between us and Richmond to the last. I shall take no backward steps." Then after various tentative thrusts by single divisions, a general assault was ordered for the afternoon. Grant himself supervising the advance by Warren and Wright. But although the Sixth Corps carried the enemy's first line of Intrenchments and captured a thousand prisoners in a most gallant assault led by Col. Emory Upton, — who was for his splendid pluck made a Brigadier General on the spot, — yet the advantage was lost by the feeble following of Mott's division; and in front of Warren the repulse was so bloody that it inflicted a loss of several thousands of his troops. General Porter tells us that in the hottest part of the afternoon's conflict General Grant sat down upon a stump to write a despatch, when a shell exploded directly in front of him. "He looked up a moment and then without the slightest change of countenance went on writing the message." On the right of the Union line was the only place where Lee's army ventured to come out of his intenchments, and here General Barlow, H. C. 1855, with two brigades was holding a crossing of the Po. Lee, noting his isolation from the main body of the Union army, sent out a whole corps to capture or annihilate him; but Barlow with splendid tenacity held his position against two fierce assaults, and inflicted great loss upon the enemy. And when Grant ordered Barlow to withdraw, he retired in good order, taking up his bridges in presence of the enemy. On the left of the Union line Burnside had advanced without much opposition to within a few hundred yards of Spottsylvania Court House, thus getting upon Lee's right flank; but he did not appreciate the importance of his position nor did he press his advantage, and at nightfall he was withdrawn to connect his corps with the Sixth on his right.

Having thus failed to pierce the enemy's line in a general assault, Grant resolved to concentrate heavily on the centre, and May 11th was spent in busy preparations to this end. He found time, however, to send off this hasty despatch to the Secretary of War: "We have now ended the sixth day of very hard fighting. The result to this time is much in our favor. Our losses have been heavy, but I think the loss of the enemy must be greater. We have taken over four thousand prisoners in battle, while he has taken from us but few except stragglers. I purpose to fight it out on this line if it takes all summer." This last sentence — now become famous — rang through the North, like a clarion, its inspiring expression of Grant's energy of patience. It relieved the general suspense, and brought the people up to Grant's grim determination to fight right through to victory regardless of cost.

Thursday, May 12th, brought a long and desperate battle in which the post of peril and of honor was given to General Hancock. He had held the same critical position at Gettysburg and had acquitted himself so splendidly that he drew the thanks of Congress and of the country. He was every inch a soldier. Tall and handsome, his majestic bearing and magnetic presence excited admiration and commanded confidence; and his flashing glance as he rode down the line of battle fired his men with his own courage and inspired them to supreme devotion. He was the idol of the infantry and its most superb corps commander. His Gettysburg wounds were still troubling him, but he did not spare himself, and he gallantly accepted the task of making the main assault on the morning of May 12th. His troops were in poor condition, one would think, for making a spirited attack; for not only were they worn with the exhausting labors of the six days' battles, but they had been tramping all night long, having been withdrawn from the right of the Union line on the evening of May 11th as soon as the darkness made a cover for their movement. To add to their discomfort the rain had poured in torrents all the day before and through this night, and the earth was so soaked it spurted water like a sponge at every pressure of the soldiers' feet. The night was so dark that all motion was made very difficult, and the locality was so little known and so thickly wooded that the direction of advance had to be determined and guided by the compass. It took till midnight for Hancock's corps to pass behind the Fifth and Sixth, and then it took till nearly morning to get them into position. Towards daybreak the rain ceased, but a dense fog lingered and concealed the assaulting column though it was only twelve hundred yards from the enemy's intrenchments. At 4.30, tired as were Hancock's men, they were ready to follow their beloved commander, and at the word they rushed forward in utter silence and without firing a shot. First they toiled through a soft marsh, then waded through a stagnant swamp, then up a thickly wooded ascent, and when they came within about four hundred yards of the Rebel line they set up a great shout and rushed forward on the double-quick up and over the breastworks, and after a short but desperate hand-to-hand contest with bayonets and clubbed muskets, captured twenty pieces of artillery, thirty stand of colors, and more than four thousand prisoners, including two generals and embracing most of Johnson's division of Ewell's corps. Hancock at once turned the captured guns against the enemy, and advanced his own line a half-mile within the Rebel intrenchments. The Second Corps was now a wedge inserted between Lee's right and centre, and if this wedge could have been driven home, it would have shattered Lee's line and put his army in jeopardy. But unfortunately Hancock was unsupported, though Warren was ordered to sustain him; and he was compelled to fall back, though disputing every inch of the ground, till he reached the breastworks he had first taken by assault. "These he turned, facing them the other way and continued to hold." Against this line Lee made five of the most terrific assaults ever flung against a heroic foe, but in vain. For twenty hours he continued the desperate struggle and then a little after midnight drew back his bleeding columns behind his second line of intrenchments and gave up all further attempt to regain his lost ground.

This was the most hotly contested field of the whole war, and Hancock's share in it was a masterpiece of brilliant execution followed by a marvel of heroic pertinacity. Over the comparatively small space where the battle raged the fiercest, more than five thousand men had fallen on the Union side alone. The ground was literally covered with the slain in piles three, four, and five deep, and sometimes the wounded lay under the dead. Sometimes the combatants were separated only by the breastworks, their rival colors almost touching in the dread encounter. The whole forest within range was mowed down by the fire of the musketry, and yet one of the trees was an oak twenty-two inches in diameter, and it was cut in two with the bullets almost as clean as with a saw. (Years after, the remaining trunk was dug up by the roots and removed to the National Museum as a curious memento.)

On the left of our line Burnside had advanced close to the enemy, and one of his divisions had climbed over the parapet but was forced back. Still he succeeded in keeping Lee from drawing away troops to reinforce his centre, which Hancock was threatening. On the right of our line, both Wright and Warren were at different times withdrawn to support Hancock. Wright, though wounded early in the day, remained on the field till midnight, and accomplished all that could be asked. But Warren's sluggish movements so nettled Grant, that he gave written orders to Meade to relieve Warren of his command if he failed again to move promptly. I believe no one ever doubted Warren's ability, but he seemed to have a constitutional incapacity for trusting his superiors and for executing their commands in the spirit in which they were given. Grant bore with him as with others with wonderful patience, but the first time Sheridan met Warren's dilatoriness, as at Five Forks, he relieved him on the spot.

In this battle at Spottsylvania Court House, though no decisive strategic advantage was gained by our arms, it was plain to be seen that our army was beginning to acquire the habit of driving the enemy instead of being driven. Meade was here prompted to issue this congratulatory order to his troops:-

"For eight days and nights almost without intermission through rain and sunshine you have been gallantly fighting a desperate foe in positions naturally strong and made doubly so by intrenchments. Your heroic deeds and noble endurance will ever be memorable, and the courage and fortitude you have displayed render your commanding General confident that your future efforts will result in success."

The next week. May 13th to 20th, was one of almost constant rain, compelling the postponement of all offensive operations, except now and then an effort to find a point where the enemy's line could be broken. But each attempt was repulsed, and on the 20th of May, Grant determined to continue the strategic movement which he had begun in the Wilderness, and by a flank march disengage the enemy from his position. This was done by taking Hancock's corps from the right of the army and marching it by night behind the other corps towards the left. It thus pushed southward as far as Milford station on the Fredericksburg & Richmond Railroad, and secured the bridge across the Mattapony at that point. But the same night on which Hancock started, Lee, apprised of the movement by his scouts, sent Longstreet with his corps down the Telegraph Road to make sure of blocking the way between Grant and Richmond. The next strategic point of importance towards which both armies now turned was Hanover Junction, where the Central Railroad of Virginia meets that leading from Richmond to Fredericksburg. It was by the Central Railroad that the Confederates received most of their supplies — for it was the most direct route of communication with the Shenandoah Valley. The advance corps of the Union army reached the North Anna, near the place where it is crossed by the Fredericksburg Railroad, on the afternoon of May 23d, but only to find Lee strongly posted on the opposite bank. Hancock's corps, however, forced a passage across; while Warren's corps crossed, wading waist-deep, at Jericho Ford five miles above, and repulsed the enemy at every point, taking nearly a thousand prisoners. The Sixth Corps followed Warren, and thus three corps were across. But when Burnside attempted to cross at Ox Ford — half-way between the other two crossings — he came upon Lee's centre strongly intrenched, and was driven back with great loss. Thus Lee had again blocked Grant's direct line of march; for the right and left wings of our army, although they had made a brilliantly successful passage of the river, were separated by several miles, and neither could reinforce the other without making a double passage of the river. Lee had formed his line very skilfully in the shape of an obtuse angle with its blunt apex thrust out to the North Anna River at Ox Ford, his right thrown back towards the Hanover marshes and his left resting on Little River. The more this position was examined, the less did Grant wish to attack it. So after spending two days in various reconnoissances and destroying many miles of the Central Railroad, he took up again his movement by the left flank in order to compel Lee to come out of his intrenchments.

Sheridan's cavalry had just returned from its raid towards Richmond, and was now ready both to cover this new move of the Army of the Potomac and to open the way before it. To cover it and deceive the enemy, Sheridan sent Wilson's division on the afternoon of May 26th to make a strong demonstration on Lee's left flank; and, under cover of this, Grant withdrew his right wing in perfect safety to the north side of the river — a very delicate and dangerous movement happily accomplished. Then Wilson's cavalry made itself a rear guard, watching all the fords until the infantry had crossed and were well on their southern march, then taking up the pontoons and destroying the other bridges. To open the way before the advance of the infantry Sheridan sent Gregg's and Torbert's divisions to demonstrate heavily at Taylor's and Littlepage's Fords as if the Army of the Potomac was to cross there, and then, leaving a small guard to keep up the semblance of a strong demonstration, both divisions pressed on to Hanovertown Ford, crossed early on the morning of the 27th and drove away the guards, and advanced to Hanovertown, driving General Gordon's brigade of Confederate cavalry in the direction of Hanover Court House. Thus an unobstructed crossing was secured for the infantry, and on the 28th it took up a position south of the river, and Grant shifted his base of supplies from Port Royal on the Rappahannock to White House on the Pamunkey, where steamers were already in waiting with rations and reinforcements that had come by way of Chesapeake Bay and York River. But though Grant thus made an easy passage of the Pamunkey, he found that he could not continue his advance over the Chickahomlny without a battle; for Lee had followed his movements on Interior and shorter lines and was now posted on his line of march near Cold Harbor and with numbers reinforced almost to the extent of making up for his losses In the Wilderness and at Spottsylvanla. Sheridan opened the way on the 28th for the Union advance towards Cold Harbor, by dislodging the Confederate cavalry which he found intrenched at Hawes' Shop, and which made a very stubborn fight under Wade Hampton and Fitzhugh Lee, repelling the first attack by Gregg's division, but yielding before their onset when reinforced by Custer's brigade.

On the 31st Sheridan advanced towards Cold Harbor — the next important strategic point, covering, as it did, the roads to White House (the new base of supplies) and also the roads along which Grant must march in his next left flank movement to the James. This movement was already determined upon on the 30th, when Grant asked General Halleck to have all available pontoons sent to City Point. Lee appreciated fully the Importance of Cold Harbor to himself as covering the roads to Richmond and threatening Grant's march in flank, and he had already sent forward both infantry and cavalry by forced marches to occupy it. But Sheridan did not hesitate to *try* to dislodge them, although he had only a part of his command at hand. He directed Torbert's division to attack the enemy in front while Merritt with two regiments of regulars passed round the enemy's left and attacked his rear This stampeded the Confederates and left Cold Harbor in his hands; but it was nine miles away from the nearest infantry support, and Sheridan knew that the enemy would return reinforced, so he sent word to Grant that he could not hold the place without support. Grant sent back word to hold it at all hazards, and at once started the Sixth Corps on a forced march to the assistance of Sheridan, who immediately utilized the Confederate lines of intrenchments by turning them the other way. He then disposed his thin line of dismounted men behind them with boxes of ammunition at hand, and passed the word that the place *must* be held. All this was done in the night. On the early morning of June 1st, as expected, the enemy returned reinforced with infantry, and advanced at once to assault Sheridan's position; but they were received with such a hot carbine-fire at close range that they recoiled; and though they rallied and made a second assault it was likewise repulsed, and before any further attempt could be made to dislodge our cavalrymen, the Sixth Corps arrived and secured the prize which Sheridan had so boldly snatched and so bravely defended. A few hours later Smith's corps arrived from Butler's command, coming by way of White House; and at six o'clock, though they were very tired and worn from their long, dusty, and hurried march, they joined with Wright's corps in an assault upon the Rebel lines, and together they captured the first line of rifle-pits and seven hundred prisoners. On the right of the Sixth Corps, Warren held a skirmish line of four miles which reached to Bethesda Church, and repulsed successfully three fierce assaults of the enemy. Grant, who had several times been vexed by Warren's sluggishness, was much gratified by his strong and determined resistance to Lee's desperate charges, and admitted that "there was no officer more capable, no one more prompt in acting, than Warren when the enemy forced him to it."

We praise the dogged persistency with which a general holds an important line, but do we appreciate the individual heroisms that are the essential elements of that success.^ Seldom, I fear, unless we have some personal knowledge of one or another who stands in the deadly breach and makes himself a shield against the shots that are aimed at the nation's life. On that line of battle that Warren that day held was posted near Bethesda Church the Thirteenth Massachusetts Infantry. Marshalled in that regiment on that fiercely contested field was my brother — dearly beloved. His bullet-pierced body, uncoffined and scarcely enwrapped by the cannon-ploughed sod, lies where he fell — the soldier's chosen resting-place. And though loving hearts would choose to have some shrine to which to make a reverent pilgrimage, and upon which to lay the offerings of affectionate remembrance, yet we know that, wherever they sleep, "the hallowed sod, unknown to men, is marked of God."

"On Fame's eternal camping-ground
  Their silent tents are spread,
And Glory guards in solemn round
  The bivouac of the dead."

"Ye unknown heroes, sleeping where ye fell
  In your forgotten graves! with secret shame
    We feel our pulses beat, our foreheads burn,
  When we remember ye have given so well
    All that ye had of life, your very name,
      And we can give you nothing in return" **(Note 9)**.

When heroic youths thus pour out their warm life-blood for freedom and fatherland, we are apt to say — What a dreadful waste! But what more could they have done for the world if they had lived a thousand years? What higher attainment could they reach if they had ages to climb? In one bound they leaped to the highest moral and spiritual elevation, and, having given all, they could no more.

June 2d was spent in making preparations for the battle which was determined on for the morrow. Lee had carefully fortified his lines with earthworks, which his army had now learned to make with great facility after the experience of the month's campaign of defence; for since the battles of the Wilderness Lee had not ventured — except in detached sallies — to take the offensive. It was much safer to fight behind breastworks. These were, first, a layer of stout logs, breast-high, forming the framework on which a thick parapet of earth would be thrown up; then in front of this line the timber for several hundred yards would be felled, making an elaborately interlaced abatis; and still in front of this almost impregnable defence would be several lines of rifle-pits from which would flame out death and destruction to any approaching force. Yet even from these jaws of hell our attacking columns had several times plucked costly victories, and it was hoped that success might now crown the efforts which sought, not without sacrifice, to reap the fruits of patriotic devotion. But besides the strong intrenchments which Lee had now thrown up, his army was posted in a most favorable position for defence, having the Chickahominy to protect both flanks and also his rear, while in front of his line were, here almost impenetrable thickets, and there almost impassable marshes. The Union forces were drawn up with the right resting on Totopotomoy Creek, and the left thrust beyond Old Cold Harbor on the road to Dispatch station.

The attack was ordered for half-past four on the morning of June 3d, and was to be, as usual, an assault along the whole line, another stroke of the hammer in the hand of Grant to crush out rebellion; but as yet the rebound of the hammer from the rebellious anvil has in almost every case in this campaign destroyed twice as many as its fall has crushed. And now, sad to tell 1 we are to see the hard necessity of weighting the hammer with ten patriots to crush one rebel, so strong was the position to be assaulted. The Union lines advanced as ordered, and swept over the first part of the space between the hostile intrenchments in as good order as tearing through thickets and wading through swamps would allow; but they were received with such a terrible fire from behind the intrenchments, that only in a few places along the whole line did any of our assaulting columns enter them, and then only to be beaten back. The utmost that could be done was to retain possession of an advanced position more or less close to the enemy's lines. The loss in this assault must have been ten thousand within an hour, and the battle was all over within two hours, with thirteen thousand as the total loss on the Union side to as many hundreds on the Confederate side. Heroic deeds of valor that cannot here be detailed were enacted in every part of the field. Sometimes our lines were advanced and maintained within fifteen yards of the enemy's earthworks, but no valor could accomplish the impossible task of taking them by direct assault; and so Grant gave up the attempt to take Richmond from the north and east. He always regretted that he made this assault at Cold Harbor, for there was no compensating gain to offset the terrible suffering and loss. These were unnecessarily aggravated by Lee's haughty and cruel refusal to let the men lying wounded between the lines be picked up by our unarmed hospital attendants. It took two days of negotiating to satisfy him as to the manner of their removal, and then all but two had died. I can imagine no more harrowing picture of the horrors of war than this of those hundreds of wounded men in mortal agony within sight of easy relief that never came. And yet this was not an uncommon experience in that fearful Wilderness campaign when for thirty days Grant had tried to get between Lee and Richmond and had been thwarted. Through a long and weary month our army had fought by day only to march southward by night and renew the fight on the morrow. But the enemy was always vigilant and marched by parallel but shorter lines; and after the battles of the Wilderness Lee followed the safe policy of fighting only behind intrenchments, or within safe distance from them. Thus this month's campaign was a running siege in which our army took constantly the risk and exposure of the offensive, and so our losses compared with that of the Confederates were as three to one, and our march from the Rapidan to the Chickahominy had left eight thousand mangled corpses in its bloody trail, while the wounded and the missing carried the fearful aggregate up to nearly sixty thousand.

"Ah! never shall the land forget
   How gushed the life-blood of her brave,
Gushed warm with hope and courage yet
   Upon the soil they fought to save."

Having thus given up the attempt to take Richmond from the north and east, Grant decided to change his base to City Point. This changing of base in the face of a vigilant enemy is the most critical of manoeuvres. It had however been safely accomplished many times in the course of this campaign — as from Alexandria to Aquia Creek, then to Port Royal, then to White House — and without the loss of a single wagon, which is very wonderful considering the immense train of four thousand teams that followed the army, and considering also that the supplies were generally drawn from great distances and over narrow roads and through a densely wooded country. The change of base from White House to City Point was accomplished in this wise: Immediately after the Battle of Cold Harbor the Ninth Corps was withdrawn from the extreme right of the line on Totopotomoy Creek and posted on the left of the Fifth Corps near Bethesda Church. Then the Fifth Corps was withdrawn and massed in rear of the centre at Cold Harbor, ready to be moved to any portion of the line if Lee should attack while this march to the left was going on. As Lee did not attack, the next day the Fifth Corps was transferred to the left flank as far as Dispatch station on the York River Railroad. In order more perfectly to cover this movement, Sheridan was sent with two divisions of cavalry to make demonstrations on the north of Richmond and to destroy more effectually the railroad connection between Richmond and the Shenandoah Valley, and Warren with the Fifth Corps and Wilson's division of cavalry was sent across the Chickahominy at Long Bridge to make a demonstration towards Richmond by the route of White Oak Swamp. Both these feints were successful, and led Lee to detach infantry and cavalry both towards the north to meet Sheridan and towards the south by way of Newmarket to meet Warren, who remained in his threatening position while the Second Corps marched across Long Bridge towards the James River by the road to Charles City Court House. The corps of Wright and Burnside reached the same point by an exterior line, crossing the Chickahominy by Jones' Bridge, while the wagon-trains crossed at Cole's Ferry, still further south, and the Eighteenth Corps, under Gen. W. F. Smith, marched to White House, where it took transports and went by water to Bermuda Hundred. Grant crossed the James at Windmill Point on pontoons, Lee crossed near Drury's Bluff, and both started on a race for Petersburg; but Lee as usual won the race by reason of his marching on interior lines and his having a lighter equipment, and this time he had besides a railroad on which he could hurry forward his men. Lee intrenched at once before Petersburg, and was able to make his works so strong that — after several attempts on the part of the Union forces to take them by assault — Grant settled down to a regular siege, and those lines were not pierced till the following spring, a few days before the end of the war, and as the result of the Battle of Five Forks.

While these grander movements of the main army of the east were going on as I have described, two other movements were progressing which were intended to contribute to the general result in Virginia. One was by General Butler with the Eighteenth Corps, under Gen. W. F. Smith, and the Tenth Corps, under Gen. Q. A. Gilmore, and a division of cavalry under General Kautz. With this force Butler started from Fortress Monroe the very day that

Grant crossed the Rapidan, ascended the James River on transports, and effected a landing at Bermuda Hundred on the 6th of May. At that moment he might very easily have taken Petersburg, and so have compelled Lee either to give up Richmond or bring his army at once to its defence; but the opportunity was not improved, and the very next day General Beauregard arrived from the South with sufficient force not only to protect Petersburg but to drive Butler behind his intrenchments and to "bottle him up" in Bermuda Hundred. Here he remained hermetically sealed till Grant uncorked him from his position by his own arrival at City Point with the Army of the Potomac.

The other movement, subsidiary to the grand one against Lee's army, was up the Shenandoah Valley, first by Sigel, who was defeated by Breckenridge at Newmarket, May 15th, and driven back to Cedar Creek; then by Hunter, who on the 5th of June met the Confederates at Piedmont and defeated them, capturing fifteen hundred prisoners. Nothing then prevented him from advancing on Lynchburg, which he reached June 16th; but here he was met by General Early, who had been detached from Lee's army with twelve thousand men. Hunter, being without sufficient ammunition to give battle, retired towards Lexington by way of Kanawha, destroying in his march the Virginia & Tennessee Railroad over an extent of one hundred and thirty-five miles.

The Shenandoah Valley being thus left unprotected. General Early seized the opportunity and made a swift and unobstructed march to Martinsburg, arriving the 3d of July. Sigel, who held post there with a small force, at once retreated across the Potomac at Shepherdstown, and Early pursued his march by way of Williamsport and Hagarstown to Frederick, arriving July 7th.

Here I will leave him to follow less important but more personally interesting events nearer Washington, where, of course, all was excitement and trepidation, as the only force at hand to protect the Capital was a body of foot-artillerists, hundred days' men, and convalescents, — a few thousand in all, and these without organization or discipline, — and a small cavalry force under Colonel Lowell, then stationed at Falls Church, about fifteen miles from Washington.

As soon as it was known in Washington on July 4, 1864, that General Early was approaching Martinsburg, orders were given to our brigade of cavalry to observe the passes of the Blue Ridge, and give notice of any approach of the enemy from that quarter. The order reached us on the afternoon of July 4th, while we were celebrating the anniversary of independence with athletic games and testing the running speed of our horses. Colonel Lowell at once ordered out Major Forbes with one hundred and fifty men, and as the surgeons were fully occupied with hospital duties, they asked me to go along and carry bandages and brandy, to be ready to care for the wounded in case of need. We started out at eight o'clock, and at midnight halted at Ball's Mill on Goose Creek, lying down under arms by the feet of our horses, and holding the bridle-rein in our hands, to be ready to remount at a moment's warning, as we were now in the region infested with guerrillas. We were ordered to be ready to march again at three, so we tried to make ourselves as comfortable as we could and to get a little sleep. I made my bed as usual with two fence rails nearly parallel and a piece of a third rail across them for a pillow, but that night I did not have my usual luck, and spent the greater part of the first hour trying vainly to find the soft side of my sharply angular pillow. I at last got up and searched out another rail with blunter edges. Then as I began to get drowsy a detail from the picket-guard brought in a guerrilla and roused us, and the Major — after getting from him all the information that he could — told our sentry to keep him under guard. Somehow I did not feel sleepy after that, for I thought — what if the sentry should relax his vigilance and the captive should butcher us in our sleep! Still, tired nature would have its way, and I began to fall off again to slumber, when I was awakened by the shaking of my bed. As I looked up, what was my horror to find that the prisoner had coolly seated himself on the bottom of my fence-rail couch, preferring it evidently to a lower seat though it be on the sacred soil of Virginia. At that moment the first sentry was relieved and a fresh guard put on duty, and, as I thus felt a little more secure, I would not disturb my guerrilla-guest, but lay down again, resolved to snatch a little sleep in the last hour of our halt. But my horse had somehow got the idea that we were going to move early, and persisted in nibbling away at the grass about my head, so as not to start without rations, and from time to time, with undue familiarity, he would pull away at my coat, — showing, as some others, little "respect for the cloth," — and so I failed to get even a wink of sleep.

We started again at three o'clock, and as the first rays of the sun began to gild the summits of the Catocktin Hills just before us we dashed into Leesburg, hoping to surprise the Rebels in their sleep; but they were all out with Mosby, and, without our knowing it, were that night only a few miles away, concealed in the woods near Waterford on the opposite slope of the mountain. We spent this day and the next scouting up and down between Aldie and Leesburg, watching the gaps of the Blue Ridge, through which Early might possibly make a descent upon Washington. At half-past five in the afternoon of the second day we stopped on the Aldie pike near Mount Zion Church, to rest and get supper. Just as we were about to remount at half-past six we were startled to hear a rapid firing by our pickets who were posted about a quarter of a mile down the pike, and the Major at once formed us in a double line of battle in the field and across the road, facing the firing. Capt. Goodwin Stone of Newburyport commanded the first rank, and Lieut. C. W. Amory of Boston and Brookline had charge of the second rank. The formation was scarcely completed before a shell (from Mosby's twelve-pounder Napoleon gun) came whizzing over the heads of the men in these two ranks, and exploded right behind them and within a few feet of where I was standing with the Major. It was the first time any of us had been treated to shells of that kind for supper, and both horses and men were very much demoralized, and the solid formation of the line was completely broken, and before it could be re-formed, Mosby and his rangers were upon us, swooping down like Indians, yelling like fiends, discharging their pistols with fearful rapidity, and threatening to completely envelop our little band. The Major tried to meet the emergency by ordering the first and third platoons of the front rank to deploy as skirmishers and so extend our line to the breadth of the attacking force. Captain Stone repeated the order, but the men were either too confused to hear it or too frightened to obey it. At this crisis, when the men were making no organized resistance and firing only at random, — some men indeed in the rear rank firing through the front rank and doing more harm to friends than to foes, — I said, "Major, what shall we do?" He answered, "We will form again — in the edge of the woods," pointing to a grove a few hundred yards to the right of our rear. Upon the word, he drew his sabre and dashed along the front of the broken line amid a shower of bullets, trying to inspire the men with courage, and shouting to them: "Form in the woods! Form in the woods!" And I echoed the shout among the men who were breaking from the ranks under the hot fire, and we all galloped across the field towards the woods. But thus presenting our flank to direct assault, Mosby saw his opportunity and ordered his reserves to charge, and thus the field for us was lost, for before we could reach the shelter of the woods, the whole force of the guerrillas was upon us, turning our retreat into a rout. No words can picture the confusion and horror of that scene, — horses madly leaping in the pangs of death, riders crushed beneath their ruthless feet; then the panic-stricken crowd galloping over their fallen companions, and closely followed by the insolent foe; here and there a rally, as some brave spirit, scorning defeat, inspired a little courage in his companions and turned to face the enemy — but only to die. One of these, and pre-eminent among the rest, was our gallant Major, who turned his horse towards the Rebels, and shouting to his men, "Now rally round your leader," attempted almost alone to stem the assault, and made a sabre thrust at Mosby himself, which would have ended the career of the most famous of the "Partisan Rangers," but for one of his faithful followers — Capt. Thomas W. Richards — throwing himself between and receiving the thrust in the shoulder. Just at that moment Mosby, aiming his six-shooter at Forbes, happily missed, though at short range; but the Major's horse was shot under him, and fell, pinning him to the ground, and he surrendered; but a hotheaded guerrilla dashed up and took aim, and would have shot the prostrate Major but for his faithful bugler, who threw himself between and delayed the fatal shot. Thus the life of the leader of each band was saved by the heroic self-devotion of one of his followers, and the dark horrors of the battlefield were illumined by the brilliant radiance of Christian self-sacrifice. "Greater love hath no man than this, that a man lay down his life for his friends."

 While this scene was enacting in one part of the field, I was trying with Captain Stone, in another part of the field and nearer the woods, to stop the flight of our men and to form them again in a defensive line; but it was impossible.

It was easy for them to persuade themselves that the day was lost, and that the nearest duty was for each to look out for himself. A demoralized cavalryman is far more unmanageable than an infantryman in the same situation; for himself and his horse are both bent on flying, and the rider easily satisfies his conscience by shifting the responsibility of retreat on his unmanageable steed. Still the Captain and I, as we galloped along, tried to reassure the men, and we shouted at the top of our lungs, "Halt! Halt!" but in vain; for every moment they heard more plainly and persuasively some whistling bullet from the pursuing guerrillas screaming, "Skedaddle! Skedaddle!" and so they did at the top of their speed. Panic knows no law either in its origin or growth, and sometimes seizes men before they are aware, and spreads from one to another like wild-fire. I would not have any one think that these flying troopers were all of them cowards. It was the first time for most of them to be under fire. We shall see later the record which they made for themselves in the Shenandoah Valley and at Five Forks, and recognize that no stouter courage and no finer devotion were ever exhibited in the annals of battle. But now the fates seemed against them, and they were flying madly from the foe, who were as madly giving us chase. Captain Stone, however, with great coolness and with splendid pluck turned, and for a moment succeeded in holding a handful of his men, who poured one volley into the ranks of the pursuers, but he himself received a bullet wound and fell forward upon his horse's neck. It was a fatal wound, as the ball lodged in his spine. But though he was partially paralyzed, he had strength enough left to hold on, and for a few moments he galloped along with me; as however the guerrillas were sharply pursuing, and he was conscious that he could do no more in the way of rallying his men, he took the first opportunity of escape, and dashed into a wood-road branching to the left, and was lost under cover of the forest. I never saw him more. I learned long after that his faithful steed carried him — helpless as he was — fourteen miles towards camp, and he was, the next day, picked up by our ambulances and taken to our camp at Fall's Church, where, though every attention that love and skill could suggest was lavished upon him, he died July 18, 1864, gladly giving his fresh young life for a cause which — as he said — was "worthy of all the sacrifice which a mysterious Providence calls upon us to make." His last word to me was, "Save *yourself*, Chaplain." But I was the only officer now left on the road, and I felt that I ought to do what I could for the men who were ahead of me galloping madly away. So I put spurs to my horse and soon caught up with them, and was advising them not to urge their horses to death, when the guerrillas were again upon us, and a volley from them brought one of our men who was in front of me to the ground, and my horse had to leap over him as he fell. Under these circumstances there was not much use advising moderation, though in a long chase it was the surest safety. We had already been pursued for three miles; and since it seemed as if the guerrillas were determined to catch us, I began, as I dashed along behind the rest of our men, to put myself and horse into the lightest running order. I pulled off my gauntlets, unstrapped my overcoat and oatbag from the saddle, and threw them away. In a few moments I came upon one of our men whose horse had been urged beyond his strength and had broken a blood-vessel and in falling had pinned his rider under him. Not recognizing me as I galloped along, he took me for one of the enemy, and shouted, "I surrender." And I heard the shout repeated behind me as the guerrillas came up, and I saw one of them — regardless of the Union soldier's defenceless condition — shoot at him as he passed. Things began to look desperate for *me*. I seemed to be chased by demons. I did not know at the time — what I learned afterwards — that the leader himself of the guerrillas — Colonel Mosby — and a dozen picked men (among them Edmonds and Munson) were pursuing *me* so persistently because they thought I was *"Yankee Davis"* — a native Virginian who knew all the country about and the haunts of the guerrillas, and who usually, though not *this* time, acted as a guide for our troopers in their raids into the enemy's country. Colonel Mosby knew his value to our side and would have given everything if he could catch and hang him. I had been thus singled out on the field and mistaken for him because I was riding a roan-colored horse, and the only other of that stripe in the brigade was "Yankee Davis'." So if I had been caught, the chances would have been — "quick shrift and short rope." But, as luck would have it, my horse was fresh and tough, and I think Mosby's must have been worn and tired. For he was said to have been the best-mounted man in Virginia, and he seldom travelled along main roads, but took a bee-line across fields regardless of walls and fences and ditches. And yet he had not overtaken me in a chase of six miles, and my horse had not been pushed beyond his mettle, and showed no signs of exhaustion. But I did not like the direction in which I was going, although it was towards camp and safety. I felt that I ought not thus to be running away from the field where the wounded needed nursing and the dying needed comfort and companionship. And as I was now alone — the rest of our flying troopers being well ahead and safe from capture — I resolved to turn into the woods at the first favorable opportunity, and if still pursued take to my legs and hide in the thickets. Among the athletes of my Class in College I was accounted the fastest runner, and I felt confident I could thus elude my pursuers without getting much farther away from the field. So, putting my horse to a final spurt to get out of sight of my pursuers if possible, just past a sharp bend in the road I dashed into the woods — lying down flat on my horse's neck, so as not to be caught, as Absalom was, by the branches. But, even thus, the low limbs caught my hat. They spared my head, however, leaving it in its place with only a few scratches; and Mosby lost my trail, and the hunt was up. More than thirty years after this adventure, I went to hear Mosby lecture in Boston in Tremont Temple, and having been introduced to him as the Chaplain of the Second Massachusetts Cavalry, I asked, "Do you remember me.?" He replied, "No, but I remember your horse." It was the uncommon color of my horse that came so near being my undoing. But having thus escaped from the open road I still feared that he might follow and search the woods. So I dismounted and hid my horse in a thicket, and going to a little distance but within sight, threw myself on the ground to listen for the first sound of any approach. Thus waiting about twenty minutes till I felt confident that the guerrillas were out of the way and had returned to the field to gather up their booty and carry off their prisoners, I started forth to find my hat. But it was now nearing eight o'clock, and I soon decided that I could not waste the precious moments in a search that promised to be fruitless in the fast-gathering darkness. So I remounted, and taking the road over which I had just galloped, I *walked* my horse that I might not pass without notice any wounded man. I felt sure that there were at least two wounded men somewhere along the road, for I had seen them fall in the chase. As I felt my way along in the darkness, I kept calling out, "Is any wounded man here?" and soon I heard a low response and found the man whose disabled horse had in falling pinned him to the ground, and who was shot after he surrendered. It was Owen Fox, a private in my regiment who had enlisted from Braintree. He was very weak, and I at once gave him some brandy, but I could not in the darkness bind up his wound. So I hurried to the nearest house and with some trembling knocked at the door. Every farmhouse in this section was a refuge for guerrillas, and every farmer was an *ally* of Mosby, and every farmer's son was with *him* or in the Confederate army. But I felt that suffering humanity would make a strong appeal, and I was not, in this case, mistaken. I induced the farmer to lend me a lantern and a blanket and to assist me in carrying the wounded man to his house. As soon as I saw the wound, I saw also that it was mortal. The cruel shot — fired after he had surrendered and while he begged for mercy — had pierced his body completely through. With wet compresses I was able to stay the flow of blood, and leaving him in charge of the farmer's wife, I sallied forth again into the darkness with lantern and blanket, the farmer accompanying me, and at last found the other soldier whom I had seen fall in the chase, and we carried him into the house. He was a New Yorker, and his wound was severe but not necessarily fatal It was now eleven o'clock, and I was several miles from the battlefield. I wanted very much to get to it, but I feared that I could not find my way in the darkness. So I concluded to watch over these two wounded men through the night, and then in the morning to press on to the care of the wounded on the field. It was not long before it became evident that Fox could not live many hours; for his strength was fast ebbing away through that ghastly wound, spite of my efforts to stanch it. I tried to get from him some message for his wife and little ones at home, but he would not — his agonies were too great; and he kept crying out even with his dying groans, "Chaplain, they shot me after I surrendered." He passed away at three o'clock. Then, having done all I could for the other wounded man, I lay down on the floor by his side — between him and the dead soldier — and snatched an hour's sleep.

I arose again at four with the first rays of dawn, and started out to see if I could find my hat, which I had lost when I dashed into the woods the night before. I could get along in the *evening* without it, as I did, and felt no harm, but I could not go forth without it under a July sun. So, though the chance of finding it seemed very small, I felt that I must make the attempt. But what was my dismay, as I sallied forth, to discover that my horse, which I had hitched just outside the house, had been stolen in the night. Not to speak of the bereavement of losing the faithful steed who had carried me through many perilous journeys and had saved my life in the chase the night before, what could I do without him, left as I was, alone in the enemy's country, and thirty miles from any possible succor? But I could not stop to question; a soldier never expects to know what a day will bring forth, and learns to scorn trifles and to make the best of what *does* come. So, weary as I was after three almost sleepless nights, I set out to *walk* over the road along which I had been pursued, thinking I might perhaps recognize the sharp turn behind which I had escaped into the woods. I bound my handkerchief over my head for protection from the morning damps, and as a safeguard I wound a white bandage about my waist and shoulder, like an officer's sash, in token of my peaceful mission, and as an extemporized flag of truce to keep guerrillas from firing upon me without warning. I soon found the advantage of this precaution, for as I was climbing a rather sharp ascent in the road I was startled with a harsh challenge from behind the crest of the hill — "Halt! Who goes there?" — and I was immediately aware of a seven-shooter carbine levelled at me, and a rough-looking guerrilla behind it with his hand on the trigger. I answered as respectfully as the occasion required, "A chaplain, looking after the wounded." As I had no arms, he allowed me to advance, and, a short parley persuading him of my humane mission and my peaceable intent, he allowed me to go my way with my simple parole of honor that I would give no information that day that would harm Mosby or his men. I soon found my hat in the woods, and immediately returned with fresh courage to my temporary hospital; and after caring for the wounded soldier, I borrowed a spade of the farmer and, selecting an attractive spot under a tree a little distance from the house, I began to dig a grave for the decent burial of the body of Owen Fox, when to my great delight I saw my horse approaching, and I said to myself. The thief has heard that I am a non-combatant and attending to the wounded, and has concluded to give me back my horse. And I laughingly said to the rider as he appreached, "Well! you've got a good horse there." But my laughter was suddenly changed to heaviness as he replied, cocking his pistol and taking aim at me, "You're my prisoner." I at once explained to him my mission, and the laws of war that shielded chaplains and surgeons in the discharge of their duties on the field; but he simply presented the shotted and unanswerable argument of his well-aimed pistol, and I yielded as gracefully as I could to the inevitable. Still I begged a few minutes to finish the burial; but he would not delay one moment, and I had to *leave* the exposed body, and the half-made grave, and the wounded soldier in the house. But I charged the farmer to care for the living and to bury the dead, and begged of him to go to the scene of the battle and with my outfit do what he could for the wounded, and then I started breakfastless on a long and tedious tramp. My captor, having no pity for the dying and no consideration for the dead, of course had no compassion for me. He made me walk in front, he keeping his pistol well in hand. My horse seemed to appreciate the shame of seeing his master driven before him, and hung his head in pity. Hungry and weary as I was, my inhuman driver urged me forward mile after mile beneath the burning sun, under the plea that I must catch up with those who had been captured the night before and so had twelve hours the start of me in their sad journey to prison. He wreaked his spite against the Union cause by singing to me Rebel songs and ballads in praise of the various Confederate leaders. He expected, by bringing in an officer as prisoner, to win favor and promotion with Mosby, and in this he succeeded. For I find, in an account of this fight written and published by one of Mosby*s aids, this entry: "There was one act of heroism of which I cannot refrain from speaking. It was the conduct of young Martin who, having his horse shot under him early in the action, pursued the enemy on foot, and returned to camp mounted on a fine horse with one prisoner." I agree with the record that he *was* "mounted on a fine horse," but if it was "an act of heroism" to *steal* that horse from his hitch outside the house on a dark night, and then to drive before the muzzle of his pistol an unarmed chaplain to prison, then we can only say that among guerrillas honors were easy. This young Martin was a typical freebooter, enjoying the service on account of its adventure and its opportunity to range freely over a country where every house was open to him, and the young ladies doted upon him as one of their fearless defenders. He took pride in stopping at the houses along our way and parading his captured horse and his clerical plunder. Although I was so exhausted before noon that I had to drag myself along very wearily, it was not, however, because I was not in the lightest marching order; for every now and then something I had about me excited my captor's thieving propensities, and he would demand it with a gesture towards his pistol that could not be denied. Thus I was relieved in succession of my watch, my gold pencil, my steel spurs, my knife, my money, my photographs of friends at home, and at last he insisted on swapping hats with me. I had always prided myself on my shrewdness at a bargain, but I must confess that in this case the Virginia chivalry got the better of me. I had now nothing left that this highway robber could take, except a memorial ring enclosing a lock of the hair of my college chum Capt. Thomas B. Fox of the Second Massachusetts Infantry, who was fatally wounded at Gettysburg. No sentiment of reverence for the honored dead kept my captor from coveting this bit of gold, so useless to him, so precious to me **(Note 10)**. But he had not the face to take it himself. About two o'clock he stopped to dine at a farmhouse, and while he was inside, the farmer was instructed to guard me and to take from me the ring. Two small biscuits were allowed me here and they were the only food I tasted that day. Fortunately for me there were many running brooks in the country through which I walked, and at every one of them I stretched myself prone upon the ground and drank my fill. There were yet ten more weary miles to travel before we should reach Rectortown, but I accomplished it by nine o'clock. The latter part of the way I was very much exhausted, and once I felt that I could go no farther. My captor, feeling the importance to himself of getting to camp and a comfortable bed, dismounted and assisted me upon Jaques, my old-time pet, and let me ride — on pain of instant death if I attempted to escape. My horse cheered up with his accustomed rider, and walked with fresh life, but only for a few minutes. Young Martin quickly concluded that the risk of losing his prisoner was too great, and making an excuse that his boots pinched, he made me dismount, and let me cling to the stirrup-strap; and so I dragged myself along the rest of the way.

Reaching Rectortown, I was locked up in a room in Mosby's headquarters, with only the bare floor to sleep upon. But I was tired enough to sleep standing, and I knew nothing till I was awakened in the early morning by Mosby's adjutant, and lectured upon the sin of invading the South and committing sacrilege upon the sacred soil of Virginia. I did not care to argue with him, but asked if I might not see Colonel Mosby, for whom I had some respect, and who, I believed, would send me back to the care of the wounded on the field of our defeat. But the Adjutant, swollen with his little brief authority, haughtily answered: "No! You're a damned abolitionist preacher, and you've got to suffer for it." This honorable impeachment was not exactly deserved; for though I respected the abolitionists individually I did not approve of their radical methods, and of course had never preached their doctrines. Still I hated slavery and was not unwilling to bear my part in expiating, even vicariously, the offence of my native State in *leading* towards its overthrow. The Adjutant then sent me out with one of his men into a field to catch a mule, as I must be mounted to overtake the other prisoners who were now several miles ahead on their way to Lynchburg. These mules in the field were the exhausted animals from the service and put out to pasture to recruit. They were mere skeletons, and to mount one was like riding a rail. Still I was compelled to ride bareback; and a fresh guard, mounted on a fresh horse, took my mule's bridle rein and led him forward as fast as he could be induced to go. This ride of fifteen miles was harder — if possible — than the thirty miles' walk of the previous day. Every added mile made the mule more excruciatingly thin. I was almost cut in twain, and as I came into camp where the other prisoners were resting at noon, the spectacle I presented should have drawn tears, but instead they all set up a great shout of laughter and cheers — of laughter at the irresistibly ludicrous sight of their chaplain balancing himself on his hands lest he should be bisected by the backbone of a broken-down mule, and of cheers because they were so glad to have unexpected companionship in their misery. The prisoners numbered fifty-five —

Major Forbes, Lieutenant Amory, Lieutenant Burns, and myself, with fifty-one privates. I at once took all their names, so that if we were separated and I should first be released, I might inform their friends of their fate. As it was, our families did not know whether we were killed, wounded, or prisoners.

We camped that night in an open field chosen so that a *few* guards only would be required to pace their beats through the night and keep any of us from running away. We had no bed but the ground, no covering but the sky. The *stars* were more companionable than our guards, and for me a few chosen constellations had happy messages of love from dear ones at home, who had promised to think of me every night they could be seen. There was need of this bread of heaven to sustain our hearts, for we had little food for any other hunger. The day before, I had — as I have said — two small biscuits. This day we had a little flour foraged from a mill near by where we camped for the night. We mixed the flour with water from the stream, and baked it over extemporized wood-fires; but it was very tough and, without salt, rather tasteless.

Next morning we started again at four o'clock without breakfast, and walked all day, with a short rest at noon, when our guards fed on the fat of the land, and each of us had a small piece of dry bread. At nine o'clock we went supperless to bed in an open field.

Next day was Sunday, and we started, without breakfast, at half-past three, and got nothing to eat till we reached Orange Court House at noon. Thus I had gone seventy miles in three and a half days, having had only three meals, and they consisted, all told, only of two biscuits, a small cake of flour and water, and a small piece of dry bread. At Orange Court House we were fed on cold corncake and uncooked pork, and then put into box cars and transported to Gordonsville. These cars had been used for carrying cattle and had not been cleaned, nor would the guards let us clean them; and at night we were herded together in a cattle-yard, and had to sleep upon the ground noisome with filth. Here we were kept till noon the next day, when we were huddled again into box cars and had a journey of seven hours to Lynchburg, where we were confined in a large tobacco-warehouse already in use as a prison. It had three floors, covered with dirt and vermin, and six hundred and fifty Union soldiers — of whom two hundred were wounded and without medical attendance, their wounds festering with gangrene from exhaustion and neglect. The upper story was a mere attic, and as it was very shallow and covered with a tin roof, it was too hot to be habitable in the daytime. So, as all the rest of the floor-space was crowded, those who slept on the upper floor at night had no refuge in the daytime but to stand or lie on the ground in the prison-yard under the direct rays of the summer sun. We, the officers, had an extra guard and were shut into a little side-room about twelve feet square and as filthy as the rest. In this, eighteen of us were to try to live we knew not how long.

I gave myself, at once, to efforts to relieve the sick and the wounded. Their first necessity was fitting food but there was no hope of getting that. I thought, however, that I might get a few simple medicines and proper bandages; and so I wrote a note describing the pitiable condition of the wounded, and I was permitted by one of the guards to send it by the hand of a friendly negro to the chief steward of College Hospital, where, a few rods away from our prison, the Confederate wounded and sick were treated. The only answer I received was this verbal message — "You shall have nothing. We must get *rid* of the Yankees in one way or another." All we could then do was to take for bandages pieces of worn-out clothing that the negroes smuggled in for us, and to keep the wounds as clean as we could by frequent washings in water. But without sufficient food and with no stimulants, the mortality was frightful, and the dead-cart trundled heavily with its daily holocaust of victims on the altar of Confederate cruelty. No words can adequately describe the horrors of that prison life. There seemed to be a studied effort to annoy us by withholding the thousand little comforts and conveniences that could easily have been given, and there was evident a deliberate plan to undermine our health by close confinement and insufficient food. The floor upon which we lay was not fit for cattle, and the meat that was served to us, a decent dog would refuse. No letters or comforts from home were allowed us, though our friends were continually sending them under promise of safe delivery by the Confederates. But the keenest torture was provided for us in the deception practised in giving us the news from the armies in the field. It was well understood that if we lost heart and hope, we should be sure to lose health and strength. At this time we were told that Early had captured Washington and that the Confederacy was about to be acknowledged. And yet the truth was that Early was then skedaddling *away* from Washington as fast as he could — barely saving the booty he had gathered in his hasty raid into Maryland.

In Lynchburg one of my messmates, Lieut. C. W. Amory, who had been wounded before he was taken prisoner, began to show signs of failing strength, and his troubles were aggravated by the coarse and unpalatable food. It seemed necessary that he should have white bread in place of the irritating corn meal. The only way to get the white bread was to buy it of the Confederates. But all our money had been filched from us by our captors. I managed, however, to get some by trading off my top-boots for a pair of shoes, and the Officer of the Guard, who was mounted, and to whom cavalry boots would be a great luxury, allowed me two hundred and fifty dollars for the difference. As the market value of shoes in Lynchburg at that time was three hundred and twenty-five dollars, this transaction showed that my boots, which cost me nine dollars in greenbacks, were worth five hundred and seventy-five dollars in Confederate currency. The prices of even the commonest articles were equally magnified in that paradise of inflation. Matches were seventy-five cents a paper. Biscuits were three for one dollar. Pies were two dollars apiece. Onions were three for one dollar. Tomatoes were ten dollars a dozen. Milk was two dollars a quart. Writing-paper was fifty cents a sheet. I was told that board in Lynchburg was thirty dollars a day. So it was essential to use great economy with my two hundred and fifty dollars to make them provide white bread for any length of time for my sick messmate. Our regular daily ration was one corn-cake baked as hard as a stone and weighing about half a pound. With this was frequently served one-third of a pound of pork, which I could never eat, as it was *always* rusty and usually rotten.

We had been in this prison six weary days when Sunday brought round its usual reminder of rest, and home, and church bells, and happy gatherings about public altars and domestic hearths. But this only made their own present misery the more intolerable to *many,* though in my own little mess of *three* it brightened our hopes to think of loved ones at home who would not forget us, and to picture to ourselves their gathering to worship a God of truth who would see that our cause should triumph; and we sung happily together the songs of church and home. It was not long, however, before a delegation from the several floors of the prison came and asked me if I would not hold a service on the middle floor so that *all* might join. Of course, I could not refuse, though I doubted if I would be permitted to speak thus openly my convictions.

At three o'clock we began the service, and I repeated the touching lament of the Hebrew captives, "By the rivers of Babylon, there we sat down, yea, we wept, when we remembered Zion," and after speaking of the comfort of the faith that our God is to be worshipped in every place, in captivity as well as when we breathed the free air of home, I dwelt on the beauty of the Hebrew's devotion, "If I forget thee, O Jerusalem, let my right hand forget her cunning," and emphasized the duty of remembering still our country's cause and serving it by patient endurance of our sufferings — as "*they* sometimes serve who only stand and wait." Then I closed with the expression of my deep conviction that the cause of the Union must triumph. We then all joined in singing "America." The only hymn-book that I could get had the *usual* words, except that the line "Land of the Pilgrims' pride" read "Land of the Southron's pride." But we sang it in the old way, only with a new kindling of devotion.

I trembled a little, after the service, to find that the Officer of the Guard and a number of his Rebel friends had been listening to all I had said; and I was not, therefore, greatly surprised, after I had lain down to sleep that night, to be summoned by the Provost Marshal of the city and to be sent to the guard-house. This was the attic of a small building, up two flights of very narrow stairs that at the bottom opened into a small yard shut in by a very high fence. At the top of the stairs stood an armed guard at the door of the room in which I was confined with fifty others who for various reasons had incurred the Confederate displeasure. The room was very low, and its superficial area was about twelve feet by thirty. At one end there were two small openings where *had* been glass, now fortunately broken. Scarcely enough air filtered through to keep us alive, and what did get in was poisoned for us by a tub of filth at the other end of the room. We begged to be allowed to remove this nuisance, but the guard was under orders not to permit it nor to let any one leave the room. Of course we could not sleep — the air was too noisome and stifling. The next morning — to add to our misery besides heaping upon us the grossest insult — forty tattered and dirty deserters from the Rebel army and a score of felons condemned and awaiting sentence were crowded in with us, and their horrid oaths and vile songs added a fiendish element to our tortures. Full daylight did not perceptibly relieve the gloom of our dungeon; only enough rays crept in to make the darkness visible; but the Southern sun shot its *heat* rays freely through the roof, and made the steaming air more noxious and repulsive. A few pieces of sour bread and rotten pork were passed in on a tray, but we could not eat. Headache and lassitude and the prisoners' scourge — diarrhoea — so reduced our vitality that all appetite was gone, and the stomach revolted from food. The second night — with the added number of prisoners — there was not room for all of us to stretch upon the floor to sleep, and I spent all night sitting with my back to the wall and hugging my knees. A second dreadful day — a little relieved by being allowed to abate the nuisance in our room and to go in turn for a few minutes into the open yard below — and then a third awful night with no relief even of sleep, and the cheerful summons came to start for Georgia. Anything was better than that living death, under whose tortures flesh and heart must soon have failed. I do not believe we could have lived there a week. So we cheerfully took up our journey, although it was to be "away down South in Dixie," and farther removed from home and from the probability of being released.

We were packed in box cars, fifty or more in each, and each man was given a ration of three pieces of hard bread which had to last us till we reached Danville at three o'clock the next morning. In the car in which I was placed, we were so crowded that we could not all lie down at once, and it was arranged that we should take turns at stretching out on the floor; but when it came my turn to lie down, I had not the heart to awaken my messmates, and I stood all night clinging to the iron rod that served as a brace at the end of the car. But this sleepless vigil was ten times more endurable than the guardhouse in Lynchburg, whose horrors have never been exceeded save by those in the Black Hole of Calcutta, and they were endured by the British garrison only for a single night.

In Danville, the abundance of cow-beans fed to us in a half-cooked soup was even more to be dreaded than the starvation rations of corn-meal that had hitherto been doled out to us. The soup, being palatable, checked the pangs of hunger, but the beans in it, being tough and indigestible, made us all sick, and only aggravated our misery. It was in Danville that I witnessed for the first time the reckless shooting of prisoners in their confinement. We were penned up in a large tobacco warehouse, and one of our men, happening to look out of a second-story window, received a shot in the head from the guard below. In this case there was no possible excuse in an attempted escape, as was urged when afterwards shooting became common along the dead-lines of the Georgia prison-pens. Here it was simple recklessness on the part of the Confederates as to the lives of their prisoners.

We were in Danville less than twenty-four hours, and were awakened at two o'clock Sunday morning and packed into filthy cattle-cars as before and transported across the State of North Carolina by way of Greensboro, Lexington, and Salisbury. In this trip there were only thirty-one in our car, and by spooning we could all lie down, though to turn over necessitated a concerted movement. I could not sleep, as I was near the side door of the car, which was partly opened and admitted a great draft and with it great quantities of cinders from the wood-burning locomotive, and I several times found my clothing on fire. As that clothing was scanty at the best, it was rather essential to keep awake to protect it.

We reached Charlotte two hours after midnight, when we were turned out into an open field, where, huddled together like sheep, it required but three or four sentinels to guard us while we slept on the ground till morning. Then we each received five hardbreads and one-third of a pound of pork for two days' rations, and were packed into the cars again and given a free ride through South Carolina. It did not help to appease our hunger to have the beauty and chivalry of the State appear as they did at every prominent station, with elegant and abundant refreshment for the guards of our train, but not one morsel for the starving prisoners. Yes! *one* morsel did get into the mouth of one of our men who, more desperate than the rest, snatched it from the bountiful supply that was being passed to our guard, but the rest of us had too much self-respect to resort to robbery, even though we felt that our rations were unreasonably slender. Our oppressors had not the justification of poverty, — in their supplies of *corn* at least, — for as we travelled through their country we could see that the fields, which before the war had yielded their rich tribute to King Cotton, now waved with abundant corn. But they were planted for other mouths than ours, and their tasselled tops only waved in mockery as we passed.

After stopping a few hours at Columbia, we started again, and travelled a day and a night till by way of Orangeburg we reached Augusta, where we encamped in an open field for ten hours. Here some of us clubbed together and invested in a watermelon, but we were so weak and exhausted that it made us all sick.

Then another day and night in box cars, tightly shut on one side, and the guard standing in the crack of the door on the other side, so that the air was stifling and the heat very oppressive, and we arrived at Macon. It had taken us six weary days and nights from Lynchburg over very rough roads that compelled a very slow and jerky motion of the trains and caused great discomfort to us their live freight. Sleep under such circumstances was always difficult, and never unbroken for any length of time. A few, driven to desperation, escaped from the train, but most of us thought it wiser to endure our confinement than to take the risk of hundreds of miles of walking through the enemy's country beset with watchful sentries and savage bloodhounds.

At Macon all *officers* were taken from the train, while the privates were carried on farther, about sixty miles, to Andersonville. Henceforth I lost sight and trace of them, and I have never learned whether any of those from my regiment survived the hardships of that frightful prison. Our own fate was only a shade more endurable. At Macon we were herded in a large pen, Camp Oglethorpe, with about sixteen hundred other officers, surrounded by a strong stockade fifteen feet high. This enclosed space was about sufficient to give each prisoner room enough for a grave. Indeed it looked much like a cemetery; for, in order to escape from the terribly intense heat of the midsummer sun, many had dug narrow trenches in which to lie down and so get a little shade. On the outside of our prison-stockade, and supported by brackets, was a shelf upon which the armed sentinels paced back and forth, their heads and shoulders just visible to us. Around the inside of the enclosure and about five yards from the stockade, was a rude railing which constituted the dead-line, beyond which the prisoners were forbidden to pass, on penalty of death. The only water for washing and drinking was furnished by a small and rather stagnant brook running through the enclosure. Of course, it received all the drainage from the prison-pen, and generally it was so sluggish that any washing in it seemed to vitiate the water up as well as down stream. It was *never* fit to drink, but I always got the supply for our mess in the very early morning before it had been disturbed, and when it was less offensive than later in the day. Our rations here were nominally issued every three days, and consisted of three pints of corn meal ("cob meal," the prisoners called it), one-half a pound of pork, one gill of beans, with a little vinegar and salt. But there were very vexatious delays in giving out the rations, so that out of this very scanty supply we lost two days' rations in every ten. Even this faint remnant of nutrition must be still farther reduced by extracting from each pint of corn meal the cob that was ground with it. At least this was our explanation of its coarseness; for when we sifted it for cooking, the quantity was reduced a full third. So far as the ration of pork was concerned, I never could eat it, but found it useful in greasing the pan in which I cooked the corn cake. Our mess-pan — which was more precious to us than gold, and which I carried with me nine hundred miles through the Confederacy — was the iron part of a broken shovel which I had picked up in Virginia. It was very convenient to hold over the fire while the cake was baking. I will confess here for the encouragement of young housekeepers that with all the care I could give I burned several cakes, but I trust they will not have to suffer for it as I did and go hungry until the next rations were issued.

Even though we were now in the heart of Georgia, we were not considered secure from Sherman's cavalry raiders. For they were only eighty miles away at Atlanta, and one day we heard the carbines of his cavalry coming to attempt our release. They were driven back, however, and their commander. General Stoneman, and a number of his officers were captured and sent to our prison. Imagine the keenness of our anxious expectation as we heard the shots of our would-be deliverers, and think of the sinking of our hearts when their efforts were frustrated by defeat.

These fresh prisoners smuggled in a little coffee concealed in their clothing. Our mess secured a teaspoonful, and though it was a small quantity to be divided among three, yet in the depressed state of our vitality it was like a rich cordial, and sent a delightful exhilaration through our frames. But it was only temporary, and resembled more the hectic flush of consumption; for it was followed by a fearful depression, which seemed as if it must shortly end in death.

It was at this time that the Inspector General of Confederate Prisons reported officially from Georgia to Jefferson Davis in these words: "My duty requires me respectfully to recommend that you put in command here some one who has some feeling of humanity and consideration for the comfort of the prisoners, some one — at least — who will not advocate deliberately and in cold blood — as the Commandant General Winder has done — the propriety of leaving them in their present condition until their number has been sufficiently reduced by death to make their present accommodations ample, and who will not consider it a matter of self-laudation and boasting that he has never been inside the stockade — a place the horrors of which it is difficult to describe, and which is a disgrace to civilization." This was said, by Col. T. D. Chandler, particularly of Andersonville, but every word of it was true of Macon, and there could be no more damning record than this which has been written by a friend and high officer of the Confederate government.

And yet this appeal of the Inspector General was utterly disregarded, and these cruelties, unabated, made the darkest blot on the escutcheon of Southern chivalry. President Lincoln could hardly persuade himself that the facts were as reported, and said with unutterable sadness: "Let us not believe them till we must. Let us hope, at least, that the crime of murdering prisoners by exposure and starvation may not be fastened on any of our people." Such crimes could only be possible to men debased by long years of familiarity with the cruelties of human slavery, and though we must forgive and should look in pity more than anger on those who were dehumanized by the institution under which they were nourished, we cannot forget the fearful price paid for its extinction not only in blood on the fields of battle but in exposure and starvation within the prison-pens of the South. Heaven save us from harboring again in our social or political system any such cruel injustice.

We remained in the prison at Macon two weeks, exposed each day to the festering rays of the Southern sun, with no variation in the monotony of suffering, except that we were several times hastily loaded upon the cars in anticipation of our attempted release by Sherman. But each time we were sadly and sullenly driven back to our pen. In this exhausting life men soon became living skeletons, and the monotony of frequent death was never relieved. What wounds and exposure and sickness did not do, starvation accomplished, and the line of stretcher-bearers to the grave never ceased to pass the gates.

At last the order came to leave this graveyard of loyal legions — a place which might fitly be called "the devil's acre" — and to get upon the cars again and be transported to Charleston to be put under the fire of the Union guns. This was a last desperate move planned and executed by Maj. Gen. Samuel Jones, then in command at Charleston. He notified the Union Commander, Major General Foster, saying, "I have confined six hundred of your officers in a part of the city which has been for many months exposed day and night to the fire of your guns." Of course the object was to compel our government to exchange prisoners with the Confederates, a thing which Secretary Stanton was constantly urging President Lincoln not to do, on the plea of military necessity, as it would be exchanging well-fed Confederate prisoners for ill-fed Union prisoners, and would be *immediately* reinforcing the Rebel armies, while it would be two months at least before any Union prisoner would be strong enough to rejoin his command, and it was doubtful if half of those released would *ever* be able to fight again. Lincoln frequently followed his heart's impulses, and asked the Commissioners of Exchange to get particular persons released; but Stanton was inflexible in his adherence to his principle that in dealing with this question, *something* should not be given for *nothing*, that a hundred thousand soldiers ready for battle *against* the Union should not be given for a hundred thousand debilitated Union men ready only for the hospital or the grave.

Our part in this arrangement was not the pleasantest. Yet when I knew that we were leaving Macon to be made to endure the last touch of cruelty by a more dangerous exposure to death, I was really glad of the change; for I felt that I could keep up a livelier courage if I were within hearing of the guns that were hammering away at the gates of the Confederacy. And it was so. When after two days and nights in the cars, packed so closely that we could not lie down to sleep, we came within sound of the Swamp Angel, and heard its defiant thundering at the bulwarks of oppression, we felt a thrill of satisfaction; for it spoke most convincingly of the steadfast determination of the Union forces to batter down all the defences of disloyalty. This gun was called the "Swamp Angel" because its foundation was built in a swamp by first driving long stout piles into the mud and then laying above them a great mound of sand-bags. It was a 200-pound Parrott and could throw its great shells into the city of Charleston, four or five miles away.

In Charleston we were confined in a large brick penitentiary, called a "workhouse." We were first registered and then searched. On being asked how much money I had, I named a sum just within the permitted limit, though I *had,* concealed about my person, quite a little more. I considered it absolutely essential to the life of my sick messmate that we should have money enough to buy wheat bread for him in place of the corn bread which was issued to us. I felt justified in deceiving those who were treating us so inhumanly. I told the truth, but not the whole truth. I believe it was the nearest I ever came to telling a lie, and if Heaven is not willing to forgive it, I am willing to suffer the consequences.

In our prison there were about three hundred officers, of all grades from major generals down to lieutenants, scattered through the cells and corridors. There were four stories to the building, and as an awful reminder of our dangerous exposure there was a gaping chasm down through the roof and every floor, marking the track along which a shot from one of our batteries had forced its way to the cellar. The Swamp Angel battery was full five miles away, and yet every fifteen minutes of my three weeks' stay in this prison, a 200-pound shell from its belching jaws burst over our heads. About every fourth shell was loaded with Greek fire, and at night by its lighted fuse we could see it rise like a star from the horizon and ascend almost to mid-heaven, then gracefully curve downwards and burst and drop its liquid flame upon the roofs of the city. Then in a few moments we would hear the bells of the fire-alarm, and we could often see the negro fire-brigade rush past our bars to try to stay the conflagration that almost inevitably ensued. The fate that awaited us if our prison caught fire was too horrible to imagine, and yet the danger was constantly before our eyes. At first the mere sound of the bursting shells — Gilmore's reports, as they were called — made us give a startled jump; but soon we got used to it, and their terrific explosion passed almost unnoticed in the daytime, and at night scarcely disturbed our dreams. Indeed I became so wonted to this fierce marking of the quarter-hours, that one night when the explosion was, for once only, intermitted, I was wakened by the unexpected silence, showing that we keep a kind of semi-consciousness even in sleep, and illustrating how we can rest amid the most disturbing sounds if they are expected. In the evening twilights we watched the bombarding with almost the heedlessness of danger that one would look upon an exhibition of fireworks, and when we gave ourselves to sleep it was with a serene satisfaction in Uncle Sam's sleepless activity, —

"For the rockets' red glare, the bombs bursting in air,
Gave proof through the night that our flag was still there."

About this time General Foster, who had command of the Federal forces about Charleston, sent the following communication to the Rebel authorities: "I must protest against your placing defenceless prisoners of war in a position exposed to constant bombardment. It is an indefensible act of cruelty. The city of Charleston is a depot for military supplies. It contains not only arsenals but foundries and factories for the manufacture of munitions of war. Its wharves and the banks of the river on both sides are lined with hostile batteries. In its shipyards armed ironclads have been built and are building. To destroy these means of continuing the war is our plain object and duty.

You seek to defeat this effort by means not known to honorable warfare — by placing unarmed and defenceless prisoners under fire. I have requested the President to place in my custody an equal number of prisoners of like grade, to be kept by me in positions exposed to the fire of your guns — so long as you continue a like course."

This request of General Foster's was granted and had the desired effect, but too late to save *me* from the exposures of the bombardment.

Jefferson Davis in a published letter, under date of January 27, 1876, tries to throw from himself the suspicion of connivance in these and like cruelties to prisoners, by rehearsing his efforts to have them exchanged. Of course he wanted them exchanged. It was at this stage of the war that he said in a speech at Macon: "We must have more men. Two-thirds of our enrolled soldiers are absent and *most* of them without leave." Davis knew very well that a general exchange of prisoners would double Lee's army in ten days, while it would be at least sixty days before Grant's army would be materially strengthened from this source. Some of *us* also understood this, and when permission came to us in Charleston to choose delegates who would be allowed to go to Washington in order to urge on Lincoln the *exchange* of prisoners that Davis wanted, although the majority favored the scheme, and I was offered my freedom and asked to go as a delegate, I could not conscientiously encourage a plan that I felt sure would not only not succeed, but if successful would damage — perhaps irreparably — the Union cause.

These sentiments I expressed when, on August 28th, at the request of General Stoneman, the ranking officer among the prisoners, I held a Sunday service in presence of all. A more novel situation for a service of religion can hardly be imagined. For an auditorium there was the filthy, noisome, prison-yard which the Confederates would not themselves, nor let *us,* keep clean. For seats there were the ground and the open windows of the prison. For a roof there was only the fragment of sky above our heads. For an altar I had a long box standing on end, and for a platform a tub, bottom upwards. To mark the time, the booming of the Swamp Angel battery told off the quarter-hours like the strokes of the clock of fate. In place of organ accompaniment there was the terrific bursting of the death-dealing shells. For an audience I had the sick and wounded prisoners, the heavy-hearted captives, the despairing victims of a remorseless cruelty. I tried to inspire a fresh confidence and hope by expressing my conviction that even then and there we could serve our country and our God, that though we would infinitely prefer to be with our brothers at the front facing the perils of the fight. Providence had evidently marked out for us as our only present duty to patiently endure the sufferings of our imprisonment, and that each one of us was thus doing more to bring the war to an end than we could by adding our enfeebled strength to the armies of the Union, since our wasted vitality would be so much overbalanced by the well-fed recruits to the Southern cause.

It may be said here that this question of duty was not wholly a new one; two hundred and forty-nine years before the Christian era, it was decided in the same way by the Roman Regulus, who advised against an exchange because, though he himself was suffering the horrors of a harsh imprisonment, he felt that his country would be defrauded by the giving up of the Carthaginian prisoners strong and well, and receiving back its own captured soldiers worn out and useless for any immediate service.

It is perhaps needless to add that no delegation went from our prison. Yet in spite of the cheering convictions that some of us cherished that we were even then serving our country, and that by our stripes her wounds might be healed, many — almost by a necessity of their physical suffering — lost all heart and hope. Those who were not already actuated by the highest motives and supported by the strongest principles, withered like broken reeds. The assured sympathy of their fellows and the known love of dear ones at home were only an added torture to them. They lost their faith in the country for which before they had been willing to risk their lives. They lost their faith in God, and forgot his ever-present care. They became sour and sad. And the sadness was the more fearful as it was really the premonition of death. For in that loathsome prison to give up cheerfulness was to give up health, to give up hope was to give up life. I have seen strong men bow themselves under this dreadful shadow of hopelessness, and one especially I recall — a young captain from Michigan — whose despair made an old man of him in a single week, changing his hair from dark to gray, and in three weeks he was an utter wreck.

As September approached we had at times quite cold nights, and, as our slender clothing was now getting worn and thin, we suffered a good deal, and our government, mindful of our needs, had a thousand changes of clothing which it tried to get to us, but the prison authorities would not allow us a thread of warmer covering.

Our drinking-water at Charleston was worse, if possible, than at Macon. Our prison-yard was very small; and well and vault were so near together that the water was thoroughly poisoned with filth and refuse, "making us by inch-meal a disease." This trial was aggravated for us by the sight of a public pump only a few rods away from our prison-gate. One day I spoke through the bars to the outside guard and told him that one of my messmates was sick and, I feared, dying; and would he be so kind as to fill for me a small pail with pure water from the pump? He sullenly got it for me, but demanded fifty cents. I paid it, for it might save a life.

Our food in Charleston was better in quality and variety than in any other prison. Our rations were three pieces of hard bread a day, or, in place of it, a pint of corn meal. To these were sometimes added a little rice and molasses. Once or twice, fresh meat was issued to us, but *pork* was the almost invariable accompaniment of our ration. How to cook the rice and meal was often a puzzle, as no firewood was given to us. I supplied this lack by tearing off pieces of wood from the partitions of the cells. I became quite skilful in boiling rice in a tin pail which I had bought. I learned to so graduate the quantities of water and rice that, after twenty minutes of boiling, each grain would be left soft and yet retain its form and individuality, which in countries where it is the staple food is the test of success in cooking. In the latter part of August *both* my messmates, Forbes and Amory, were sick, and the money of our common purse was used to buy for them white bread, which with flour at one hundred dollars a barrel had to be used sparingly. I fed them for ten days on dry toast and beef-tea varied with boiled rice and sometimes a little coffee and a boiled egg. When my patients improved sufficiently, I celebrated by giving them a surprise — breakfast of griddle-cakes, which I made of corn-meal, rice, and flour, in equal parts, with one beaten egg. I ought perhaps to call them shovel-cakes from the utensil — the iron part of a shovel — on which they were cooked. Spite of the rough utensil the cakes were pronounced very good.

At last the day of my deliverance was at hand, and the order came that all chaplains and surgeons should be released. It was very hard for me to leave my two messmates in exile — especially as one of them was slowly wasting away under the hardships of his prison life. But I resolved to do everything in my power to get him released, and, as the only thing I could do for him *then*, I stripped myself of all my underclothing and left it for him, as he needed its extra warmth. I also, as a parting service, boiled in a great iron kettle all the clothing of my messmates in order to clean it and to kill out the vermin that it was our daily practice to skirmish for with thumb and forefinger. I then scrubbed the pieces, using a window-blind for a washboard. My washing water was so brackish that it curdled the soap, and I have since learned that I reversed the proper order of washing-day by boiling before rinsing. But I rubbed away on my thirteen pieces for two hours under a boiling sun, my two messmates meanwhile waiting in their cell in the only garments the Confederates could not steal.

As the time came to say farewell we sang once more the hymn that we had sung together almost every day of our imprisonment, and that had done a great deal to keep up our spirits, — the hymn called "God of the fatherless" to the tune "Day slowly declining" by Von Weber, — and then with many a warm embrace, not without tears, we parted.

We were put upon a Confederate steamer, and as it approached Fort Sumter we were ordered to sit on the deck with our backs to the bulwarks, that we might not see its battered condition. But while the guard's face was turned I caught with great satisfaction a glimpse of its completely demolished wall on the side towards our guns, and it was to me an augury of our sure triumph. Only two weeks before, the commander of Fort Sumter, Capt. John C. Mitchell, was killed by a shell from Morris Island, and now the force within the fortress was commanded by Captain Huguenin, only twenty-six years of age. No wonder it was said of the Confederate government that to support its tottering pillars it robbed the cradle and the grave.

At the mouth of the harbor we were met by a United States steamer and transferred to its protection. How can I tell my joy when at last I stood once more under the old flag? How beautiful to my long-exiled vision was every waving of its folds! I have seen the gorgeous sunsets of the Bay of Naples, where the golden haze of the atmosphere unites in one indistinguishable glory the flaming mirror of the sea and the flaming canopy of the clouds, and I have felt the finer fascination of the moon at midnight on the canals at Venice as they mirrored its silvery splendor in the magnificent framework of cathedrals and palaces, but the loveliest vision upon which my eyes ever lingered was the flag of my country as it gleamed at the masthead of the steamer that waited in the distance to receive me out of prison. Its stars calmed my anxious spirit, as they told of the steadfast endurance of the nation's life, and every streaming fold wrapped me in its sure protection.

"Its hues were ail of heaven —
  The red of sunset's dye,
The whiteness of the moonlit cloud,
  The blue of morning's sky."

Under its starry benediction it seemed as if every faculty of my being was distended with the fulness of delight. It was so splendid to breathe again the free and unpolluted air! So glorious to see the whole expanse of the heavens! So heart-quickening to feel that I was again among friends! For days it all seemed like a splendid dream, and every moment I felt a quivering fear lest the vision should break and I should awake to find myself again in Rebel hands.

I made it my first duty to acquaint General Saxton — then in command of the besieging forces — with the fact that the shells from his batteries were bursting directly over the prison in which our men were confined, and that a slight change of direction would relieve them; and he at once ordered the change to be made. I then sought by every possible means, and at last successfully, to send money and clothing back to my messmates. But I was most pleased to be able to interest the Commissioner of Exchange in my sick companion, Lieut. C. W. Amory, and to get him released in time to save his life, though with a broken constitution that never was made whole **(Note 11)**.

Then I sought for the headquarters of the Provost Marshal to report to him; and as I inquired the way of a negro, he seemed struck with my pitiful appearance. Perhaps he saw by my sallow complexion and sunken cheeks that I was just from prison. At least he was led in some way to suspect that I *had* seen better days, and he said, "Massa! you wants better hat. Dat hat good enub for nigger" — and with that he took off his own and insisted upon swapping, as my Rebel captor had before, only the cavalier urged his suit with a loaded pistol, the negro with a full heart. The former I would not refuse for the sake of my life, the latter I *could* not for the sake of humanity; and

I have kept the hat these fifty-three years as a memento of those deep chords of sympathy that, beneath all disguises of ignorance, misery, and degradation, thrill to the touch of human need.

I soon found the Provost Marshal and tried to get my back pay. But he required some proof of my identity, and I knew no one at Hilton Head. So I took the boat for Morris Island, where was stationed the Fifty-fifth Massachusetts Infantry, many of whose officers (among them Col. A. S. Hartwell, H. C. 1858; Lieut. Col. C. B. Fox; and Capt. C. S. Soule, H. C. 1862) were my personal friends. On the boat were many Sanitary Commission supplies and I recall the eagerness with which I dipped into a bottle of delicious lemon jelly; but, like all other things that I ate in my then weakened condition, it palled upon my stomach. I did *not,* however, lose the sense of delightful satisfaction in tasting of something that was provided, not, as for two months past, by the grudging hands of the enemies of the Union, but by the loving devotion of friends at home. At Morris Island I got a full outfit of government clothing, and after a bath in the ocean made a glad offering to Neptune of my prison garb. As soon as I got my pay I took a steamer for New York, and reached my home in Dorchester, September 17th. *There* and in the delightful companionship and refreshment of the island of Naushon, with Mr. and Mrs. John M. Forbes, I spent nearly four weeks trying to recuperate my strength sufficiently to return to the seat of war, which I did October 13th, but I never recovered the vigor which was so severely drained by the exposures and starvation of Southern prisons. I was more fortunate, however, than most in that it was possible for me to return to the front and take an active part in the closing scenes of the war; and to these scenes we will now direct our attention.

The Campaign of the Shenandoah Valley may be dated from the 7th of July, when General Early made his appearance at Frederick, threatening at the same time both Baltimore and Washington. On the 8th he advanced towards Washington. Gen. Lew Wallace, then in command at Baltimore, hurried forward with a small extemporized force of raw troops, and, though sure of defeat, he with the help of Rickett's division of the Sixth Corps blocked Early's path for a few hours at the Monocacy and so accomplished more than is sometimes gained by a victory. Early pushed on as far as Fort Stevens, one of the outermost defences of the Federal Capital. He might then have dashed into the city and have gained the empty glory of holding It a few hours. But he delayed, and made a reconnaissance with a view to attacking on the next morning; but that very afternoon — thanks to the energy of John Garrett, president of the Baltimore & Ohio Railroad — the rest of the Sixth Corps under General Wright, who had by the foresight of General Grant been detached for this purpose from the Army of the Potomac, arrived, and was soon followed by the Nineteenth Corps under General Emory, and when General Early, on the morning of July 12th, found the defences of the city well manned, his eagerness to attack was at once changed into anxiety for his own safety, and he began to retire towards the Potomac. As It happened, the Second

Massachusetts Cavalry Regiment was then the only one available for pursuit, and It started Immediately to harass the Rebel retreat. Our advance battalion led by Colonel Crowninshleld came upon Early's extreme rear guard — composed of Jackson's cavalry brigade — just beyond Rockville, and charged upon them gallantly. The Rebel Gen. B. T. Johnson says, "The Second Massachusetts Cavalry hung upon our rear and made It very uncomfortable for us generally." The discrepancy of numbers suggests the likeness of a small fly hanging upon the flanks of a large horse, but even thus a good deal of annoyance can be given. The Rebels were soon provoked to turn, resolved to *wipe out* our regiment. They drew up two of their best brigades — one of them known as the Maryland Line — and made a heavy counter-charge, overpowering our advance squadron, and hurling it back upon the rest of the regiment just as it was being led by Colonel Lowell through the centre of the town. There was not time for the Colonel even to turn his column, and it was overwhelmed by the numbers and fury of the onset, and forced back in confusion towards Washington. But Colonel Lowell was not the man thus to give up the day. At the very first favorable position, with a splendid audacity, and a voice sure to be obeyed, he shouted the order — "Halt! Dismount!" The men in a moment sprang from their saddles, in another moment they were in line, and in the next moment poured such a hot volley into the pursuing column that it recoiled in confusion. Then with his small force — just before routed and in full retreat — he held the ground against four impetuous charges till the enemy were forced to retire without dislodging him from his position. This was a marked instance of his genius for command. Other leaders might give the proper orders, but not one in a thousand could thus make them instantly obeyed. Colonel Lowell's control over his men on this occasion has not inaptly been compared to Sheridan's more famous rally of his broken columns at the battle of Cedar Creek.

General Early now hurriedly crossed the Potomac at Edwards Ferry, taking with him an immense train of horses, cattle, hogs, and sheep, and wagons loaded with grain, groceries, and clothing, and, besides, several hundred thousand dollars which he had levied upon the citizens of Hagarstown and Frederick. But although he had made such desperate efforts, marching his men four hundred and ninety-seven miles in twenty-five days, he had utterly failed in the main object of his expedition, which was to so threaten Washington that Grant would be compelled to relax his hold on Petersburg. The same tactics had succeeded several times before when other generals were in command of the Union forces, but Grant had that dogged persistency that he could not be shaken from the grip he had taken in the throat of the Confederacy; he simply detached one corps that he could afford to spare, and so kept Lee in his intrenchments.

Shortly after this abortive attempt to frighten Grant, Early made another on July 25th, and this time penetrated into Pennsylvania as far as Chambersburg, and laid the town in ashes. This sent great consternation through the

North, and determined Grant to clear the Shenandoah Valley. This beautiful valley was an immense granary for feeding the armies about Richmond, and its high bastions of hills on either side furnished an easy and safe path for an invading army to penetrate into Pennsylvania or Maryland or to threaten Washington. Twice before, Lee had thus used it, — in the Maryland invasion of 1862 which ended in the Battle of Antietam, and in the Pennsylvania invasion of 1863 which ended in the Battle of Gettysburg. At all times it had been necessary to employ a considerable army to guard the Valley and its passes, and now Grant determined to clear it out and lay it waste, that it might no longer distract his attention from the main army of Virginia in its intrenchments before Petersburg. To this end he consolidated the four geographical districts — West Virginia, Washington, the Susquehanna, and the Middle Department — into one, styled the Middle Military Division, and put it under the command of Maj. Gen. Philip H. Sheridan on the 7th of August, 1864. Both Lincoln and Stanton thought him too young for such a responsibility, as he was then only thirty-three; but Grant saw in him just the leader he wanted, and General Hunter, with pure and patriotic disinterestedness, withdrew from the chief command of the department in order to give Sheridan free play. Taking only three days to get his troops in hand, Sheridan began on the 10th of August to move up the Valley, Colonel Lowell's provisional brigade leading the advance. This brigade had been hastily made up of the Second Massachusetts Cavalry and detached portions of nearly every other cavalry regiment in the service swept together from the dismounted camps near Washington. And yet in less than two weeks Colonel Lowell moulded this heterogeneous mass into a well-disciplined troop and held it in the position of greatest peril, opening the way for Sheridan's advance. Lowell's brigade was under fire every day for the next month, on the 11th of August driving the enemy pell-mell through Winchester and along the Valley pike southward as far as Fisher's Hill, and on the 16th guarding Sheridan's rear as he retired down the Valley again to Halltown and Harpers Ferry. This retrograde movement was determined upon by Sheridan when he learned by his scouts that Lee had detached from his army about Richmond two divisions of infantry under General Anderson, two brigades of cavalry under Fitzhugh Lee, and twenty pieces of artillery, and that they were hurrying to Early's assistance by the way of Front Royal. Sheridan sent Merritt's division to watch their movements, and it was attacked by Kershaw's division of infantry and Fitzhugh Lee's division of cavalry, but it handsomely repelled the attack, Devin's brigade taking the honors — two battle-flags and three hundred prisoners. Devin won his star in this fight.

On the 26th of August, Lowell led his two regiments of troopers in an attack on the advance line of the enemy's infantry and charged up to a rail fence behind which they were intrenched, and while he and a few of his men held them there — he himself actually whacking their levelled muskets with his sabre — the rest tore down the barrier, and then they all charged again, and captured one colonel, three captains, five lieutenants, and seventy-four men. Such a noble scorn of danger and death inspired our men with a perfect obedience, and a courage that quailed at nothing. Lowell's daring and skill in this attack made a deep impression on Sheridan, and as an expression of his confidence he took the brigade of Regular Cavalry — First, Second, Fifth, and Sixth — and Artillery that had been raised for General Buford, and which was called the finest in the service, and put with it the Second Massachusetts Cavalry Volunteers, and, designating them all as the Reserve Brigade, gave the command of it to Colonel Lowell. While the main army remained near Harpers Ferry several weeks with no important movement, the cavalry was employed every day in harassing the enemy, its opponents being principally infantry. Sheridan wanted to "educate them" — as he said — "to attack infantry lines."

On the 16th of September, Grant visited General Sheridan at Charlestown and brought with him a plan for a campaign against Early. But he found Sheridan so much master of the situation, and so confident of what he could do if he only had the authority, that without even taking the plan out of his pocket he said simply, "Go *in*." And Sheridan did go in, and only three days after initiated the famous Battle of Winchester by moving against Early, who was posted with about 26,000 infantry and 4,000 cavalry on the opposite side of the Opequan. Sheridan had learned through a loyal lady in Winchester that Lee had recalled Anderson with Kershaw's division of infantry and twelve pieces of artillery; and besides he learned through his own scouts that Early had just then divided his forces to try again one of those raids on the Baltimore & Ohio Railroad which had so often created a panic in Washington and among the Union generals. But Sheridan was made of other stuff, and saw his opportunity, and at once determined on assault.

On the morning of September 19th the movement began. The plan was for Wilson's division of cavalry to force the passage of the Opequan where it is crossed by the Berryville pike and open the way for Sheridan with the Sixth and Nineteenth Corps and General Crook's command to move upon General Ramseur's two divisions that had been left to guard that crossing while Early with three divisions under Gordon, Rodes, and Breckenridge were off on a raid into Maryland. But Early on reaching Martinsburg had learned on the morning of the 18th of September of Grant's visit to Sheridan, and, suspecting a movement, immediately started back, and by night his advance divisions under Breckenridge and Rodes had reached Stephenson's station while Gordon's division had reached Bunker's hill. Fitzhugh Lee's cavalry, near Breckenridge, guarded the left of Early's extended line, and Lomax's cavalry guarded its right adjoining Ramseur's infantry. Although Wilson's cavalry started betimes and carried the Berryville crossing at dawn, yet the gorge fronting Ramseur's position was so narrow that Sheridan found it impossible to march his army through and get into position before ten o'clock, and by that time Early by forced marches with the divisions of Gordon and Rodes had come within supporting distance of Ramseur's left and so made Sheridan's task harder than he expected, and compelled him to give up the plan which he had first entertained of putting Crook's command south of Winchester to cut off Early's retreat. Instead, he held it in reserve to be used at the crisis of the battle. His line was formed with the Sixth Corps at the left supported by Wilson's cavalry, and the Nineteenth Corps holding the centre and right. The enemy's resistance was very stubborn, and about noon, in an impetuous charge upon the right of the Sixth and the left of the Nineteenth Corps, they pressed back our line and threatened to break it, using for this purpose the divisions of Gordon and Rodes, who had just arrived for the succor of Ramseur. But Sheridan, nothing disconcerted, holding Russell's brigade of the Sixth Corps in hand, waited till the enemy's advance opened their flank to attack, and then unleashed Russell's men upon them, and drove them back in confusion and re-formed his own line. Sheridan now delayed the final blow till he should hear of the success of Merritt on his extreme right, and he did not have to wait long. Merritt had started from Summit Point at three o'clock in the morning and with Devin's and Lowell's brigades had carried Seaver's ford a little before sunrise. The enemy's infantry was posted on the opposite side of the Opequan at that crossing, and their fire was simply terrific; but Colonel Lowell, having the advance, threw over dismounted men as skirmishers, and closely supported them with the Fifth United States and Second Massachusetts Cavalry, and soon by a brilliant charge gained the crest and captured a body of infantry. General Merritt then connected Lowell's line on the right with that of General Custer who had gallantly carried Locke's ford three-quarters of a mile below, and on the left with the line of General Devin, and the three brigades now advanced together, with orders to press the enemy vigorously. Soon the line of Breckenridge's infantry was seen in the edge of the woods, protected by rail barricades. Major Smith of the Second United States Cavalry says, "It seemed rash, yes! foolhardy to charge a line of infantry so well posted; but we did, Colonel Lowell leading the charge with the Second United States Cavalry in column of squadrons." Nothing could exceed the brilliant heroism of this assault. "Cannon in front of them volleyed and thundered." The long-range muskets of the infantry on either side poured upon them showers of leaden hail, which could not be returned by the cavalry's short-range carbines till Lowell had brought his men within a few hundred yards of the barricade. Then, forming his column in line, Lowell led them up to the very muzzles of the enemy's guns. But no human power could take such a position against such fearful odds. Many fell never to rise again. But the moral effect of this charge was equal to a victory, as was plainly to be seen in the subsequent events of the day, and Sheridan's object was gained in keeping Breckenridge, whose attention was thus taken up with our cavalry, from sending his corps to reinforce Early near Winchester.

Merritt's cavalry now formed a junction with General Averell, who had moved his division of cavalry up the valley from Darksville and had taken a position near Stephenson's station, ready to form with Merritt a turning column at the crisis of the battle. This time came about four o'clock when Sheridan pressed the enemy in front with the Sixth and Nineteenth Corps, and let loose Crook and Merritt upon his left flank, routing his whole command and driving them in great confusion through Winchester and for miles up the pike, and capturing twenty-five hundred prisoners, five pieces of artillery, and nine battle-flags. In this final charge, the open country on either side of the Valley pike offered an opportunity such as seldom came during the war for an attack with a broad front of mounted troops. The Confederate line at this point constituted the left flank of Early's army and was held by Breckenridge's infantry and Fitzhugh Lee's cavalry. General Torbert's line was all cavalry and was made up of five brigades abreast, Lowell's Reserve Brigade on the left, connecting with Crook's infantry, then on the right in succession Devin's and Custer's brigades, and still to the right Averell's division. These all moved by brigade front with single regiments in column of squadrons. One continuous and heavy line of skirmishers covered the advance, using only the carbine, while the line of brigades as they advanced across the open country, the bands playing the national airs, presented in the sunlight one moving mass of glittering sabres intermingled here and there with bright-colored banners and battle-flags. It was one of the most inspiring and imposing scenes of martial grandeur ever witnessed.

Little effective opposition to this charge was made till near Winchester. Here the Reserve Brigade was exposed, without cover, to the severe fire of a well-posted line of the enemy's infantry. Yet — though now reduced to about six hundred men — it rode up fearlessly within five hundred yards of the enemy, who had on their left a two-gun battery resting on an old earthwork. The order was given to charge the line and get the guns. The brigade was in column of squadrons, the Second United States Cavalry in front. General Rodenbough of this regiment says: "At the sound of the bugle we took the trot, then the gallop, then the charge. As we neared their line we were welcomed by a fearful musketry fire, which threw the leading squadron into temporary confusion. But the instant shouts of the officers — 'Forward! Forward!' brought a response of deafening cheers, and without breaking front the column leaped a blind ditch and we were face to face with the enemy. They seemed to stand a moment, as in awe of the heroism of the brigade, and then broke at once into complete rout, our men sabring them as they vainly sought safety in flight. I" — continues the General — "I was taken prisoner just in front of the second line of the enemy's works, my horse being shot under me. As my captors surrounded me, they cried — 'Great God! what a fearful charge! what brigade was that?' The confusion, disorder, and actual rout produced by the successive charges of Merritt's cavalry division would appear incredible did I not actually witness them."

In this superb charge, Colonel Lowell achieved new distinction. In the confusion of the onset, at one time he found himself with only Captain Rodenbough and four men face to face with one of Breckenridge's guns whose first discharge killed Billy — Major Forbes' favorite horse, which Lowell was then riding— tore off the Captain's arm, and wounded two of the men. Yet the Colonel would not retreat, but quietly mounted the first horse that came up and soon the gun was his. "A little more spunk," said Lowell, not even then satisfied that enough had been done, "and we should have had all their colors." A member of Sheridan's staff answered, "A little more *go,* and you would have been in Richmond."

Sheridan telegraphed from the field to Washington, "We have just sent the enemy whirling through Winchester, and shall be after them to-morrow." Custer says, "This was the first decisive field victory won in the war, and was made decisive only by the proper use of cavalry." In this battle Sheridan again justified his boast to Meade in the Wilderness that he could accomplish something worth while if Meade would let him have the cavalry in mass instead of in small detachments. The news of this victory in the North gave unbounded joy, and it relieved Maryland and Pennsylvania from any further fears of invasion. Of course the cost of the victory was great, the Union loss amounting to about 4,500 in killed, wounded, and missing.

General Early did not pause in his flight till he reached Strasburg, and took up a very strong position reaching across the Valley from Fisher's Hill to North Mountain. Here Sheridan assaulted his front with the Sixth and Nineteenth Corps, and again, as at Winchester, used Crook's infantry as a turning column, and sent it under cover of the woods along the slopes of North Mountain upon the Rebel left and rear, and so routed Early again and in greater disorder than before, and his army fled, leaving behind sixteen pieces of artillery and several hundred prisoners. Sheridan still kept up the pursuit through Woodstock, Mount Jackson, Harrisonburg, and Staunton, till Early took refuge in the gaps of the Blue Ridge, and then, not caring to subsist his army so far from its base of supplies, Sheridan slowly retired down the Valley, spreading his cavalry so that they swept in all useful supplies, and leaving the country waste. At first the Rebel cavalry kept at a respectful distance; but later they took courage from the arrival of General Rosser with a fresh brigade from Richmond, and began to annoy Sheridan's rear guard. On the third day Sheridan determined to halt his army and teach Rosser a lesson that would check his presumption. So he ordered General Torbert to engage the enemy next morning and added in his brusque way, "Either whip him or get whipped."

At daylight on the 9th, Torbert advanced with Custer on the back road facing the Rebel General Rosser — who had been heralded as the savior of the Valley — and with Merritt on the pike facing the Rebel Generals Lomax and Johnson. Colonel Lowell and the Second Massachusetts had the advance along the pike, and as the Colonel led forward his dismounted skirmish line, his men crouched behind trees, rocks, and fences, or anything that promised shelter. But the Colonel *rode* fearlessly along the line, and, though he was thus a conspicuous target for the enemy's musketry, he seemed not to mind it, and coolly directed every movement of his men. The enemy soon grew tremulous at this bold advance, and Lowell, seeing it, ordered the bugles to sound the charge, upon which the Confederate lines broke in utter confusion, and a hot pursuit was made for twenty-six miles as far as Mount Jackson, where they found protection behind Early's infantry.

Custer had a like success on the back road about three miles away and parallel to the pike. He chased Rosser and his "Laurel Brigade" — as it was called — beyond Columbia Furnaces. The captures of the day were eleven pieces of artillery and three hundred prisoners. The engagement was afterwards known as the Woodstock races, and in many respects was the most brilliant cavalry fight of the war. All the early part of it was along "Toms Brook" which gives the official name to the battle, and Sheridan witnessed the charges and counter-charges from the summit of Round Top Mountain. The honors of the day were about even between Lowell and Custer, but a friend and follower of Custer could not say too much in praise of what he styles "the steady old Reserve Brigade — the regulars under Lowell." The only volunteer regiment in this brigade was the Second Massachusetts, and equalled in discipline and effectiveness the best of the regulars.

Sheridan now retired to Strasburg and took position on the north bank of Cedar Creek. He reports that in this movement from Staunton to Strasburg, in carrying out his orders to destroy everything that could subsist the Rebel army, he burned over two thousand barns filled with wheat and hay, and over seventy mills filled with flour, and drove before the army more than five thousand head of cattle and three thousand sheep. Such is the desolation that lies in the track of war.

But spite of this desolation and his frequent defeats, General Early soon returned down the Valley with reinforcements of infantry and cavalry, and took position behind the intrenchments at Fishers Hill. Sheridan had not believed that Early would again take the offensive in full force, and so had detached the Sixth Corps and started it towards Ashby's Gap to join the Army of the Potomac. But a bold demonstration by Early on the 13th of October against our lines led Sheridan to recall the Sixth Corps, and it took position on the right of the Nineteenth Corps, which was holding the north bank of Cedar Creek west of the Valley pike. General Crook held the position east of the Valley pike as far as the junction of Cedar Creek and the Shenandoah River.

At this time Sheridan was summoned by the Secretary of War to Washington for a consultation, and started October 16th and proceeded as far as Front Royal with the whole cavalry corps, meaning to send it through Chester Gap to Charlottesville to destroy the Virginia Central Railroad, while he himself went through Manassas Gap with a small escort to Washington. But at Front Royal a courier from General Wright brought the following despatch which had been read by our scouts from the Rebel signal flag on Three Top Mountain: "To Lieutenant General Early. Be ready to move as soon as my forces join you, and we will crush Sheridan. Longstreet, Lieutenant General." Sheridan, suspecting it was a ruse, could not believe it, yet to be on the safe side ordered back all the cavalry to General Wright with the word to "look well to his ground and be prepared." Sheridan then hastened to Washington, arriving about eight o'clock on the morning of the 17th. Wishing to get back to his army as soon as possible, he asked Secretary Stanton to have a special train ready at twelve o'clock to take him to Martinsburg, which he reached that evening, and the next morning started with his escort for Winchester, twenty-eight miles away, and reached there about three o'clock. Hearing that all was quiet at the front, he took a quiet night's sleep, while Early was planning to surprise his command and was moving his troops all night from the intrenchments at Fishers Hill, going himself with Kershaw's division through Strasburg towards Roberts' ford, sending Wharton's division by the Valley pike to where it crosses Cedar Creek, and directing General Gordon to lead his division with those of Ramseur and Pegram along the road leading to Front Royal till it reached Bowman's ford then to cross the Shenandoah and under cover of the darkness strike the rear of Crook's division, which formed the left of the Union line. This left of the infantry, for some unaccountable reason, was exposed without cavalry protection, although Sheridan had specially directed General Wright to close in Powell's division, which was then at Front Royal. Had this been done the disaster of the early morning would have been averted. As it was, Gordon's Confederate column, covered by the fog as well as the darkness, rushed in upon Crook's sleeping camp, capturing eighteen pieces of artillery and more than a thousand prisoners, thus crushing completely the whole left of our army. At the same time, with this rolling up of our left flank, Early made a direct attack upon our centre, where the Nineteenth Corps was posted, and this also gave way in the confusion. There remained then of the infantry only the Sixth Corps not yet engaged, and that, as often before, stood like a tower of defence, as did also the cavalry on the right. It happened that morning that in prompt obedience to orders of the previous evening to make a reconnaissance as soon as the fog broke, Colonel Lowell caused reveille to be sounded at four o'clock, and at 4.30, spite of the fog, his brigade was in motion. Crossing the creek, he found the enemy in force directly in his front, and began to skirmish sharply with him, and held his position till 7.30, when he was relieved by Infantry. His punctuality in making this reconnaissance and then the tenacity with which he held his position saved our right from surprise and disaster possibly as great as that which befell the other end of the line. This stand of the cavalry and of the Sixth Corps saved the army from utter rout, and allowed the broken divisions of the other corps to form again a few miles back in and about the village of Middletown. Here again, before a strong line of defense could be made, Early assaulted our left and threw it again Into confusion, and the whole Union line fell back about a mile and a half beyond Middletown to a position just secured by our cavalry, which had at about nine o'clock been moved, with Getty's division of Infantry, from the right to the left of our line, and which now opposed an Impregnable front to the advance of the enemy beyond the town. Here, too, Colonel Lowell held our advance line, and while the infantry were retreating in confusion, dismounted his little band of cavalry and pressed forward under a heavy fire to a strong position behind a stone wall, and held it spite of the enemy's repeated and desperate attempts to dislodge him with heavy assaulting columns and with artillery. Here, as usual, he attended in person to the disposition of his men, riding backwards and forwards along the line of skirmishers, a conspicuous mark for the sharpshooters on the roofs of the village of Middletown. Colonel Lowell not only held this line, but led his men in several gallant charges. In the third charge he had his horse shot under him, — which was the thirteenth horse he had thus lost in this campaign of three months, — and here he received his first wound — from a spent ball; but he would not leave the field, although the force of the blow against his lungs caused internal hemorrhage which was likely to prove fatal. Torbert's cavalry line was thus held with dogged persistency, and with a gallantry that has never been surpassed, till the broken ranks of the infantry were re-formed several miles to the right and rear. The Commanding General says in his official report, "The cavalry held their ground like men of steel; officers and men seemed to know and to feel that the safety of the army depended in no small degree on their holding their position, and they can never receive too much credit for the manner in which they did their duty." General Wright had given the order to retreat to Winchester, and our six or seven thousand cavalry kept the roads open by checking the enemy and repulsing charge after charge hurled upon them by an army of nearly twenty thousand infantry flushed with the morning's victory. The only supporting infantry on this front line with Custer and Merritt was Getty's division of the Sixth Corps, and it seemed, as the morning wore away, as if their united gallantry could not much longer stem the tide of the Rebel advance which rolled in heavier and still heavier waves towards our position. But just at this juncture, while every prospect was so threatening, unexpected succor was at hand, not in the shape of large reinforcements, but in the form of one man.

"Up from the south at break of day,
Bringing to Winchester fresh dismay,
The affrighted air with a shudder bore.
Like a herald in haste to the Chieftain's door,
The terrible grumbling and rumble and roar,
Telling the battle was on once more
    And Sheridan twenty miles away."

Sheridan, who had reached Winchester the night before on his way back from Washington, had slept in the Logan House, then occupied by Col. Oliver

Edwards, commanding the brigade posted there. Before six o'clock in the morning, the picket-guards nearest Cedar Creek had heard the guns and reported it to Sheridan. He thought it was all right and took it to be the sound of General Grover's guns feeling the position of the enemy. A little later report came that the firing was continuous. Upon that he arose and ordered breakfast and that the horses be saddled. Still he did not even suspect any ill-fortune, and started off leisurely at about nine o'clock for the front, mounted on Rienzi, his coal-black steed. He had not gone half a mile before he came to a crest just beyond Mill Creek, and there broke upon his astonished gaze the appalling spectacle of frightened herds of runaways, and broken and demoralized regiments and wagon trains, all skedaddling towards Winchester. Sheridan at once sent word to Colonel Edwards to stretch out his brigade across the country back of Mill Creek and stop all fugitives and to park the wagon trains north of Winchester. Then he detached most of his staff and escort, telling them to stretch out in as long a line as they could and drive in the stragglers; and then he took Maj. George A. Forsythe and Capt. Joseph O'Keefe of his staff and twenty men from his escort and with them galloped up the pike towards the front, himself shouting to the crowds he met: "Face the other way, boys! Face the other way! It's all right! We're going to lick them out of their boots! We'll be back in our camps to-night!" At times Sheridan had to leave the pike, it was so blocked by retreating wagons and flying troopers. But whether along the pike or through the fields, his presence infused new courage, and even the skedaddlers began to turn about and to cheer. His black steed was a magnificent animal, sixteen hands high, five years old, full of fire, and seemingly infused with Sheridan's spirit. Every one recognized the horse and knew that he was carrying his master to the front and to victory, if victory were possible. Every one resolved to follow such a gallant leader even to death, and whereas before all were discouraged and many were covered with conscious disgrace, now all were jubilant with hope and intent on wiping out the morning's record of demoralization and retreat. Pretty soon the shouts of the newly inspirited stragglers reached the anxious line of battle, where the heroic cavalry, with General Getty's division of the Sixth Corps, were making a stand against the enemy. When Sheridan and his foam-flecked charger wheeled from the pike and galloped down in front of these serried ranks, they at once broke into the most tumultuous enthusiasm. General Torbert, not satisfied with the formal soldier's salute, rode up exultingly and exclaimed, "My God, I'm glad you've come!" Such scenes as his coming produced and such emotions as it awakened are not realized once in a century. There was immediately a revulsion of feeling from doubt and almost despair to faith and almost triumph. As Sheridan rode along, whole lines of battle-flags rose up as if out of the ground. "General, we're glad to see you," was the welcome frequently shouted to him. "Well, I'm glad to be here," was the cheerful response. One group of officers — deserted by their men — had clung to their regimental colors, and waved them in the air to greet him.

Sheridan recognized one of these as Colonel Hayes, afterwards President of the United States, and then as always utterly faithful. For two hours, from ten o'clock till noon, Sheridan rode up and down inspiring the men and re-forming their broken lines. He ordered General Wright to bring up the Nineteenth Corps and the two divisions of the Sixth Corps that had been halted in the rear of Getty's division, and to form them on Getty's right. Then he sent Major Forsythe to Getty's left to inquire of Lowell if he could hold on there, and Lowell gallantly said he could. Sheridan then sent Custer's division back to the right flank, ordered General Wright to take his old command the Sixth Corps, and, accepting the suggestion of Major Forsythe, rode along in front of the whole of the new line of battle, that his men who had only heard of his return might see him and take new courage. It was about noon when Sheridan observed that Early was getting ready to assault, and to meet it he strengthened the Nineteenth Corps with Getty's division of the Sixth. Early's victorious army moved forward in magnificent order, utterly confident that they would now wipe out the remnant of Sheridan's troopers; but they did not measure rightly the reinforcement that one man had brought. With this fresh alliance the Nineteenth Corps bravely stood its ground and repelled Early's impetuous assault. Sheridan now rested his men and waited till the fugitives of the morning could get back to the front. Meanwhile, fearing that Early might also be reinforced by the expected arrival of Longstreet, Sheridan ordered Merritt to take a small body of his cavalry on the extreme left of the line, and charge upon an exposed battery of the enemy and capture some prisoners. This was at once done and the prisoners assured Sheridan that Longstreet had not arrived. The way was now clear for Sheridan to take the offensive. At about half-past three the order was given for an advance along the whole line of infantry, the cavalry being held back for a charge after the Rebel line should be broken. It happened, however, that the left of the Rebel infantry line overlapped our right, so that for a few moments disaster threatened in the shape of this flanking column of the enemy. But in this Sheridan saw his opportunity and ordered a charge against the open angle of the Rebel line. "That order," says Colonel Whitaker, "was the death-knell of the Confederacy." It cut off the flanking column, while a general advance swept back the rest of the Rebel army.

> "Now in the tumult of the battle's van
> Shone Fortune's darling, mounted Sheridan.
> Rapid to plan and peerless In the fight,
> He plucked Fame's chaplet as by sovereign right;
> Emerged triumphant from a wild retreat,
> And blazoned victory's colors on defeat."

Sheridan was everywhere. He had mounted a fresh horse just before this final charge, and galloped from one place to another wherever his men needed stimulus or direction. While he was watching the charge of the infantry that cut off the flanking column of the enemy, Custer, who was about to charge and gobble them up, delayed a moment to dash up to Sheridan and hug and kiss him in his rapturous delight. Sheridan says, "I forgave him the delay, as he at once swooped down upon the enemy and took many of them prisoners." The rout was utter. Not only did Sheridan regain the camps from which Wright had been driven in the morning, but he captured the lost guns, and besides all of Early's camp equipage, caissons, artillery, ambulances, and thousands of prisoners, among them Major General Ramseur.

Thus in thirty days, by three brilliant victories, Sheridan had almost annihilated an army of twenty thousand men, having captured thirteen thousand prisoners, a hundred pieces of artillery, and thousands of small arms. In the last battle he had by his personal magnetism and all-conquering energy turned back the overwhelming flood of defeat and lifted the whole army on a refluent wave of victory that engulfed the shattered remnants of Confederate resistance, and raised the trembling hopes of patriots throughout the land to a vantage-ground of confidence and security.

"Hurrah! hurrah, for Sheridan!
Hurrah! hurrah, for horse and man!
And when their statues are placed on high
Under the dome of the Union sky —
The American soldier's Temple of Fame —
There, with the glorious General's name,
Be it said in letters both bold and bright, —
Here is the steed that saved the day
By carrying Sheridan into the fight
From Winchester, twenty miles away."

This ride of twenty miles is a poetic license for about twelve miles — the distance between Winchester and Middletown. But Rienzi carried his master more than twenty miles that day in his mad galloping back and forth along the line of battle and in the personal visits to various sections of the command. Rienzi was christened "Winchester" after this battle. He carried his master through ninety engagements, but though he survived the war thirteen years and reached the age of nineteen, Sheridan never mounted him after the war, but committed him to a faithful groom with directions to surround him with all the care and comfort that his faithful services deserved. The noble animal died in 1878 and Sheridan told me that he had ordered his skin to be stuffed for preservation.

Of course this victory of Cedar Creek and Sheridan's wonderful personal achievement of re-creating an army out of a broken, dispirited mob of flying fugitives electrified the whole country. General Grant ordered a salute of one hundred guns. President Lincoln wrote to Sheridan a letter of thanks, and in a few days he was promoted to the major generalship made vacant by General McClellan's resignation. This victory closed the campaign of the Shenandoah.

Let us now turn aside for a few moments to meditate upon something of the price that must be paid for such a victory, and to speak of one only among the many who gladly gave their lives that we might enjoy ours in peace; one, however, whom none could surpass in the preciousness of the voluntary offering or the completeness of the heroic sacrifice.

I have already told how my gallant Colonel, in this month's campaign in which he was every day under fire, seemed to bear a charmed life, having had thirteen horses shot under him — one of them struck in seven places — and his clothes riddled with bullets. He had not himself been touched till the third charge in the Battle of Cedar Creek, when a spent ball for a moment took away his breath and afterwards left him voiceless. General Torbert urged that he be taken from the field. But Lowell whispered: "No! It is only my poor lung. I have not lost a drop of blood yet. I want to lead in the final charge." So a little parapet of earth was thrown up to shield him from the bullets of the enemy, and he lay there motionless for two hours, having exacted a promise that he should be told when the charge was ordered. This came about three o'clock. Then, though too weak to mount his horse without assistance, he said, "I am well, now," and allowed his faithful men to lift him into the saddle, and he rode to the front amid the cheers of his troops. Then his strength rose with the occasion, and though the death flush was on his cheeks he rode firm and erect as ever, and though he could only whisper his commands to his aids, all saw by the pointing of his sword that he meant Forward to victory or death.

Just as they were in the thickest of the fight, Lowell — still leading on his men — was pierced by a bullet from shoulder to shoulder and fell into the arms of his aids. Yet even thus he would not check the vigor of the assault, but allowed himself to be carried forward in the track of his rapidly advancing brigade till he reached the village of Middletown and saw that the battle was won. Then he lay down upon his death-couch as calmly as to a night's repose, and, though partially paralyzed, he remained for a time conscious, and gave minute directions about the business of his command, dictated some private messages of affection, and twice directed his surgeon to leave him to look to the wounds of other officers and of some wounded prisoners whose cries of pain he overheard, and then quietly and contendedly went to sleep and waked no more on earth.

I need hardly say that Charles Russell Lowell was the most brilliant officer I ever met. He was one of an eminently patriotic family, of whose members eight, under thirty years of age, were killed in the war. Life opened for him with exceptional promise. In his college class he was pre-eminent above all rivalry, yet, while marvellously apt in the direction of literature and philosophy, his stronger bent was towards the mechanic arts and practical life, and in this direction he easily and quickly attained high responsibilities, and the breaking out of the war found him managing the Mount Savage Iron Works at Cumberland, Md., but on hearing of the attack in Baltimore upon the Massachusetts troops he dropped his work instantly and took the first train for that city. There he decided to offer his services to the government, and, as railway and telegraphic communication with Washington was cut off, he set out on foot, and by devious paths and shrewd stratagems made his way to the Capital, reaching it only two days after the attack in Baltimore. With keen, prophetic eye he saw that the struggle must be a long one, but with wise judgment and characteristic modesty he chose to learn the art of war from the beginning, and applied for the lowest office in the Regular Artillery. While waiting for his commission, he busied himself with organizing means for the care of Massachusetts troops and for gathering military stores, and found time to scout beyond our lines and inspect the preparations of the Confederates.

I think it was a good fortune that turned Lowell to the cavalry service. I can hardly imagine his being satisfied with any less venturous command. He was a born cavalier, high-spirited, quick, flashing his plans into instant orders and pushing his orders to prompt execution; yet, with all this dashing, chivalrous spirit, he was always calm and self-possessed. Some one in authority, seeing these traits, offered Lowell a captaincy in the Sixth United States Cavalry, and he instantly accepted, and soon made himself such a master of the tactics that his Colonel regarded him as "the best officer appointed from civil life, that he had ever known."

His regiment fought under General Stoneman through the Peninsula Campaign, and Lowell was constantly in action, and for distinguished service at Williamsburg and Slatersville was nominated for the brevet of Major. His brother James, referring to the affair at Slatersville, writes: "Charley was charging, and came upon a man who was aiming a double-barrelled carbine at him. Charley called out to him, 'Drop that!' and he lowered it enough to blow to pieces Charley's coat, which was strapped on his saddle behind him." His fellow-officers recall many such instances of the irresistible power of his commands.

On the 10th of July, 1862, Lowell was ordered to the staff of General McClellan, where he remained till November, achieving marvels of energetic devotion to perilous duties, and seeming to bear a charmed life in the hottest actions. In the Battle of Antietam he enacted the miracle that Sheridan repeated on a larger scale at Cedar Creek. Sent with orders to General Sedgwick's division, Lowell found it recoiling in confusion under a hot fire. He at once set himself to check the retreat. He seemed to fly from point to point, his eyes flashed fire, his voice shouted defiance, his sword pointed towards the foe, his horse caught his master's spirit, and they two, as one, put new courage into the flying troops, and so checked the rout which threatened disaster to the right of the Union line. Shortly after, Lowell's horse, pierced with seven bullets, fell under him, while a rifle ball passed through his own coat and another broke the scabbard of his sabre. In recognition of his gallantry in this battle, Lowell was intrusted by General McClellan with the office of bearing to Washington, and presenting to President Lincoln, the thirty-nine standards captured in that campaign.

In November, 1862, Lowell was ordered to report to Governor Andrew, and was commissioned as Colonel to organize the Second Massachusetts Cavalry, and was engaged in this service till May, 1863, when he took his regiment to Washington, and was assigned to the command of all the cavalry of the department, with headquarters at Vienna. Here was spent the winter of 1863-64, in the very unpleasant but very responsible service of guarding a line of thirty or forty miles of the exposed front of Washington from the incursions of Mosby's Partisan Rangers and other unorganized guerrillas. To do this effectually, Lowell made constant counter-incursions — some of which I have already detailed — into the surrounding country, and broke up the haunts of the guerrillas wherever his scouts discovered their camps. Though the country was necessarily unfamiliar to him, and almost every engagement was with unknown forces in their own chosen positions, he never hesitated to dash right up to their intrenchments, and by the boldness of his onset seldom failed to strike confusion into their ranks. The movements of Lowell's thought were like flashes of lightning. He took in the situation by a seemingly intuitive discernment. He knew not only how he should deploy his own troops, but how the enemy would deploy theirs. Orderlies would dash up to him in the thick of battle from various sections of his extended lines, reporting an advance here and a retreat there, and his frequent response was: "I know it. I have given the necessary orders." In the wild whirl of battle his eyes glistened with flashing thought, and his face shone with keen intelligence. Horse and rider seemed one being, instinct with bounding life. As Shakespeare says of the Norman Horseman: "This gallant had witchcraft in his riding. He grew into his seat, and to such wondrous doing brought his horse as he had been incorpsed with the brave beast." Lowell had travelled much on horseback in pursuit of health, and in Algiers his equestrian skill had excited the admiration even of the Arabs. He had a closely knit, wiry frame and a light delicate figure, and his intense vitality and exhaustless energy achieved what seemed impossible to others. I have followed him wearily sixty miles in a day and he has come in at night seemingly as fresh as when he set out. He was easily the first in anything to which he laid his hand. He had studied carefully the military systems of the European nations and so was a master in the science, as well as the art, of war. His Reserve Brigade was admitted by many to have been the most superb body of cavalry in the service. He could lead them anywhere. With the regulars of his command it may have been the prompt obedience of discipline, but with the Massachusetts Volunteers it was the perfect obedience of trust. He was always ready to expose himself when the occasion demanded, and once with his own sabre he cut down a Rebel who stretched out his hand to seize a color.

Yet, with all this overflowing energy of action, Lowell had a deep repose of thought, and delighted in nothing more than in philosophic contemplations.

How often on the march, in scouts after guerrillas, and even in the near presence of danger, have I listened with wonder to his subtle speculations in metaphysics, and his keen insights in social science! He kept always his refined taste and his scholarly habit. He dwelt always in the purest atmosphere of high thought and delicate feeling. Few men have combined so many talents of such brilliant lustre. Few men sacrificed so much that was fascinating In liberal studies and refined activities, for the rough pursuits of war. The soldier's life had for him no attractions other than the fulfilment of a high ideal of service to his country and humanity. Yet no one surpassed him in soldierly qualities, whether in prompt movement and fearless daring or in tactical skill and readiness for emergencies.

> "I do not think a braver gentleman,
> More active valiant or more valiant young,
> More daring or more bold, hath ever lived
> To grace the world with noble deeds."

His virtues were not without distinguished recognition. A high official said, "I do not think there was any officer in all the army so much beloved as Lowell." "We all shed tears," said Custer, "when we knew we had lost him. It is the greatest loss the Cavalry Corps ever suffered." Major General Torbert — the leader of the Cavalry Corps — says in his official report: "Thus the service lost one of the most gallant and accomplished soldiers. He was the beau-ideal of a cavalry officer, and his memory will never die in the command." Said General Sheridan: "I do not think there was a quality I could have added to Lowell. He was the perfection of a man and a soldier. I could have been better spared."

His commission as Brigadier General of Volunteers — "for gallant and meritorious services at the Battles of Winchester and Fishers Hill" — was signed only the day before his death, too late for him to wear the honors that he had earned so well; but he wears the immortal glory of his heroic devotion, and he can well spare the sounding titles that echo our mortal praise.

> "He in warm life-blood wrote a nobler verse"
> Than poets sing, or tuneful lips rehearse;
> "Lived battle-odes whose lines were steel and fire,
> And shaped in squadron-strophes his desire."

In a niche at the west end of Memorial Hall in Cambridge is a marble bust of Charles Russell Lowell sculptured by Daniel C. French. Upon the bracket that supports the bust is carved in wood the descriptive motto — "A knightly soldier, bravely dead," and upon the panel beneath the bracket is cast in bronze the inscription — "Charles Russell Lowell, born at Boston, Jan. 2, 1835, graduated at Cambridge, 1854, Captain 6th U. S. Cavalry May 14, 1861, Colonel 2nd Mass. Cavalry, April 15, 1863, Brigadier General of Volunteers,

Oct. 19, 1864. After thirteen horses had been shot under him, he received his mortal wound at Cedar Creek Oct. 19, 1864, and never wore his 'star.'"

Beneath these words is the shield of the University Seal with its motto "Veritas," and then follow these lines from James Russell Lowell's Commemoration Ode: —

"He followed Truth and found her
With danger's sweetness round her;
So loved her that he died for her."

At the bottom — with the date 1885 — are these words: "This bust is the gift of his fellow-officers of the 2nd Mass. Cav., and other admirers of his brilliant leadership, his heroic gallantry and his self-sacrificing Patriotism."

James Russell Lowell wrote me under date July 16, 1885: "I looked at the bust of my nephew on Commencement Day and thought it very good. The pose of the head struck me as particularly characteristic. What touched me most of all in looking at it, however, was the pious and affectionate impulse that had wrought with you in having it done.

"As to the verses for the inscription, I have been hoping that some would come to me that I should like better than those you have chosen. But as yet I am like an augur gaping in vain for the birds that will not come. Perhaps some fine day I may be luckier."

That day never came, and Lowell suggested that I take some lines from Emerson, but it seemed to me more fitting to take them from that Ode which is the finest literary monument not only of the poet himself but of the heroes whom he commemorated.

Because Lowell's star as Brigadier General did not reach him before his death, I suggested to the sculptor to put it in a spray of laurel under his bust, and there it may be seen in **Note 12**.

After the Battle of Cedar Creek nothing of importance occurred in the Valley till November 27th, when General Merritt, the commander of our division of cavalry, received this order from General Sheridan: "You are hereby directed to take your command beyond the Blue Ridge by way of Ashby's and Snicker's Gaps, and operate against the guerrillas in the region between Rectortown and the Potomac, and between the Blue Ridge and the Bull Run mountains. This section has been the hotbed of lawless bands who have from time to time depredated upon small parties on the line of our communications, and upon safeguards left at houses. Their real object is plunder and highway robbery. To clear the country of these parties, you will consume and destroy all forage and subsistence, burn all barns and mills and their contents, and drive off all the live-stock. This order must be literally executed, bearing in mind, however, that no dwellings are to be burned, and that no personal violence be offered the citizens. The responsibility for this destruction must rest with the authorities at Richmond who have acknowledged the legitimacy of guerrilla bands."

This necessity of destruction is one of the many dark phases of war. As we descended the eastern slope of the Blue Ridge, nothing could be more beautiful than that garden of Virginia flanked on the further side by the Bull Run mountains. It is one of the richest counties in cattle and pasturage, with splendid stock in horses and sheep. It fell to the lot of our brigade to go through the beautiful Valley between Loudon Heights and the Short Hills, and flankers were sent out so as to sweep the whole Valley. Some idea of the general destruction may be formed when I relate that in one day two regiments of our brigade burned more than one hundred and fifty barns, a thousand stacks of hay, and six flour-mills, besides driving off fifty horses and three hundred head of cattle. This was the most unpleasant task we were ever compelled to undertake. It was heart-piercing to hear the shrieks of women and children, and to see even men crying and beating their breasts, supplicating for mercy on bended knees, begging that at least one cow — an only support — might be left. But no mercy was allowed. Orders must be obeyed. All that could subsist guerrillas must be destroyed. If citizens would not of themselves cease harboring guerrillas, then we must compel them to desist in the only way open to us. It was a terrible retribution on the county that had for three years supported and lodged the guerrilla bands and sent them out to plunder and murder.

In this expedition I got even with the Confederacy on the score of horses, and made up for the one the guerrillas had taken from me when I was captured in July, by securing a young but very fine animal, tall and graceful, and with a very dainty step, as if dancing to music, and she carried me to the end of the war.

Our winter camp in the Shenandoah Valley was not permanently fixed till the middle of December; and horses and men were compelled to endure great hardships from exposure to wind and cold. Our brigade was employed to guard the construction corps that was engaged in rebuilding the railroad from Harpers Ferry to Winchester.

When we were stationed at Charlestown, the dreary monotony of our regular rations of hard-tack and pork was for a single occasion delightfully varied by an elegant breakfast at the house of George Lafayette Washington, a great-grand-nephew of the "Father of his Country." His good lady entertained a few of the officers of my regiment with Southern profuseness, setting before us hoe-cakes and corn cakes in almost endless variety, with honey and apple-butter to make them still more appetizing, and cider to make them more grateful. Since the war, our hostess of that occasion has been compelled by the impoverishment of her resources to part with the medal presented to George Washington, March 27, 1776, by the Continental Congress in commemoration of the evacuation of Boston by the British. Some wealthy and patriotic citizens of Boston contributed five thousand dollars for the purchase of this precious family heirloom, that it might be preserved in the city that owed its safety to Washington's military skill.

Our camp at Charlestown was on ground made historic not only by its former ownership by Charles, the younger brother of George Washington, and by having been for a time the resting-place of Braddock's boastful army, but also by the trial and execution here of John Brown. The house in which we were entertained was once the home of Samuel Washington, elder brother of George, and many men known to fame have enjoyed its hospitality, among them Louis Philippe — afterwards King of France — and his younger brothers the Duke de Montpensier and the Count de Beaujolaix.

The rest of the winter would have been passed quietly in the Valley but for the desire of General Grant to have the railroads about Gordonsville destroyed. To this end we were awakened at half-past four o'clock on the 19th of December — a cold, dismal, rainy morning — and ordered to put up four days' rations and forage, and to be ready to move at 6. The expedition consisted of two divisions of cavalry — Merritt's and Powell's, in all about five thousand men, and twenty-four wagons — and made a column about five miles long, under the command of General Torbert. My regiment led the advance the first day, and we took the direction of Front Royal. It was a very picturesque sight to look back from some commanding hill and see the column winding like an immense serpent through the Valley. After we passed Front Royal we began to ascend the western slope of the Blue Ridge, and when we had penetrated about half-way through Chester Gap, we were halted for the night. And such a night! A bleaker camp could not be imagined. The winter as a whole was exceptionally severe for Virginia, snow falling frequently, and the mercury sinking sometimes to zero. It was excruciating at the climax of this inclement season to be perched at the top of a pass in the Blue Ridge and to face the icy blasts as they sucked and swirled through the narrow gorge. We made a large fire of logs, and after a supper of hard-bread and coffee, lay down upon blankets, with our saddles for pillows, and our feet towards the fire, which the guard was directed to keep bright. I was so weary with the long day that I slept from nine to twelve o'clock, when the extreme cold awakened me. I got up and paced back and forth for an hour trying to get warm; but I could not, the wind was so piercing. So I huddled up again under the blankets as near as possible to the fire; but, do my best, the wind would creep in, and blew away all sleep. I never appreciated so keenly how eager must be their waiting that is said to be "more than they that watch for the morning." It seemed as if the cold Pleiads would never set. Reveille at 5 was a relief, — anything rather than stay longer upon those cold heights in the clouds. We descended the eastern slope of the Blue Ridge, and were soon in a warmer atmosphere. Our course was now south-west, right under the Ridge and hugging it all the way. We made about thirty-five miles between sunrise and sunset, halting for ten minutes every two hours. That night it threatened rain, and I went in with the Major under a shelter-tent, and had a good sleep till 4.30, when to our great surprise we waked to find four inches of snow on the ground. My surprise was soon turned to dismay when I found that my mare Loudon — whom I had named after the county of her birth — was so stiff from yesterday's exertion and from lying on the cold, wet ground, that she could hardly move. I was afraid every moment that she would give out, and then what could I do? Early in the day the storm changed from snow to sleet and then to a very cold rain, and as we dismounted to rest our horses we wet our feet and could not get them warm again. We halted at four o'clock on the summit of one of a circle of hills encompassing the town of Criglersville, and there I beheld the grandest cloud-scenery that I had ever witnessed. The whole valley was a vast amphitheatre in the hills, whose sides and summits were heavily hung with thick clouds big with storm and tempest. The firmament above our heads was perfectly clear, and we stood upon the one elevation of all around that was open to the eye of heaven. It was very grand, but I have enjoyed the pictured memory of it more than I did the actual sight, as I was suffering so much from the cold, and was so anxious about my horse. I was frightened to think of having to walk the rest of the journey, as many were already dismounted from like cause, and were wearily dragging their way through the slush and mud, vainly trying to keep up with the fast-passing column. As we descended from this summit, it grew colder, and before we had gone many miles, the ground was frozen and our ears and feet almost so.

We soon approached Madison Court House, and here we first struck the enemy and skirmished. It was now eight o'clock, and our brigade was drawn up in line of battle for an hour, waiting till our advance developed the force of the enemy. It was a bitterly cold and most cheerless hour. The thought of the night before us was enough to freeze the blood. But soon the order came to fall back into the woods and encamp. Fortunately it was a pine forest into which we now entered, and the thick boughs broke the force of the wind. We cut down small pine-trees and taking their flat-spreading branches laid them upon the snow for a bed, and then built a fire and surrounded ourselves with a barricade of boughs stuck in the snow. It was eleven o'clock before we had supper, and as we had not eaten anything since six in the morning, of course we were very hungry. That night we had a splendid sleep. Pine boughs were as grateful as mattresses to our chilled and tired frames. We slept within two feet of the fire and so kept warm. Five hours of rest, and reveille called us to go again on our journey. We passed through Madison Court House and took the road to Gordonsville. It was very cold, and the horses slipped round on the frozen snow like hogs on ice. But we pressed on to the Rapidan, broke through the ice and forded the river, and made a reconnoissance towards Gordonsville, driving in the enemy's advance guards and capturing from Johnson's and McCausland's brigades two pieces of artillery. In this way we discovered that reinforcements had already reached Gordonsville from Richmond, and that the place was too strong to be attacked. We also learned that Wharton's division of infantry had been detached from Early's forces at Staunton in order to check Torbert, and that they were approaching by way of Charlottesville. So we were forced to give up the object of the expedition and to retreat as fast as possible. That night we encamped again in the woods the same way as the night before, only we had become so chilled through the exposures of the day that it was almost impossible to get warm. The nearer I got to the fire, the more I would shiver. My blood seemed curdled with the cold, and as it crept slowly through my veins, made me shake in every fibre.

Friday, December 23d, reveille sounded at 5 again, and, with a breakfast of coffee alone, we started. Our rations and forage were now exhausted, and for the rest of our journey we must live on the country. In the course of the day our headquarters forager brought in two hams, a spare-rib, and enough flour for several days. We marched until eleven o'clock that night, and encamped under the cold light of stars on a side hill so steep that we had to crawl on our hands and knees to keep from falling. The top of the snow was frozen into a hard crust which the horses' hoofs scarcely broke. However we made ourselves comfortable with a log fire, a supper of coffee, ham, and griddle-cakes, and a bed of boughs, and after five hours we started again.

Our regimental position this day was in the rear of the column, a very uncomfortable place to be in when the column is long and the roads are bad. There were many places where an obstruction or break in the road made it impossible for more than two horses to pass abreast; and, as we generally marched by fours, the column at such places would be drawn out to twice its normal length; and if the advance moved steadily it would get away eight or ten miles from the rear at such an obstruction, and then the rear companies, after having waited to let the others pass the obstacle, would have to gallop to close up the column. Generally, however, at such a place, the advance waits for the rear to catch up, as a caterpillar when it meets an obstruction huddles up, fixes its tail, then lengthens out over the obstacle, fixes its head and, drawing in its lengthened body, huddles up again, and then creeps on as before with equal length. Besides this unevenness of motion, a position in the rear is also unpleasant from the sights one has to witness. On this day we passed hundreds of horses worn out by the toilsome march and left dead by the side of the road; and we kept passing dismounted men who could not keep up with the column, some of them with boots worn through and a few barefoot and leaving tracks of blood in the frozen crust. That night we got into camp at nine o'clock, cold, tired, and hungry; still we brightened up a little to think it was Christmas Eve, and that our friends at home were enjoying it in quiet comfort and happy meetings, even though we could not enjoy it, but must spread our cold and cheerless tables in the presence of those enemies who otherwise would make our home firesides cold and cheerless as our own.

Next day was Sunday — December 25th — and as we woke, the "Merry Christmas" wishes went around, but always with the added wish for a merrier Christmas next year.

We forded, this day, the two branches of the Rappahannock, having first to cut a passage through the ice that covered the river. In our march we often had to dismount and to lead our horses down the steep hills, sliding with them most of the way. Their shoes were now so smooth that they with difficulty kept from falling even on level ground. Our sufferings this day from the cold were very severe. Our feet were almost frozen, encased as they were in wet and frozen boots, and dangling in the frosty air. There is not sufficient exercise in the slow motion of a cavalry column to send the warm blood away down to the feet. Our only relief was a partial one when the column halted — in stamping upon the ground.

Next day — December 26th — we passed through Sulphur Springs, whose once magnificent hotel, where the beauty and chivalry of Virginia used to gather and revel, was now a mass of ruins, and the place was almost utterly deserted. We drank of the waters, without however renewing our youth. In the course of this day the column marched over a part of the way along which five months before I had wearily walked as a prisoner, and I noted several places where I had sunk down by the road exhausted. It brought the thought of my deliverance vividly home to me, and cheered me with thankfulness. As we passed through Warrenton, General Torbert narrowly escaped being killed by a shot fired by a guerrilla from some safe concealment. Leaving Warrenton, we took the road to White Plains, and went into camp in that region infested with guerrillas.

Next day — December 27th — we marched through Middleburg and Upperville, and recrossed the Blue Ridge at Ashby's Gap, being fired upon several times by guerrillas concealed in the woods. We forded the Shenandoah with difficulty in its winter flood, and went into camp on its north bank at ten o'clock. After we got asleep a heavy rain began to fall, and I awoke at three o'clock to find myself lying in a puddle of water safely held in the hollows of my rubber blanket. I got up and readjusted it and lay down again, but was too chilled to sleep.

An early breakfast and a short march brought us back to our old camps near Winchester, thankful to have escaped from the hardships and exposures of the hardest expedition of the war with only a few painful reminders of it in chilblains, shivers, and twinges of rheumatism.

We now tried to make our horses and ourselves comfortable for the rest of the winter. For me it was very slow work, as I did not wish to take any of the men from their work on their own quarters to help me on mine. So it was nearly two months before my quarters were made comfortable; and I was settled in them only two days when the order came to have all the horses shod with steel corks, all unserviceable horses turned in to the Quartermaster, five days' rations in haversacks, eight rounds of ammunition in cartridge-boxes, thirty pounds of forage on each horse, fifteen days' rations in the wagons, and all to be in readiness to start on the morning of February 27th upon an expedition towards Lynchburg. Grant's instructions were to destroy the

Virginia Central Railroad and the James River Canal, capture Lynchburg if practicable, and then either to join General Sherman in North Carolina or return to Winchester as Sheridan should think best.

But for the constant schooling of a soldier's life in the virtue of equanimity, taking things as they come without complaint, it would have been a sore trial to give up so hastily the preparations of months. I had received from friends at home and had just finished cataloguing a soldier's library of several hundred volumes, and I had begun to distribute them among the men when this order came, and I was compelled to box them up immediately. In order that they might not fail utterly of their mission, I sent them to the Agent of the United States Sanitary Commission in Winchester, who saw that they were distributed through the hospitals. But I never saw them more.

The morning of February 27, 1865, was cold and rainy, and snow still covered the ground, but we started punctually as ordered, and took the turnpike towards Strasburg. The column was about ten miles long. The First Division, in which was my regiment, consisted of 4,787 men and was commanded by General Devin. The other division, of 4,600 men, was led by General Custer. Each division had one section of artillery. The train consisted of four baggage wagons, sixteen ammunition wagons, eight ambulances, eight pontoons, and about three miles of pack-mules carrying fifteen days' rations of coffee, sugar, and salt. General Merritt was made Chief of Cavalry and General Sheridan directed in person the movement. Never was a more superb body of cavalry sent into the field, and never were any more ably commanded. These ten thousand cavaliers were as one in their fearless devotion to any duty set before them by their admired leader. They were almost all veterans, toughened to war's exposures, disciplined to its sternest demands, fearless of its dangers, and heedless of its alarms. And they were superbly mounted, not a halting animal in the miles on miles of thick-ranked steeds. Alas! that thousands of these horses were never to reach that journey's end!

We made thirty miles the first day, passing over the familiar battlefields about Newtown, Middletown, Cedar Creek, and Strasburg, and encamped near Woodstock. We found the streams much swollen with the rains that were still pouring down and washing the gathered snow into the rivers, but our pontoon boats bore us safely and easily over them. The second day we made twenty-nine miles and approached Harrisonburg. The third day brought us to Mount Crawford, where General Rosser's cavalry attempted to delay our column by trying to burn the bridges over Middle River. But two of Colonel Capehart's regiments swam the stream — a terribly cold swim on March 1st, but they routed Rosser and captured thirty prisoners and twenty ambulances and wagons. After crossing the river, we went into camp near Staunton where General Early had made his winter quarters. The fourth day, without any delay for reconnoitering, the column pushed right on and entered Staunton, which General Early had hastily evacuated in order to make a stand in a more favorable position at Waynesboro, where he could have the

Blue Ridge at his back to flee to in case of defeat. And well he did this, for it was the only way he saved himself and Wharton and two other of his Generals. Custer had the advance that day and found the enemy in his chosen position with two brigades of infantry behind breastworks flanked by artillery and cavalry. Custer made his dispositions to attack at once, sending Pennington's brigade dismounted around the left flank of the enemy, while he with the other two brigades, partly mounted and partly dismounted, boldly attacked and impetuously carried the works in his front. Then he immediately ordered two regiments — the Eighth New York and First Connecticut — to charge in column of fours through the broken line of the enemy. This they did gallantly and pressed on through the town and across the South Fork of the Shenandoah, where they spread out in a thin long line ready to scoop up the retreating enemy. But there was little need of using force to this end, as the Rebels at once threw down their arms, and surrendered, with cheers at the brilliant stroke by which they were captured. The substantial results of this victory were eleven pieces of artillery with horses and caissons complete, two hundred wagons loaded with subsistence, seventeen battle-flags, and sixteen hundred prisoners. The results from a military point of view were much greater, as the Shenandoah Valley was thus cleared of all enemies, and the undisturbed crossing of the Blue Ridge was secured at Rockfish Gap, the only pass that at this season was free from snow.

The next day — March 3d — our brigade destroyed the iron bridge at Waynesboro by heaping up railroad ties at intervals upon it and then setting them on fire, thus allowing the heat to warp the bridge to destruction. Then we took up our march through Rockfish Gap towards Charlottesville, having the hardest and most destructive day's tramp I ever knew; for the rain had been pouring in torrents through three days, and the roads were bad beyond description, and horses and men could hardly be recognized for the mud which covered them. As the horses by their tramping kneaded out the water from the clayey mud, and as each successive rank of fours naturally stepped in the hollows made by the rank in front of it, the mud soon lay in ridges a foot and a half to two feet high like heavy beams across the road, and the horses who were unfortunate enough to be at the end of the moving column had to step very high and with great labor over these barriers, soon exhausting themselves. We were always glad, on these muddy days especially, when it came our turn to lead the column; and then too it was quite an advantage to get into camp at reasonable hours at night. On one of these days when we brought up the rear we did not bivouac till four o'clock in the morning.

As we approached Charlottesville the mayor of the city met us at the outskirts and with profuse ceremony delivered up the keys of the public buildings. But General Custer, who was in the advance, waived all formalities and dashed through the town and gobbled up some cavalry and artillery that were attempting to escape.

Sheridan ordered a halt of two days for the cavalry at Charlottesville to wait for the wagons to extricate themselves from the mud and to catch up with us. Still we were not idle, but spent the time in destroying the Orange & Alexandria Railroad for fifteen miles in either direction towards Gordonsville and towards Lynchburg. This was done to prevent troops from Richmond and from Lynchburg from massing in our rear when we should go forward to the James River. We also took advantage of the rich country about — as yet unwasted with war's desolations — to gather large quantities of forage and subsistence. Thus our enforced delay was an unfortunate one for the city and its vicinity. Our appetites, never feeble, were doubly whetted by the keen mountain air, and broiled chicken and roast pig were luxuries not to be passed untasted. Then too the wine-cellars of the gentry disgorged for us their precious treasures covered with the dust of years, since they were gathered from the sunny banks of the Rhine and the Danube. Many of the men took more perilous tastes of apple-jack — warranted, it was said, to kill at forty paces — and sure enough they who touched it to their lips would fall as if shot, so overmastering was the potent draught. The foragers for pork had great sport in gathering their unctuous supplies. I *saw* some of them, just as they struck the trail of a sow and a litter of eight fat pigs rooting in the woods. Alas! poor pigs! Not one was left to tell the harrowing tale or squeal his lonely woe. The eager foragers charged with drawn sabres upon the porcine pack, and though the pigs' swift wheelings drew many an ineffectual thrust, yet in a very few minutes the cavaliers secured their booty, and were soon distributing the unusually savory rations among their companions.

This delay by reason of mud and rain compelled the abandonment of the plan to capture Lynchburg, as it was already being reinforced. But Sheridan determined to destroy the railroad as far towards Lynchburg as Amherst Court House, and the James River Canal as far as Newmarket. Custer was assigned to the first labor, and his men made short work of it. They would build up a large mound of sleepers and then cross the rails on top of them so that when the fire was kindled they would bend with their own weight; and then, to destroy them even more completely, the men would draw them with their red hot centres from the flames and wind them about telegraph poles. A regiment could thus destroy in a day a whole mile of railroad. Devin's division was assigned the task of destroying the canal by opening and disabling the locks; and they also burned all the mills and factories along the banks. One squadron of the Second Massachusetts Cavalry was sent forward to secure the bridge over the James at Duguidsville in order that Sheridan might cross and make a raid towards Appomattox Court House, and destroy the South Side Railroad from that point to Farmville and so cut off *all* of Lee's sources of supply. But the Confederates had anticipated this design and had covered the bridge with combustible materials which they kindled at our first approach. One of our companies then reconnoitred towards Lynchburg and went within sight of the city and found that it was strongly fortified and occupied by a heavy force of infantry, which was just as Young's scouts had already reported to Sheridan. These facts together with the burning by the enemy of the bridge at Hardwicksville and the impossibility of crossing the James in its then swollen condition with the eight pontoons at our command made Sheridan give up his plan of destroying the South Side Railroad. And of course he could not join Sherman even if he wanted to — which he didn't. Neither did he care to return to Winchester, as the whole country north of the James was now open to him and he might continue his destruction of the northern lines of Lee's supply. Besides he wanted to be in with Grant at the death of the Confederacy and to have his cavalry share the honors of the final victory, which he believed to be very near. So we faced about and marched towards Richmond along the James River, reaching Columbia on the 10th of March, having destroyed on the way the canal and all the mills with immense quantities of tobacco, flour, and bacon, and having captured many canal-boats loaded with shot and shell for the Rebel army. The enemy's cavalry kept up a constant fire upon us from safe retreats on the southern bank of the river, but with little or no effect, and they burned every bridge to prevent our crossing. One of our brigades pressed on as far as Goochland and eight miles beyond, destroying the canal the whole distance.

Sheridan halted one day at Columbia to let the trains catch up. For the rain and the mud were still delaying them, and the mules were getting exhausted. But the thousands of tired mules found helpful friends in thousands of negroes who gladly joined our column, and with a will put their sturdy shoulders to the wheels, and lifted along the stalled wagons so that we were not long delayed. At Columbia, Sheridan sent despatches to Grant notifying him of our success, position, and condition, and our intention to join him, and requesting that supplies be sent to meet us at White House Landing, and a pontoon bridge to take us over the Pamunkey. These despatches were so important that they were sent in duplicate by two sets of scouts, — one set by land around the Rebel lines, the other set down the James River through the Rebel lines. Both were safely delivered; but, as in many another instance, the farthest way round was the nearest way home. The shorter way through Richmond and Petersburg was beset with dangers, and suspicious questionings had to be answered at every turn. The danger on both sides — on one side of being shot as a deserter and on the other of being shot as an invader — in passing from the Rebel to the Union lines at Petersburg was not the least that was encountered.

But how was Sheridan to get to White House without a very long and wearisome march? The railroad from Richmond to Gordonsville was still intact, and Lee — already aware of our presence — could throw his infantry on our front or flank or rear as he chose. He had shown himself able to keep his line of defence before Grant and at the same time to detach large bodies of infantry to assist in the defence of more distant places that were exposed to the raids of Sheridan's cavalry. And now Sheridan was not many miles away, and threatening all the northern sources of supply for Lee's army. It was certain that Lee would make a desperate effort to disable Sheridan. In this emergency, Sheridan decided first to prevent the enemy from getting in our rear. This he accomplished by sending Devin's division to Louisa Court House to destroy the Virginia Central Railroad as far as Frederick's Hall, and Custer's division to destroy it from Frederick's Hall to Beaver Dam station. Then fighting his way as far as he could towards Richmond till he should encounter Lee's infantry, Sheridan, under cover of this pretended attack upon Richmond, would withdraw and march by a short detour on the north side of the Pamunkey to White House Landing. This bold plan was fully carried out. It took but two days to destroy the railroad completely for thirty-five miles. Then both divisions marched by different routes towards Richmond, meaning to come together at Ashland. The first determined opposition that Devin's division met was developed at the bridge over the South Anna. Here the Second Massachusetts Cavalry, having the advance, dismounted and charged up to the bridge and then dashed across it, driving away the artillerists posted to defend it, and turned their own guns — four 20-pound Parrotts — upon them, causing fearful havoc. Custer's division marched by way of Ground Squirrel Bridge, but before he got there he intercepted a telegram from General Early to Lee, stating that he was following Sheridan with two hundred cavalry and intended to strike him in the rear at daylight. Custer, without delaying his main column, sent out a single regiment after him. It soon scattered the party, capturing two of Early's staff officers and most of the men. Early himself escaped by swimming the South Anna River. Thus ingloriously ended his Valley Campaign in which he had lost all his army, every piece of artillery, and all his trains. Thus ended also what had been for many months our frequent joke: "What's the *news* from Sheridan this morning?" "He's gone to *press* Early."

The whole cavalry force reached Ashland on the morning of March 15th, and found the enemy in force under Longstreet with Pickett's and Johnson's divisions of infantry and Fitzhugh Lee's cavalry. These had been sent out by General Lee with orders to annihilate Sheridan and his rangers. We skirmished with them till dusk, and then Sheridan, leaving Colonel Pennington of Custer's division with one brigade to keep up the show of an intended advance, withdrew the rest of his command, and marching northward recrossed the South Anna River and pressed on over Little River and the North Anna. Colonel Pennington withdrew after dusk, and by midnight the whole command was in camp near Mount Carmel Church, and Sheridan slept quietly, as there was now a clear road before him north of the Pamunkey.

But there was one of the command who, though off duty, did *not* sleep quietly, and who looked more like a drowned rat than anything else. And he *felt* so too. It happened that evening that the Second Massachusetts Cavalry came to the ford of the North Anna about eight o'clock, and, as it was rainy and very dark, the marks of the ford as it rose from the opposite side of the river had for some time been invisible from the southern bank. So the only guide to the ford for each cavalry-man was the horse in front of him, and, without suspecting it, this was another instance of the blind leading the blind. For the unconscious pressure of the current upon the legs of the horses had slowly but persistently pushed each successive rank farther and farther down the stream and away from the only practicable ford. Thus it came to pass that when we entered the river, the column's line of crossing had been pushed so far down that our horses began to flounder wildly in the deep water, and they pressed confusedly for the nearest point of the opposite bank, which at this place was so steep that my Colonel's powerful stallion just before me, in his mad efforts to climb with his rider the precipitous shore, fell over backward and knocked me off my horse, and before I could clutch the bank, I was trampled upon by the swimming horses behind me and crushed down under the water to the bed of the river; and there I was, my back prone upon the mud and sand, and my face and front exposed to the merciless kicks of the frantic beasts who were unwittingly making a stepping-stone of my pummelled body to assist them up the treacherous muddy bank. I was only saved from broken bones by the fortunate depth of the water, which buoyed up the otherwise crushing weight of the struggling steeds. My escape from a watery grave was due chiefly to the happy chance that before I was pushed under the river, I had noticed a flat boat moored only a few feet away. Happily, too, I had sense enough left to know that my only chance of escape was to get under its protection away from the horses' feet. So I wriggled along on the river bottom in that direction, pulling myself by laying hold of what seemed, and I doubt not were, the roots of the trees growing on the bank. While thus struggling for dear life, I experienced that miracle of thought that, in such fateful moments when the soul enters the shadow of instant dissolution, flashes its lightning-like illumination through the dark chambers of the memory, bringing into clear view many a long-forgotten scene, and presenting in a moment the whole drama of life. It seems as if I could fill an hour with the mere enumeration of the vivid recollections of those few moments when the waters drew their black pall over my outward sight only to flash more clearly upon the inner vision the instantaneous picture of the past. Even this supreme crisis of intensest life with its thousand thronging memories and its unspeakably solemn anticipations was relieved with a touch of humor as I thought of the unheroic homeliness of my being smothered there alone in the river's moist shroud as contrasted with the sustaining inspirations in meeting death with brave companions on the field of glorious war. I said to myself: "This inglorious taking off is hardly what I anticipated in coming out to fight for my country. None will know whether I made a brave ending, or *where* I met my death. I shall not even be missed till daylight, and if my body should chance to be picked up downstream, it will be labelled 'unknown,' and no 'monument more lasting than brass' will tell to the coming generations of the heroism of the soldier's sacrifice." At this harmless temptation of the devil I laughed inwardly, and then went on with my wriggling, and as soon as I was free from the legs of the horses, rose under the scow and struck out for the farther side, and had just strength enough left to pull myself out of the river into the friendly boat. As soon as I had disgorged some of the water and sand, and could speak, I shouted for Colonel Crowninshield, fearing that he had shared my unwilling baptism without my fortunate escape; for there, right before me, was his riderless horse struggling with mine and others to clamber up the steep and muddy bank. But no answer came to my shouting and I learned soon after that the Colonel had — with his usual quickness of insight — seen the cause of the danger we were in, and, leaving his horse to shift for himself, had hurried to the ford to make a fire for a beacon light and so save the rest of the column from our misfortune. I at once gave myself to the task of extricating the horses from their perilous situation, and with the aid of two of our men we managed, by getting a purchase on the trees growing by the bank, to pull them out by their bridle-reins. My horse and myself presented, as may be imagined, a sorry spectacle. Her saddle had been turned under her by my overturning, and in her struggles the blanket had become detached and had gone down stream, and in her pawing away at the bank she had completely covered herself with its reddish clay. I was dripping with water and weighted down with unmeasured quantities of mud and sand. I counted *thirteen* pocketsful, as I emptied them one after another. Every front button of my overcoat had been torn off by the horses' hoofs, my poor hatless head bore the marks of my pummelling in many a bump, and my hair, mouth, nose, and ears were filled with sand and plastered with mud. After a long search in the darkness, I found my regiment encamped not far from the ford, and the officers sleeping around a faint fire of logs struggling to burn in the drizzling rain. I did not dare to lie down in my wet clothes, this chilly night of the 15th of March, so I stood through the rest of its slow-moving hours, turning round and round as on a spit before the fire, trying vainly to thaw out the shivers and dry my dripping garments. The world's record for a willing stay under water was in 1910 three minutes and six seconds. What in 1864 my unwilling record was I cannot tell, but I know the time I went under, as my watch stopped at 8.25, and according to my feelings the water must have got to it only a few seconds before.

We took an early start in the morning in the direction of Mangohick Church, and next day — March 17th — reached King William Court House. Both these days were cloudy, and though March winds might stiffen they could not dry my clothing. Yet, thanks to the vigor nourished by our outdoor life, I caught no cold, and felt almost as well as ever after a few days.

We reached White House on the 18th of March, tired and dirty and tattered and torn, but thankful for preservation from a thousand perils, and ready after a few days' refitting to undertake new labors.

Sheridan said in his official report: "There was never a march where nature offered such impediments and shrouded herself in such gloom as upon this." "Sixteen out of the twenty days we were drenched with almost incessant rains." "Swollen and almost impassable streams, bottomless swamps, and well-nigh bottomless roads opposed our way." "But both officers and men were buoyed up by the thought that we were on our way to help our brothers in arms before Petersburg in the final struggle."

It was very unselfish in Sheridan, who had had full command of a department, to go to Grant and to take the risk of being put under commanders of much less experience. To be sure, he was immediately rewarded by an enlarged and independent command, but that does not detract from the disinterested patriotism of his motives.

We found at White House not nearly enough horses to supply our losses. We had left nearly four thousand by the way, nearly all of them disabled by hoof-rot or grease-heel and scratches. I lost one the tenth day out. In the wading through the mud the horses were apt to scratch themselves in the unaccustomed effort, and, as we could not stop to wash the wound, every slightest scratch would be aggravated by constant contact with the mud till in two or three days the horse would be useless, and have to be shot to prevent his afterwards reviving and becoming of service to the enemy. So our way was strewn with the dead bodies of these dumb but heroic partners in our toils and perils. Most who lost their horses obtained a remount from the captured horses and mules. But many were compelled to walk long distances. We had marched about four hundred miles in twenty days, and by the destruction of hundreds of miles of railway and canal made it impossible for Lee to campaign or get supplies any more north of the James. The threatening advance upon Ashland and the quick retreat in the night foiled Lee's plan to cut us off from joining Grant; for though Longstreet, on discovering the next morning that we had vanished from his front, marched at once to Hanover Court House, he could not at that point cross the Pamunkey to again block our advance, and after that he could not get to White House as quickly as we. So without further efforts to check us he returned to Richmond.

Our entire loss in *men* in the whole expedition did not exceed a hundred, and thousands of negroes, looking upon us as their deliverers, followed our column into White House.

The rich results of this campaign show the advantage of delegating discretionary powers to leaders who are trusty. The original plan of joining Sherman could not have borne half the fruits. Grant had discovered that Sheridan was not only a brilliant raider and an impetuous fighter, but also a deliberate strategist and a careful handler of his men. So In giving his instructions at Winchester, Grant left to Sheridan to determine his course by the light he should get on the way. And Sheridan chose, as we all did, to throw our lot with our fellow-soldiers of the Army of the Potomac.

It took us six days to get ready again for the field; and even then many for lack of equipment had to be sent to dismounted camp. For the horses were still dying daily by hundreds from the exhaustion of the march. Our camp was on the border of an immense swamp which before we left became nearly filled with dead horses unburied, whose noisome and noxious stench had already begun to poison our men, many of whom were suddenly seized with chills and fever. It was a perfect paradise for turkey buzzards, but a hungry graveyard for horse and man.

On the morning of March 25th at 6.30 we started from White House on the march that in sixteen days was to end at Appomattox. The first day brought us by way of Charles City Court House to Harrisons Landing. The second day we skirted the north bank of the James past Malvern Hill to Deep Bottom, where we crossed the river and went into camp on the southern bank. The night was intensely cold, and when we started again at 6 our march was over frozen ground. We soon reached the Appomattox River near Point of Rocks and crossed on two pontoon bridges, passed through Fort Cummings near the southern bank of the river and then through Forts Haskell and Stedman. We had thus been near enough to the Rebel batteries to be under their fire at times, and could see in the distance the church spires of Petersburg. That night we went into camp near Hancock station on Grant's extreme left at the terminus of the military railroad which ran for fifteen miles from flank to flank of the Union Army.

We now enter upon the closing scenes of this bloody drama of rebellion. When Grant learned that Sheridan was approaching by way of the White House, he delayed the final movement in order that he might have the cavalry at hand for a decisive stroke. He felt that the force of the rebellion was nearly spent. By the capture of Atlanta, Sherman had severed the Confederacy in twain, and had destroyed one of its chief sources for the supply of food and ammunition; and he was now sweeping a wide swath of desolation northward towards Virginia, threatening disaster to any force that might escape from before Grant's tightening clutches. By the crushing defeat of Hood before Nashville, Thomas had practically annihilated the Army of the West, and so put an end to the hopes of the Confederacy beyond the Alleghenies. And now Sheridan had destroyed those main branches of Lee's communications — the Lynchburg Railroad and the James River Canal. The effective forces of the Rebellion were thus confined to the small region between the Neuse and the James, the Blue Ridge and the Atlantic. And even there its life was flickering; for it had lost its hold upon the people. They could no longer be drawn into enlistment by bribes nor threats. They could not be made to contribute even the necessary supplies for the army, except by forced levies. The excitement and enthusiasm that had taken them out of the Union had long since cooled. The fair fields of Virginia, which were now to drink the last drops of sacrificial blood, had already swallowed up nearly one-half of the dreadful holocaust of precious lives — estimated at two millions wounded or disabled and half a million killed in the whole war over the whole extent of the country. How this proud State would have hesitated before throwing down the gage of battle, had she known how War with horrid front would stalk across her borders, trampling into barrenness her fruitful fields, felling her forests to give clearer sweep to his fiery coursers of destruction, reddening her streams with the blood of her chosen sons, and leaving her maimed and exhausted, her pride and her power crushed in a common ruin. Up to the 1st of April, 1865, she had withstood, or driven back, or only partially yielded before, the furious onsets of the Union forces led successively by McDowell, McClellan, Pope, Burnside, Hooker, and Meade. But now Grant, with a more dogged persistency of purpose, was pushing a cordon of impregnable force about the shattered remnants of the once proud Army of Northern Virginia, and nine days, only, served to crush them completely.

Lee's forces at this time numbered on paper one hundred and sixty thousand men, but really he had only about fifty thousand effective troops. Still they had a marvellous energy of despair, and, though poorly clothed and fed, they were sustained by the brilliant record which their army had made; and Lee still hoped to prolong the war till terms more favorable to the Confederacy could be extorted from the Federal government.

To this end there was but one course open to him — to retreat from Petersburg and Richmond, and unite with Johnston's army, which was now at Raleigh, and together to attack the separate armies of the Union, or, failing in that, to flee into the mountains, and from them to sally forth at favorable opportunities and worry the national government into satisfactory terms of peace. This course was indeed decided upon, and the line of retreat along the South Side Railroad was fixed, as being very much shorter than any other, and orders were issued to accumulate rations at Amelia Court House, which was to be the first base of supplies for the new movement. But Grant's left was already threatening this line of retreat. So Lee resorted to a demonstration against the Union right in order to compel Grant to withdraw his left. But though in a fierce and swift assault the Confederates carried the first line of works and captured Fort Stedman near City Point, they had neither the impetus to push on to the second line nor the strength to hold the first; and they lost in this action five thousand effectives which they could by no means afford to spare, and they relaxed not by one iota the grip which Grant was gaining on their line of retreat.

On the 24th of March, 1865, the day before this last offensive movement of Lee, Grant had issued orders for a movement, by the left, on the *29th*, and on that morning at three o'clock the movement began. Our cavalry from the Shenandoah, now united with our comrades of the Second Division under General Crook, which had been serving since the previous August with the Army of the Potomac, entered upon this campaign as a separate army, reporting directly to General Grant. This arrangement had been made by Grant in the way of a reward to Sheridan for voluntarily yielding up his independence as a department commander. Our line of march was first southward towards Reams station on the Weldon Railroad and then westward towards Dinwiddie Court House, with instructions to destroy the two main roads now left for the supply of Lee's army — the Danville and the South Side Railroads. But before night, a carrier from Grant countermanded the order to cut the railroads, and directed Sheridan to follow his own *strongly expressed* desire to "push around the enemy and get upon his right rear"; and the message declared also in characteristic terms, "I now feel like *ending* the matter."

Grant accordingly began to move the infantry in the direction *we* had taken. The Second Corps under General Humphreys, leaving their intrenchments on the extreme left of Grant's fortified line, crossed Hatchers Run by the Vaughan Road, and then marched in a northwesterly direction through the woods and marshes towards the enemy's fortified line along the White Oak Road. Following the Second Corps, the Fifth, under General Warren, crossed Hatchers Run four miles farther down, and marched by the Stage Road towards Dinwiddie as far as the Quaker Road, when it turned northward and crossed Gravelly Run in order to put itself on the left of the Second Corps. Meanwhile, the place of these two corps had been supplied from the north side of the James by General Ord with two divisions of the Twenty-fourth Corps, Major General Gibbon commanding, and one division of the Twenty-fifth Corps, Brigadier General Birney commanding, and also by Mackenzie's cavalry. Thus on the night of March 29th there was a continuous line of infantry from Gravelly Run to Petersburg, Warren commanding the extreme left, and the other corps commanders to the right being Humphreys, Ord, Wright, and Parke, with Weitzel commanding the remnant of the Army of the James north of that river. As this new extension of the army to the left advanced beyond Gravelly Run, Griffin's division of Warren's corps came upon the enemy at the site of Dabney's saw-mill, and a warm engagement ensued, in which the Confederates were driven back — with a loss of several hundred — as far as the junction of the Quaker Road with the Boydton Plank Road. Here darkness stopped farther advance; but the next day — the 30th — although a heavy rain was falling continuously, Griffin's division was still farther advanced with heavy skirmishing till the enemy were driven within their breastworks near Burgess' Mill; and at the same time, Ayres' division was pushed forward along the Claiborne Road to the White Oak Road near Mrs. Butler's.

By reason of the fearful state of the roads, the next day — March 31st — would have passed without any forward movement of the infantry. But Lee, with an audacity born of desperation, was already, without our knowledge, taking the initiative, and had detached every man he could spare from the trenches about Petersburg and was even now massing fifteen thousand men upon his extreme right to drive back the Union left; and on the morning of the 31st he made a furious attack upon the advanced position of the Second and Fifth Corps, at first driving them back in confusion almost to the Boydton Plank Road; but here our line rallied, and again drove the enemy back into his intrenchments.

In this desperate action my friend and classmate Charles J. Mills was killed. He was serving on the staff of General Humphreys, and had just written home this frank confession: "To die for one's country is all very well, but it is a contingency to be avoided if possible; and the more battles one goes through, the less inclined one is to come to grief." Still he kept up his manly courage, and blenched not at any danger. A solid shot struck him from his horse and he died instantly.

While affairs thus passed with the infantry, our cavalry under Sheridan had swept round in a wider curve past Reams station, as I have said, and across Rowanty Creek where — the bridge having been destroyed by the enemy — some of the Maine cavalry dismounted and took up the axe which they had been accustomed to swing so deftly in their native forests, and very quickly knocked together a bridge upon which we crossed by fours. While we were waiting for the bridge to be built, I saw a cavalryman, more venturesome than the rest, try to cross. He was deceived by there being very little water in the stream. There had not been rain for several days. But the treacherous mud was there, and his horse plunged into it, and with every struggle sank deeper and deeper into the slime till nothing but his ears were visible, and his rider was barely rescued from being buried alive.

After crossing the Rowanty, our column pressed on rapidly, having learned that the Confederate cavalry under Generals W. H. F. Lee and Rosser were south of us marching on parallel roads to secure if possible Dinwiddie Court House. But our advance entered it first, reaching it at five o'clock, and so gained and held a point of great strategic importance, as the intersection of four roads — Flatfoot running south, Vaughan running east, Boydton running northeast and southwest, and Five Forks running north — along which the enemy's cavalry might have reached the rear of Warren's corps in its present position across the Boydton Road, or upon which Sheridan might get out to destroy the Danville and South Side Railroads, or, on the other hand, strike Lee's right flank at Five Forks. Sheridan's first move was to send Gregg's brigade down the Boydton Plank Road to destroy the bridge over Stony Creek, and thus compel the Confederate cavalry, which was threatening our flank and rear, to keep off, and to make a wide detour beyond Chamberlain Creek before they could form a junction with the Confederate infantry.

So matters stood the night of the 29th, which was one of the most dismal imaginable. The rain began to fall early in the evening, and was soon pouring down in sheets. We had *no* tents, and very *little* supper. Our supply train was stuck in the mud and scattered all the way from Malons Crossing of Rowanty Creek to the Jerusalem Plank Road. Every field became a pool, and every road a quagmire. But with fence-rails *under* us, and rubber ponchos *over* us, we managed to get a little sleep.

The next morning, March 30th, although the rain was still falling, and our horses were deeply mired in the swamps and quicksands, Sheridan ordered Merritt to send Devin's division on a reconnoissance to Five Forks, and to feel the enemy's position. My regiment happened that morning to have the advance, and we had hardly left our camp, before we came upon the enemy's cavalry, and charging upon them drove them back in confusion as far as the White Oak Road. Here our skirmishers, under Captain Kuhls, rebounded from a deadly fire of infantry from behind the Confederate earthworks. We had unconsciously struck Lee's new fortified line. But still, thinking the earthworks might be thinly manned, our regiment, led by Colonel Crowninshield, formed a compact line of battle, and made a gallant charge; only, however, to be hurled back again by a bristling line of fire.

Here, Captain Kuhls, an enthusiastic, hot-blooded German, who seemed crazed by the excitement of the onset, refused to quail before that belching blaze of death, and I could see him as, without a follower, he galloped his horse defiantly up to and over the breastworks, utterly oblivious of the fact that alone he was charging upon Pickett's division of ten thousand veteran infantry. I think that his daring must have struck such amazement into the enemy that they refrained from shooting him at such close range; for the mad Captain escaped with his life, though we never saw him more. I have heard that he died in 1883 in Idaho. At this juncture the Sixth Pennsylvania Cavalry came to our support, and, with them on our left, we formed a line of defence along Chamberlain Run, near where it crosses the White Oak Road, and held this position till the next day.

While *we* had thus been busy through the day, *Sheridan* was busy in the effort to persuade Grant not to delay the movement of the infantry, as he was feeling compelled to do by reason of the rain and the mud. Grant had written to Sheridan *that* morning, saying that it seemed "impossible to do much." But Sheridan had already set his own troops in motion, and was greatly troubled lest any advantage he might gain should be lost for lack of support. So, with his impetuous spirit, he resolved to appeal to Grant in person. Mounting his powerful gray pacer, Breckenridge, he struggled mile after mile through the mud to Grant's headquarters on the Vaughan Road south of Gravelly Run. Grant had been so beset with complaints of the difficulties in the way of moving the trains and other impedimenta of the army, that, though it was against his wishes, he had consented to delay. But Sheridan's earnest confidence soon brought him to his better judgment, and he said, "We will go on." Sheridan then hurried back and made his dispositions to attack on the morrow. He knew, by *our* reconnoissance, that the enemy meant to hold the White Oak Road, and he learned by his scouts that Fitzhugh Lee's cavalry and five brigades of infantry under Pickett and Johnson had joined the forces threatening his front and left flank. Feeling the immense importance of Five Forks as a strategic position, he gave directions, early on the morning of the 31st, that Merritt should, with two brigades of Devin's division and Davies' brigade of Crook's division, pass through the line that we of the Second Massachusetts and Sixth Pennsylvania had been holding, and try to gain the White Oak Road, while Crook, with his other two brigades under Smith and Gregg, was ordered to turn to the left and watch the crossings of Chamberlain Creek, on the opposite side of which the cavalry divisions of W. H. F. Lee and Rosser had been seen the day before. Merritt succeeded this time in reaching the White Oak Road, and captured the coveted position at Five Forks; for the intrenchments were thinly manned at that point, as the enemy's infantry were now concentrated farther to the right in the attempt of Lee, which I have already described, to drive back the advance of Warren and Humphreys. But our cavalry could not hold the Forks long; for Lee, failing in his attempt to drive back our *infantry*, and appreciating the necessity of holding Five Forks, sent back the infantry under Pickett, who soon, though not without stubborn resistance, dislodged our troopers from the crossroads. At the same time, the Confederate *cavalry* made a desperate attempt to force the crossing of Fitzgerald's Ford on Chamberlain Creek, but were driven back by Smith's brigade. They then attempted to cross farther up where Davies' brigade was posted; and here, aided by infantry from Five Forks, they succeeded, and pressed back our thin line till they broke it and crowded Davies' troops against Devin's left flank, which itself had been pushed back by the Confederate infantry nearly to the place where the Forks Road branches, about halfway to Dinwiddie. This break in the line separated Devin and Davies from the rest of our cavalry, and left *them* no recourse but to retreat, and by the Boydton Plank Road rejoin the main body at Dinwiddie. When Devin began to execute this movement, the Confederates set upon him with all possible vigor, and thought to cut him off utterly; but in following *him* they exposed their own flank to Sheridan's advance, now held by the Reserve Brigade, to which my regiment belonged; and we were ordered to charge upon them at once, while Gregg, who had been sent to our assistance, assaulted their rear. This unlooked-for sally compelled the Confederates to give up the pursuit of Devin, and to face about by the rear rank to defend *themselves*. As soon as they had re-formed their lines, they again pressed forward towards *us,* and with ranks reinforced by infantry from Five Forks. Sheridan, perceiving now that he would have a difficult task even to hold his own against this overwhelming force, sent off rapid riders to General Custer, who had been laboring all day in the rear to bring the supply trains over the bottomless bogs at Malons Crossing, and ordered him to take two brigades and come with all haste to the front. The Confederate infantry now before us were not accustomed to be delayed in their advance by cavalry. They were the flower of the Army of Northern Virginia, and were led by one of its best fighting Generals — Pickett. They seemed to us utterly reckless of death. In the face of our severest fire they would swoop down upon us across an open field with such a careless swing, it seemed as if they enjoyed being on the skirmish line, and we suspected that they had such a miserable time of it in camp that they preferred standing up to be shot at. Ours was now the toughest task of the day, to hold them at bay till we could be reinforced. To accomplish this most effectually, three of every four of our men dismounted, the fourth leading the three riderless horses to the rear. A cavalryman feels somewhat lost fighting on his legs, but our men formed as broad a line as they could with their small numbers, and, though armed with short-range carbines, they were able, by deliberate aim and quick discharges, to make the Confederate advance exceedingly slow, and to give Sheridan time to make a new line of defence in our rear. It was now nearly dusk, and we could not hold out much longer against the long-range rifles and heavy columns of the Confederate infantry; for, though our Spencer carbines were puffing out shots like flashing stars from a Roman candle, the enemy's onset was in a heavier line of more fatal flame, and we were yielding step by step, when up dashed Custer on a gallop with Capehart's brigade taken from the guard of the belated wagon train. One of these troopers was Wilmon W. Blackmar, then a lieutenant and on the eve of winning a "medal of honor," afterwards one of the most honored citizens of Massachusetts. Custer at once set his band to playing his favorite charging tune, "Garry Owen," in order to inspire us at the front, and to strike terror into Confederate hearts. Then he dismounted his troopers, and set them to gathering fence rails to make a temporary breastwork. We caught the favorable omen, and held on a little more courageously to our advance line. But more inspiring than martial music was the presence of Sheridan, as he now appeared on the field at the critical moment, as was his wont, and with Custer and Merritt, and his own glittering staff, dashed at a gallop with flying colors and clanging sabres along the front of battle between the skirmish line which our brigade was slowly drawing in and the rail barricade which Custer's men were putting up; and with waving hats and resounding hurrahs they cheered us again and again, while the band played "Hail, Columbia," all together raising our spirits to the highest enthusiasm, and making us almost unmindful of the air thick with the missives of death. It was the very intoxication of battle, and it reveals the secret of much of Sheridan's brilliant success; for his own dashing bravery inspired his men with confidence, and made them fearless in the extremest perils. This daring ride of Sheridan drew an increasing blaze of musketry along the enemy's advancing line, and It emptied several saddles of the dashing cavalcade; and It wounded Theodore Wilson, a too venturesome reporter of the New York *Herald,* — an incident which Sheridan long years after recalled to me with some glee, as he felt that the reporter was out of place. But *our brigade* had the worst of the fire, for we were nearer the jaws of death. It was the hottest fire I was ever in, and It was the harder for me to face, as I had no definite place to hold, and no specific instructions to fulfil. Wherever I stood it seemed as If I ought to be somewhere else. Many of our men fell, and It was with difficulty that I could help even a few of the wounded off the field. Contesting every Inch of ground, our advance line was steadily withdrawn by our commanders Gibbs and Gregg, till they took up and held a new line resting on the Boydton Plank Road with Pennington's brigade at their left, and beyond his, Capehart's and then Smith's, all together forming an unbroken defence in a semicircle covering Dinwiddie. The chief force of Pickett's last desperate onslaught, that night, was thrown over the open field from which our skirmish line was just withdrawn. It was made with heavy columns of infantry greatly outnumbering our thin lines of defence. Custer's men, behind the barricades, waited until the enemy came within close range, and then poured upon them from their repeating rifles such a hot fire that they recoiled in dismay; and for that night, at least, Dinwiddie was safe.

But what a night! "Confusion worse confounded!" Blackness like Erebus! Roads like a "boggy Syrtis, neither sea nor good dry land"! Nothing can exceed the stickiness of the clayey soil of Virginia on the breaking up of winter. Our horses, almost exhausted for lack of food after their life-and-death exertions, toiled along but slowly through the mud. The vicissitudes of battle — waged chiefly in the woods and much of it after dusk — separated men from their companies and officers from their commands. And no quiet came even with the thick darkness. For above all the frequent shouting by bewildered wanderers, "What regiment is this?" arose the screams of the drivers urging their struggling teams to the front, that we and our horses might have something to eat the next morning. And yet in that blackest of nights, order must be brought out of all this chaos, that we might be ready to oppose a compact front to the expected advance of the enemy in the morning.

I worked till midnight getting the wounded to the hospital. One of these was Captain Papanti of my regiment, whom I supported on his horse for nearly four miles, that he might have a safe resting-place. By one of those peculiar chances that seem like humors of fate, this son of a dancing-master was wounded through both feet, and some one said facetiously, "I guess *his* dancing days are over." But he recovered, and for many years conducted one of the most fashionable schools of dancing in Boston. But that night things looked a little dubious about his pedals, and it was with great difficulty that I got him to the hospital.

Early that evening Sheridan sent this word to Grant: "We have been fighting all day with Pickett's infantry, and with Fitzhugh Lee's, Rosser's, and W. H. F. Lee's cavalry. Our men have behaved splendidly, but this force is too strong for us. I will hold on to Dinwiddie till I am compelled to leave." Grant had already suspected our perilous position, and had ordered Warren to come to our support *immediately* with the Fifth Corps, and sent word to Sheridan that they would probably reach him at midnight; but Warren was very slow in starting, and none of his infantry appeared till late the next morning after our cavalry had already been engaged several hours and had driven the enemy a long way towards Five Forks. This was a great disappointment to Sheridan, and it was the first great provocation he received in Warren's seeming lack of heartiness in his support. At 10.15 P.M., March 31st, Grant gave the order to Warren to attack Pickett in the rear the next morning, and he might easily have done so by coming in on the Crump Road any time that night with the division which he had already posted at Dr.

Boisseau's. Sheridan waited till 3 a.m., April 1st, and then, as no sign of the Fifth Corps appeared, he sent an urgent order to Warren to attack Pickett's rear at daylight. Our *cavalry* was up betimes, and began to press Pickett back, — as it was hoped, upon Warren's infantry; but we drove the enemy long past where he *could* be taken in the rear, before any of the Fifth Corps appeared; and so Sheridan lost the coveted opportunity to cut off Pickett's force before it could get behind its intrenchments on the White Oak Road. In this emergency Sheridan, though greatly annoyed, lost not heart, but shifted his plans, and as soon as the Fifth Corps came up, halted them at J. Boisseau's, where the Five Forks Road branches, and set out with the cavalry alone to drive the enemy to a standstill; meaning *then* to make a feint to turn their right flank, while he should quietly move up the Fifth Corps to attack their left flank and if possible drive them westward, and so isolate them from the rest of Lee's army, whose right flank was only three miles away near the Butler House at the junction of the Claiborne and White Oak Roads. Sheridan accomplished the first part of this plan by two o'clock with Merritt's dismounted cavalrymen, Custer with spirited charges pushing the enemy back along the Scott Road, and Devin with equal persistency driving them along the Boisseau Road to Five Forks. The Confederates hotly disputed every inch of the ground, and were dislodged with great difficulty from two temporary lines of defence. Their musketry fire seemed absolutely continuous. A lieutenant of my regiment, Huntington F. Wolcott (brother of Gov. Roger Wolcott), was sent forward by General Gibbs, commander of our Reserve Brigade, to advance the skirmish line, and found many giving way before the terrible fire, but he *did* rally them though he was compelled to draw his sabre upon some of them to drive them back. He said, "The Rebel bullets seemed to strike everywhere." Thus this boy of nineteen, — tenderly reared, who had never left his home till he could no longer refuse his country's call, who joined us only three days before, and who was now for the first time under fire, — with a noble scorn of death, was humbly doing his duty, and teaching greybeards the way of heroism and self-sacrifice. His first battle was his last. His young life was laid on his country's altar. The sacrifice was accepted. O precious offering!

> "We cannot say thy life was short,
> For *noble* death is length of days."
>
> "Thy youth was soon perfected."
>
> "Being made perfect in a short time, thou didst fulfil a long time."

Soldier, farewell! **(Note 13.)**

I spent nearly all the day dismounted, following as best I could through the thick woods the line of our advancing brigade, and helping wounded men from the front to the ambulances which came up as far as where the Five Forks Road meets the Gravelly Run Church Road. But even here the ambulances were only just beyond the range of the enemy's fire. It was the twenty-seventh anniversary of my birth, and though the noise of battle hurtled in the air, I snatched one moment to write to my home a word of loving remembrance, and happy farewell if I should not see it again, and then hurried off once more to my sad work.

Soon I came upon one of our brigade, a wounded captain of the Fifth United States Cavalry. We wrapped *him* like the rest, in a blanket, and bore him toward the rear to get out of the range of the musketry. But oh, it was sad to see the struggling of that soul, tossed as it was by a tempest of doubt and fear! While yet we were bearing him along, I could see by his ejaculations that he was trembling with apprehension before the awful mystery of death and expected judgment. His conception of God was evidently of a being terrible in wrath, inexorable to entreaty, arbitrary in his judgments, and unmoved by anything akin to human pity; and he dreaded to come into such a presence. His faithful men who were carrying him so tenderly tried to comfort him by telling him he would probably get well from his wound; but he was already *grappling* with death, and their suggestions of earthly hope were as idle words, and he said, "I wish I could see a chaplain." I did not yet reveal myself to him, for we were still amid the noise and confusion of the battle. When we came to the ambulance-station we laid him down upon the ground and the surgeon bent over him to bind up his wounds; but the captain was more anxious about his soul than about his body, and said to the surgeon, "I wish you would send for a chaplain." Then I revealed myself, and told him that I had been with him all the time, and spoke a few words of good cheer. And he said, "Chaplain, I wish you would pray with me." Then I knelt and with his hand in mine I prayed, thanking God that he had put it into the heart of his young servant to give himself to his country, and that He had sustained him through so many hardships and trials, and now in this last, greatest trial I prayed that God would still sustain and cheer him, and lead him gently through the valley of the death-shadow to the bright regions of heavenly peace. As I finished he said, "Chaplain, I have been a bad man, a very bad man; but do you think God will be merciful?" I said, "Are you *willing* to die for your country?" He answered: "Oh, yes! I *am* willing." Then out of the fulness of my faith, and the sure prophecy in my soul that God *was* a God of mercy, I said, "With such sacrifices God is well pleased, and they will cover a multitude of sins." This thought seemed to give him some foundation for a brighter faith. For though faith have wings like a dove, it yet needs some solid ground to stand upon, as the dove let loose from the ark soon returned because it found no place to rest its feet. But this soldier's trembling faith found a sure support in the thought that he had done *one* thing at least, had made one sacrifice, which the great God, whom before he had known only to fear, would accept as a fitting service. Then I repeated the Twenty-third Psalm — "The Lord is my shepherd," and at its close said, "It is sweet and pleasant to die for one's country." Upon the word his face lit up with an almost unearthly brightness, as he felt the uplifting glory of a willing sacrifice, and he exultantly repeated the old motto in the Latin original — *"Dulce et decorum est pro patria mori"* — a line which he had probably translated as a *task* at school, but which now he was translating eagerly into immortal life.

The captain was now quite calm, and permitted the doctor to dress his wound. Then he bade an affectionate farewell to his men, who, he said, had always been faithful to him; and we lifted him into an ambulance. As I was about to depart, he said, "I wish you would stay with me a little longer; I shall not need you long." Then as I sat alone with him in the ambulance he said, "I wish you would administer to me the sacrament." I answered: "There is no need of a sacrament. The sacrifices of God are a broken spirit." And again he caught the inspiration of the thought, and took the words from my lips, and continued — "a broken and a contrite heart, O God, thou wilt not despise." Then again he was calm, and gave me messages for his wife and little ones. He would have his sabre given to his boy; and if, when he grew up, his country should have need of *his* services, he would have him to be a soldier too. He gave me his two rings, — one for his wife, the other for his little girl. He said they would know which was for each. Then I took him by the hand and bade him "Good-bye, keep up good courage," and his last, brave words were, "Tell them I was willing to die for my country."

But we must hasten again to the front to see how fares the battle. About 1 p.m. Merritt's two divisions of dismounted carbineers, under Custer and Devin, had succeeded by resolute advances in driving in Pickett's whole skirmish line, and so had shut the Confederates within their intrenchments along the White Oak Road. It will remain a wonder to the end of time that this could have been done by less than six thousand cavalry against sixteen thousand of the flower of the Virginia infantry besides two divisions of Confederate *cavalry*. But the greater task was yet before us, to *keep* them there till our infantry could be brought *up* on their flank. This, Sheridan proceeded to do. He first ordered Merritt to keep up a hot fire all along the line, but to demonstrate most heavily on the enemy's right flank, so as to draw his attention away from the intended assault of our infantry upon his left flank. He then ordered Warren to move as promptly as possible on the road to Gravelly Run Church, and there form with Ayres on the left, Crawford on the right, and Griffin behind Crawford in reserve, and then by a left wheel strike the enemy in flank. He at the same time ordered McKenzie's cavalry to protect the *right flank* of the Fifth Corps as it swung round to the left, and to drive whatever opposing force it found, towards Petersburg, and then countermarch and assist the infantry in its flanking movement. Sheridan waited as patiently as he could for Warren to bring his corps into action. He had tried to inspire him with something of his own zeal, but Warren was offish, and seemed indifferent. There is no doubt that he was personally brave, and a *very* able officer; but his cold nature was so different from that of the fiery Sheridan that they not only could not assimilate, but they could not understand each other. Grant had noted this, and had, through Colonel Babcock, sent authority to Sheridan to relieve Warren. But Sheridan did not like to do this so near the crisis of the battle, although his patience with Warren was nearly exhausted when after three hours he had moved his troops only two miles and had not yet engaged the enemy. When Sheridan rode round to Gravelly Run Church to see what was the matter, he found Warren sitting under a tree drawing a rough sketch of the ground instead of hurrying his men into the battle along the lines that Sheridan had already marked out. This nettled Sheridan terribly. Yet still he restrained himself from displacing Warren, and resolved to throw his own personal presence into the scale on the side of the infantry, which was now directly on the left flank of the Confederates. In the forward movement, Ayres' division was the first to receive the enemy's fire. In fact, it was the only one that faced the enemy's intrenchments, as by a mistake of Crawford his division swerved to the *right* as soon as it struck Mumford's Confederate cavalry, and thus made a gap between him and Ayres; and the enemy at once took advantage of it, and began to overwhelm the exposed right of Ayres' division. Sheridan at once perceived the danger, and sent word to Warren to recall Crawford from his too wide detour; but Warren could not be found. Then he sent two messengers to Griffin, who had followed Crawford, directing him to return and succor Ayres. But more important than the aid of either Crawford's or Griffin's division was his own personal presence at this *"return"* in the enemy's works, which was indeed the key to their position. Sheridan knew that Pickett would fight desperately for the protection of this flank towards Petersburg, and had intended, as I have said, that Ayres and Crawford, and Griffin in Crawford's support, and McKenzie guarding the infantry's right flank, should sweep round in unbroken order and overwhelm the enemy's left at this point and cut it off from Petersburg. But instead of that, he had at hand only Ayres' division, and that was giving way. Nothing daunted, however, Sheridan threw himself into the battle like a Viking, and, galloping everywhere, soon brought order out of confusion by his magnetic example; and by his fiery enthusiasm, his reckless disregard of danger, and his evident entire belief in victory, he reassured the panic-stricken regiments, and again turned their faces towards the foe. Then, taking his colors into his own hand and waving them in air, he led the men on, where the fire was hottest, his eyes glowing like live coals, his face flushed like a flame, his short but stocky form radiating defiance. And his superb black charger Rienzi, — afterwards named "Winchester," the same that Buchanan Read has immortalized in his poem "Sheridan's Ride," — and whose body now stands, stuffed, in the Museum on Governor's Island in New York Harbor, he having died in 1878 in his twentieth year — this noble steed caught the inspiration of the fray, and plunged and curvetted, champing his impatient bit, as Sheridan dashed along the lines, drawing from the enemy a blaze of musketry that pierced the colors and wounded several of his staff, but filling the soldiers with such enthusiasm that they made an impetuous charge upon the breastworks and carried them at the point of the bayonet, capturing over a thousand prisoners and many battle-flags.

At the same time that Sheridan with Ayres' division was making this assault on Pickett's left flank, Merritt's dismounted cavalry was making an assault all along the front, and Devin and Custer, at the head of their respective divisions, contended for the honor of the first foothold within the enemy's works. On the right of our line, Devin's carbineers with the Reserve Brigade at the right centre carried the intrenchments in front at the same time that Ayres' division carried the "return"; and *together* they drove the enemy back upon Griffin, who, hearing the hot fire, decided, before Sheridan's messengers came up, to turn his brigade from following after Crawford, and made a left wheel across Crawford's rear, and swept into the meshes of his advancing lines more than fifteen hundred Confederates whom *we* had dislodged from their works. And now Griffin and Ayres with their two divisions of infantry, and Devin with his division of dismounted cavalry, are pressing the remnants of the enemy along the White Oak Road towards Five Forks; and Crawford's division of infantry and McKenzie's division of cavalry, having reached the Ford Road, are advancing upon the *rear* of the enemy's line at the Forks. The whole centre of Pickett's position was thus surrounded by an ambuscade of flame, and most of its defenders threw down their arms and surrendered. A few attempted to make a stand on the Ford Road, but Griffin soon dislodged them, and they fell into the hands of Crawford. After this, only a short stand was made on the Confederate right. Here Custer had fought desperately for hours, holding Terry's and Corse's brigades of Confederate infantry in check with Pennington's dismounted brigade of cavalry, and with his other two brigades, Wells' and Capehart's, mounted, tackling the whole of W. H. F. Lee's division of cavalry. But he could not move them from their position till Sheridan had begun to sweep down upon them in flank and rear. Then they cleared out, and took up a new position along the west side of the Gillian field. But just at dusk, Custer with the co-operation of a few regiments of infantry drove them from this position, and then there was nothing left but for the cavalry to swoop down upon the disorganized fragments of the Confederate regiments and gobble up as many prisoners as they could find in the gathering darkness. The trophies of the whole day were six guns, thirteen battle-flags, and nearly six thousand prisoners, while our *losses* in killed and wounded did not reach one thousand.

Thus the most important gateway to the stronghold of the Confederacy had been opened by Sheridan in one of the most complete victories as well as one of the most hotly contested battles of the war. It annihilated the right of Lee's projected line of defence and destroyed the last of his communications except the Richmond & Danville Railroad. It was also one of the most skilfully managed battles, both in bold dash and deliberate strategy. Especial credit is due to the cavalry for their part in the brilliant results. It is very much against the spirit and training of a cavalryman to dismount and fight at necessarily great odds with infantry solidly massed against him. Not only is there the disadvantage of the unaccustomed position and movement, but also the *greater* disadvantage of the short range of his carbine as compared with the muskets of the infantry. Still, our men counterbalanced all these permanent disadvantages, and the incidental weariness of long marches and hard fighting for two days before, with a heroic courage and an impetuous valor caught from their admired commanders, and they kept their lines unbroken before the hottest and most continuous musketry fire. We of the First Division felt a thrill of proud satisfaction that our men were first within the enemy's works, as it was announced to the country by Abraham Lincoln in an official bulletin, "The Five Forks, strongly barricaded, were carried by Devin's First Division of Cavalry."

Although the Confederate defeat seemed to us utterly irretrievable, yet Sheridan feared that Lee would sally out from the right of his fortified line which was only three miles away, and make a desperate attempt to cripple him, separated as he was from the Army of the Potomac. Fearing in such an event to depend upon the sluggish support of Warren, Sheridan relieved him of his command and advanced Griffin to his place and directed him to form Ayres and Crawford in line of battle near Gravelly Run Church and facing toward the enemy at the junction of the White Oak and the Claiborne Roads. But Lee had no disposition after this for offensive movements, and Grant looked upon our victory as the beginning of the end for the Confederacy. The echoes of the musketry fire at Five Forks had hardly died away before there began a general bombardment along the Petersburg lines of investment, from all the batteries and all the forts and all the gunboats and monitors — an unbroken roll of thunder, the death-knell of the Confederacy. This was kept up through the night till four o'clock on the morning of April 2d, when a general assault was made along the whole line. Parke on the right with the Ninth Corps carried the first line of intrenchments, but failed to take the second. Next him, Wright with the Sixth Corps carried everything before him, capturing many arms and about three thousand prisoners. Ord with the Twenty-fourth Corps carried the lines near Hatcher's Run, and Humphreys with the Second Corps, the whole right of the enemy's fortified line. But when Grant's lines, contracting as they came towards Petersburg, reached the inner line of defence, the Confederates with desperate courage put a stop to further advance that day, except at the extreme southern salient below Petersburg, where Fort Gregg was defended by Harris' Mississippi Brigade numbering only two hundred and fifty men. This handful of troops with determined valor resisted the surging ranks of assault until they had inflicted a loss of twice their own numbers, and had left themselves only thirty men to be taken prisoners. But the rest of the inner line of defence could not be pierced, and under cover of this resistance and the darkness of the hastening night, Lee gathered together the remnants of his army — the Richmond Garrison under Mahone, and Longstreet's corps from the north side of the James, and at break of day — April 3d — had advanced sixteen miles from Petersburg on the only road still open to him, north of the Appomattox.

Let us now turn to the cavalry. Tired as we were with the Herculean labors of Saturday, April 1st, shattered as we were by the losses of battle, we yet were started under General Merritt at four o'clock Sunday morning, and reached Ford station on the South Side Railroad at ten o'clock. Here we found that a division of the Confederates had thrown up intrenchments during the night with the intention of making a stand. The earth was yet damp on the breastworks as we rode through unchallenged, and ungreeted except by some grinning darkies, almost beside themselves with joy, who shouted, "Dem Rebs is done took out two hours ago!" Then we pressed on to Scotts Corner on Namozine Creek, and about nightfall came up with the rear of the Confederate infantry that had been at 3 p.m. driven from their intrenchments at Sutherland station by General Miles and his gallant division, and had taken the river road westward, leaving behind their artillery and many prisoners. We bagged a good many stragglers, but darkness prevented any decisive assault.

The next day, Monday, April 3d, the cavalry led the advance towards Deep Creek with occasional skirmishing; but we were chiefly occupied with destroying guns, wagons, forges, caissons, and small arms abandoned by the Confederates in their precipitate flight. Arriving at Deep Creek, we encountered a strong body of the enemy's infantry, which Merritt at once attacked and drove from the ford. But darkness again prevented our further advance.

At daylight on April 4th we again started in pursuit of those whom we had the night before driven from the ford, and who were hastening to join the main body of Lee's army, which was now heading from the other side of the Appomattox towards Amelia Court House, where Lee had ordered supplies from Lynchburg and Danville to be ready for his famished men. We caught up with the Confederates at Tabernacle Church, where we had a severe fight with two divisions of their cavalry and one division of their infantry. As *we* had only one division of cavalry we found it impossible to break the enemy's lines, which were held with great tenacity as being absolutely essential to the safe passage of the main army of Lee, whose flankers we could now see. Under these circumstances we fell back, crossed Beaver Brook, and let on the water from the dam to prevent the enemy from harassing our rear. [It was here that Major William H. Forbes rejoined us after his five months in prison. I had left him on the boat that had taken us to Fort Sumter to be exchanged, but, sad to tell, he was taken back to prison for lack of some formality in the terms of exchange, and was later taken to Columbia and was paroled from there In December, 1864; but it was not till April 2, 1865, that the formalities of exchange were completed and he was allowed to rejoin his command. He hastened at once to the front and delighted us on April 4th by his cheering presence. It was a great joy to him that he could be in with us at the death of the Confederacy.] All we could do now was to annoy and delay Lee's progress, to hang on the flanks of his retreating columns and at times dash in and capture what we could. That day we took hundreds of Confederate stragglers; but at night we received orders from Sheridan to join him at Jetersville station, at which place he had arrived that evening with the Fifth Corps and Crook's division of cavalry, after a forced march, with the hope of blocking Lee's escape by the Danville Railroad. Sheridan felt that Lee would make a great effort, and might easily break through the thin lines of cavalry which as yet had been disposed in his front facing Amelia Court House; and in order to have sufficient force to block this contemplated advance, he had selected Jetersville as the point to defend, occupied it first with his bodyguard (the First United States Cavalry), and at once sent off couriers to gather in the scattered commands of cavalry, and to hurry up the slowly advancing infantry. On receiving the order, we at once set out, marching all night, thus making thirty-two hours that we had been in the saddle without intermission. In the early morning we took position on the left of Sheridan's line, and breakfasted.

General Meade received the urgent solicitation to hasten his advance, just after his men had gone into camp at Deep Creek. Still, appreciating the necessity, he at once issued orders to his army to be ready to march two hours after midnight.

Thus on the evening of April 4th Sheridan was preparing to dispute the enemy's advance. In a few more hours he could confidently challenge Lee with his "Thus far and no farther." These few hours constituted Lee's great opportunity. If he had pushed foreward at once he could easily have brushed away the single corps of infantry — the Fifth — and the single division of cavalry — Crook's — that alone opposed his path to Danville and a junction with Johnston. But he did not. There was an obstacle in his path harder to overcome than our victorious columns. It was hunger. When Lee determined to evacuate Petersburg, he despatched orders that large supplies of commissary and quartermaster's stores should be sent forward from Danville to Amelia Court House, there to await the arrival of his columns. When, however, on Sunday afternoon the loaded trains came in, the officer in charge was met by an order to bring on the train (meaning the empty train) to Richmond to help transport Jeff. Davis and his cabinet with the property of the government. The officer — mistaking the intent of the order — started at once for Richmond without unloading the cars, and there the supplies were consumed in the general conflagration. This was a severer blow to Lee than a defeat in battle. For, being obliged to halt at Amelia Court House and send out foraging parties into the country round to feed his men, he gave Grant time to bring to Sheridan's succor the rest of the Army of the Potomac and so to cut off Lee's line of retreat.

At Jetersville, Sheridan intercepted this telegram from Lee's Commissary General: "The army is at Amelia Court House short of provisions. Send 300,000 rations quickly to Burkesville Junction." This telegram was in duplicate, one copy addressed to Danville the other to Lynchburg. They were found in the boots of a messenger who had been sent forward to telegraph them from Burkesville. Sheridan saved him the trouble, and intrusted them to Young's scouts, who easily persuaded the unsuspecting telegraph agent to forward them, only we planned to eat them ourselves. And we did secure those from Lynchburg, as the sequel will show.

When on the 5th of April, Sheridan began to suspect, by Lee's not appearing in his front, that he had abandoned the attempt to reach Danville, and might be trying to escape to Lynchburg by making a detour northward, he sent out Davies' brigade to Paine's Crossroads to reconnoitre. Davies, who was of the Class of 1856 H. C, found that Sheridan's suspicions were true, for Lee's wagons were already rumbling along the Crossroads in advance of the army. *Davies* at once set upon them pellmell, and destroyed more than one hundred and fifty wagons — some of them belonging to Lee's headquarters — and scooped up nearly a thousand prisoners, including two Confederate generals, with five pieces of artillery and several hundred mules, all of which he started at once towards our camp at Jetersville. Davies found hot work enough to do to protect his small command from the hordes of Confederates who set upon him as soon as it became known that he was in their front, but shortly the rest of our cavalry came to his succor and he maintained his ground. Thus passed the 5th of April, with the cavalry, while Meade's infantry were hurrying to reach Jetersville. The Second Corps came up at 3 p.m. and Sheridan wanted to attack Lee at once, but Meade wanted to wait till the Sixth Corps should arrive and so the opportunity was lost to end the war then and there. Sheridan was so troubled by this that he sent to Grant couriers urging his personal presence at the front. Grant was then about fifteen miles away with the Army of the James, which was marching towards Burkesville along the South Side Railroad. Leaving orders for General Ord to push on to Burkesville and intrench for the night. Grant started off with a small escort across country for Sheridan's headquarters and reached there a little before midnight. It took but a few minutes to persuade Grant that Meade's suggested strategy would give Lee his coveted chance to escape. So Grant and Sheridan went together to Meade's headquarters, and he changed his orders at once, and all were prepared in the early morning of April 6th to follow Sheridan's flanking strategy instead of a stern chase. Meade's desires were followed to the extent of returning to him the Fifth Corps, and McKenzie's cavalry was returned to the Army of the James, so Sheridan was left with only the rest of the cavalry.

On the morning of April 6th, instead of following Meade in a useless advance towards Amelia Court House — already deserted in the night by the enemy, Sheridan struck off by the left towards Deatonsville, where we again caught sight of Lee's wagon trains, and Crook's division set upon them as Davies had done the day before, but with very different result. For now Lee was aware of his danger. He knew that he must make a flank march in the face of a vigilant enemy, and so had doubly guarded his trains; and as soon as Crook advanced, he was received with a terribly destructive fire and hurled back in confusion. Sheridan thus found that he was not to be allowed to make any more captures without hard fighting or skilful strategy, but, both being in his line, he at once formed the combinations to accomplish his purpose.

Leaving Stagg's brigade and Miller's battery about three miles from Deatonsville to threaten Lee's columns as they moved on the road to Rice's station and at any favorable opportunity to break through their line at the point where the road to Rice's station forks with the road to Appomattox River, Sheridan ordered Crook to lead off to the left parallel with the enemy's line of march, and Merritt to follow, and both to seek for some vulnerable point of attack and try to gain the Deatonsville road. Such a point seemed to present itself just south of Sailor's Creek, a small tributary of the Appomattox. Custer's division happened to be just opposite this point, and he began to skirmish with the flankers of the Confederate wagon train, and drove them up to the road along which the train was moving. But here his troopers were met by a line of *infantry* fire, from behind a low stone wall, that made many a rider bite the dust, and sent the whole column staggering back. Custer, however, was not the kind of leader to be balked by a single defeat. As soon as he could form his men again he made the assaulting column more solid by doubling it, and then sent it off up the slope on a gallop.

There is no more thrilling spectacle than a cavalry charge with drawn sabres, the scabbards clanking against the saddles, the steeds champing their foaming bits, the earth thundering beneath their heavy tread, the air alive with gleaming blades and flying colors. Add to this the enthusiasm of the onset rising at times almost to madness, horse and rider sharing and mutually increasing its intoxication up to the point of collision, and you have a scene that is terribly grand. But who shall picture on canvas or portray in words the awful scene which I then witnessed when this advancing array of galloping steeds and fearless riders was hurled back by the belching thunderbolts of war? It is like the proud ocean-wave mounting the shallower shore, and tossing its white crest in confidence of its irresistible might, but as soon as it beats upon the rocky ledges, it is broken and hurled back in forceless foam. So was this second wave of defiant assault broken and flung back in forceless fragments of defeated valor, and the earth was strewn with death. Earlier in the war this second attempt would not have been made. The sacrifice would have been thought too great. Even at this time, by most leaders no third attempt would have been considered. But not so thought Custer or Sheridan. Without a moment's delay Custer asked for the Reserve Brigade in which was my regiment, massed it with his own troops in ranks twice as heavy as before, formed them within a few hundred yards of the enemy's line in solid front across the whole breadth of the open field, and then, drawing his sword and putting spurs to his steed, he dashed along the front of the whole line of serried soldiery, his brown sombrero turning up its broad brim from his bronzed forehead, his long yellow curls floating on the wind, the ends of his crimson cravat flying like tongues of fire over his shoulders, his face aflame with the eager joy of battle. He seemed utterly oblivious to danger and to bear a charmed life amid the shower of bullets, and gave us an inspiring example of death-defying valor. Then the bugles sounded "Forward!" the bands struck up "Yankee Doodle," and this third wave of gallant cavaliers swept forward with resistless might and carried everything before it.

These stirring events, which seem to the younger generation so far away, seem but as yesterday to those who took part in their exciting scenes. To a cavalryman, the sound of the bugle, although heard amid peaceful surroundings, brings back vividly the old thrill of battle under heroic leaders and with faithful companions.

"In the hush of the calm and peaceful night
    When all is lone and still,
I think I hear an old-time strain.
    An echo from the hill;
My heart beats fast, my pulses bound,
    Old friends I seem to see;
The ringing, singing bugle brings
    The old days back to me."

The days of grand, heroic souls
    "Crowd back from buried years,"
And Custer's face again doth flame,
    "And Lowell's name brings tears."
"And Bayard, Buford, and the rest"
    All ride again so free
"When the ringing, singing bugle brings
    The old days back to me."

"Kilpatrick, daring, gallant soul,
    And Dahlgren's graceful shade,
And Sheridan, still in the van"
    With spirit undismayed: —
"They've ridden to the silent night,
    Yet oft their forms I see —
When the ringing, singing bugle brings
    The old days back to me."

[Richard Henry Savage — *adapted.*]

But let us go back to the field. Devin and Crook, farther to the left, at the same time gained the road, and, swinging round to the right, bagged unnumbered prisoners, captured sixteen pieces of artillery, and destroyed four hundred wagons. Thus our cavalry stood athwart Lee's line of march and separated Ewell's Corps, which was astride Sailors Creek, from Longstreet's

Corps, which was waiting at Rice's station. Meanwhile Stagg's brigade and Miller's battery had, by sharp sabre-thrust and the rough rending of solid shot and shell, hewn another gap behind Ewell, between him and Gordon, thus forcing Gordon's corps to turn to the right at the forks towards the Appomattox River, whither it was followed by the Second Corps under General Humphreys. Thus was isolated from the rest of Lee's army, General Ewell with Anderson's, Kershaw's, and Custis Lee's divisions, and they fought with the greatest desperation to keep themselves from capture. Anderson's division was advanced to some favorable ground and intrenched facing Merritt and Crook in the hope of covering the escape of the other divisions through the woods towards the Appomattox. But Crook, who held our extreme left with two brigades dismounted and one mounted, cut off the possibility of retreat in that direction by overlapping Anderson's right, and, by assaulting at the same time with Merritt, compelled Ewell to stand still in defence. This holding of Ewell by our cavalry gave time for Sheridan to bring up the Sixth Corps — a consummation he most devoutly wished. It had been in the Shenandoah Valley his main reliance in support of his cavalry, and ever since he joined Grant before Petersburg he had begged to have it assigned to him. It now went in under Sheridan with its old alacrity, and to meet it Ewell faced about Kershaw's and Custis Lee's divisions, leaving Anderson to hold back our cavalry. The Confederates, thus hemmed in, fought like fiends. Seymour's division of the Sixth Corps was for a time checked and pushed back, but, Getty's division coming up, again drove the enemy, and at all other points they had already given way. This was not, however, known to Ewell till he caught sight of his burning supply trains, and saw the drawn sabres of our cavalry men issuing out of the woods from which Anderson's corps had been driven by Merritt and Crook. So, beset in front, left flank, and rear, Ewell, after a short but heroic defence, gives up his sword to Sheridan, and surrenders his whole corps of more than nine thousand men. On one of the captured wagons was found the inscription, "We uns has found the last ditch." And Ewell must have *thought* so, although he *said* little; he only begged Sheridan to send a flag of truce to Lee to demand his surrender in order to save any further useless sacrifice of precious lives. Sheridan wrote at once to Grant — "Up to this time, we have captured Generals Ewell, Kershaw, Barton, Defoe, Corse and Custis Lee. If the thing is pressed, I think Lee will surrender."

After the battle, which continued till dusk, our division under Devin was pushed on for more than two miles through the woods in pursuit of the remnants of Anderson's corps, which had fled in a disorganized mass towards the Appomattox. But it was too dark to bag many more that night, and we dismounted and lay down overwearied and went to sleep at our horses' feet, holding the bridle-reins in our hands. Soon a terrible explosion awoke us, and we discovered a hostile battery in position only a few hundred yards away shelling with "spherical case" the woods in which we were encamped;

but they were giving us only a few parting shots, and we turned over and soon were asleep again.

This battle of Sailors Creek, so desperately contested by Ewell, so sharply and successfully fought by Sheridan, not only eventuated in the capture of Ewell's corps, but compelled Longstreet's column in his front and Gordon's column in his rear to give up all hope of escape to Danville. Longstreet's column took the road from Rice's station to High Bridge closely followed by detachments from the Army of the James, and Gordon's column took the road to the Appomattox closely followed by the Second Corps.

While Sheridan was thus cutting out a large section of Lee's retreating army, its advance was approaching High Bridge over the Appomattox, meaning to follow the railroad to Farmville, where Lee could feed his army with supplies from Lynchburg and then make that fortified city his centre of defence, or, failing in that, to escape into the mountains.

Capt. Francis Washburn

But as the advance guard of Confederate cavalry approached High Bridge, what was their surprise to find a squadron of Union cavalry and a line of infantry disputing their passage! Lee could not think it a large force, still he began to make dispositions for a serious attack; but before his lines were fully formed, the squadron of cavalry charged and broke through his first line, and was only stopped by a second and stronger line posted in the edge of the woods where our men could not effectively use the sabre. This squadron of horse which thus defiantly threw down the gage of battle before two divisions of Confederate cavalry, under Rosser and Fitzhugh Lee, was a part of a single battalion of the Fourth Massachusetts Cavalry numbering only 12 officers and 67 men under command of Col. Francis Washburn of Worcester, of the Class of 1859 Lawrence Scientific School. He had lately been promoted from a captaincy in my regiment, where he had proved one of the best officers of the line. He had been sent forward with his squadron and 800 infantry from Burkesville by General Ord of the Army of the James to destroy High Bridge. But before he could execute the order. General Ord, learning of Lee's advance, sent Col. Theodore Read with 80 cavalrymen to bring him back. To return was then impossible without cutting their way through Lee's advancing lines. Colonel Read was killed in the first charge; but Washburn, undiscouraged at the first vain attempt to drive back the cavalry in his front, made another impetuous charge, and this time broke through the enemy's line, and might have made his escape back to Burkesville, but he would not desert the infantry, who were now completely surrounded by the swarming Confederate troopers. Accordingly he made his third charge; and in this, while crossing sabres with a Confederate officer whom he had nearly disarmed, he was shot in the head by another, and after he had fallen received a sabre-cut on the skull. Both General Grant and General Ord bore testimony to his heroic daring, and I am proud to have known him as a fellow-officer and a friend. In this engagement eight out of twelve of his officers were disabled, and the rest were completely surrounded; but, says an officer on Lee's staff, "to the sharpness of that fight, the cutting off of Lee's army at Appomattox was probably owing. So fierce were the charges of Colonel Washburn and his men that General Lee — although at first supposing it was a small force — concluded that they must be supported by a large part of the army," and so stopped to throw up a line of breastworks, and ordered three trains of provisions, forage, and clothing, which had been sent from Lynchburg over the South Side Railroad, to be sent back to prevent them from falling into our hands. Thus his army was deprived of the supplies from the want of which they were already nearly exhausted. And besides, this delay of Lee's advance gave time for Ord to come up with the Twenty-fourth Corps of Infantry, and so to cut off the last possible chance for Lee to escape southward to Danville, and compelled him to make another detour northward and westward.

The sufferings of Lee's retreating army at this time can be compared to nothing in the annals of history, unless perhaps to the retreat of the French from Moscow, where the element of intense cold was added to the hunger and fatigue of the march harassed night and day by pursuing Cossacks. Lee had now twice missed his expected supplies — first at Amelia Court House and now at Farmville, — and his men kept themselves alive by eating whole corn and such buds or young shoots as they could tear from the branches in their hurried flight. Years afterwards, in the island of Teneriffe, I met Col. Robert Renshaw, H. C. '51, a classmate of my Colonel Charles Russell Lowell. He was Lee's nephew and had been quartermaster on his staff. He told me that his headquarters forager came in, one of those evenings, his eyes beaming with delight, and drew from his pocket four onions, more proudly than if they had been nuggets of gold; and the Colonel said they were the first food of any kind he had seen that day, and he distributed them — one to each of the three constituting his mess, and one to the darky as a reward for his devotion. Soldiers fell out of the ranks by hundreds from sheer exhaustion, and threw down their arms by thousands from utter inability to carry them. They were driven like sheep before howling wolves, and, fearing to be shot at by their eager pursuers, many struggled on till they fell to the ground from the combined effects of hunger, fatigue, and sleeplessness. For at night they had no rest. They had to march on, if only to get a little respite from fighting. And even that did not save them. For our cavalry also marched at night, and were all ready to set upon them, however far they had toiled forward. For lack of forage, the horses and mules perished by hundreds, and this compelled the burning of a great part of their wagons, and the spiking of many of their guns. The straits to which the Confederates were thus reduced led the subordinate officers of Lee's army to an almost unanimous decision that there was no alternative but surrender. Lee, however, thought otherwise. Still there was no time now for consultation; for early on the morning of April 7th, just as Lee's rear guard were setting fire to the wagon-road bridge near High Bridge over which he had crossed in the night, General Humphreys with the Second Corps came up and extinguished the flames. This was a great good fortune for us, as the river was unfordable at that point. Humphreys immediately crossed, and took up the pursuit with two divisions along the old stage-road to Appomattox Court House, sending Barlow with one division towards Farmville. This was Maj. Gen. Francis C. Barlow of the Class of 1855 H. C. He found a considerable force of the enemy here burning the bridges and guarding a wagon train. He at once attacked and dislodged them, and destroyed one hundred and thirty wagons. He then rejoined the rest of the Second Corps, which had overtaken Lee's army at Cumberland Church, and found it in a strongly intrenched position. Humphreys had the audacity to attack, but was repulsed so severely that he waited then for reinforcements. He was in a critical position, but the enemy had not confidence to attack him. Night soon came on, and Lee again took up his line of retreat, after, however, writing this note to Grant: "General: I have received your note of to-day [this note was brought through the lines by my classmate Gen. Charles A. Whittier of General Humphrey's staff] asking of me the surrender of the Army of Northern Virginia. Though not entertaining the opinion you express of the hopelessness of further resistance, I reciprocate your desire to avoid useless effusion of blood, and therefore ask what are your terms of surrender." Without waiting for an answer Lee retreated, as I have said, under cover of the darkness.

While Humphreys and the Second Corps were thus fiercely following the rear of Lee's columns on the 7th of April, Sheridan was moving with Merritt and McKenzie towards Prince Edward Court House on the pike to Danville, while Crook's cavalry went to Farmville, where Gregg's brigade had a severe tussle with the enemy on the north side of the river, and Gregg was taken prisoner. When Sheridan heard of this engagement he decided that Lee was directing all his energies now towards reaching Lynchburg, and resolved to throw his cavalry athwart Lee's new path of retreat. So during the night of the 7th he recalled Crook to Prospect station, and sent Merritt forward to Buffalo Creek and McKenzie to the Lynchburg Railroad. The Fifth Corps followed the cavalry as fast as it could and went into camp at Prince Edward Court House. Ord with the Army of the James pushed towards Lynchburg by way of Farmville and between the Fifth Corps and the Appomattox. Wright and the Sixth Corps built a bridge across the river at Farmville and hurried to the support of Humphreys and the Second Corps.

Early on the morning of the 8th, Sheridan gathered all his cavalry at Prospect station and started for Appomattox station, where he hoped to block Lee's last and only chance of escape by the narrow neck of land between the Appomattox River and the James. Shortly after our march commenced, one of Major Young's scouts met us, riding in hot haste, and reported that there were four trains of cars at Appomattox station loaded with supplies for Lee's famished troops. These supplies were sent in response to the telegram which we had captured on the 4th of April and had forwarded in the hope of getting the provisions for ourselves. Sergeant White — of Young's scouts — had been on the watch for them, and induced the officer in charge to halt them at Appomattox. Then he galloped off to tell Sheridan. Sheridan at once ordered that our column should push on as briskly as possible, for, as he said, "supper is awaiting us twenty-five miles away." General Custer had the advance, and about sunset came in sight of the station and the curling smoke of the locomotives, and quickly surrounded the trains and captured the engineers; then, calling for engineers and brakemen from his own ranks, he ordered the trains towards Farmville to get them under the safe cover of the approaching infantry of Ord and Griffin. As he was attending to these details, unconscious of danger, there suddenly opened upon him a banging of batteries, going off like myriad bunches of cannon crackers; but, nothing disconcerted, he dashed in upon the gunners with the men that he had about him, and before the other divisions could reach the field, he had captured twenty-five guns, a hospital train, a large number of wagons, and nearly a thousand prisoners. These were the advance guard of Lee's army, who had been hurried forward to secure the trains, and for the third time in six days they lost their coveted supplies. Soon our whole cavalry corps came up, and Sheridan disposed them in line of battle with Devin on the right of Custer and Crook to the left, and advanced on the road to Appomattox Court House, which is about five miles from the station, pushing Lee's advance guards back upon the main body.

At twenty minutes past nine that evening, Sheridan sent this despatch to Grant, who was then at Farmville: "We are pushing the enemy towards Appomattox Court House, having cut off his expected supplies. If the infantry can get up to-night, we will perhaps finish the job in the morning. I do not think Lee means to surrender until compelled to do so." Sheridan also sent word to Ord and Griffin that if they would press on with their corps, there would be no escape for the enemy, who had now reached the last ditch.

That night Sheridan did not sleep, but most of us got about three hours' rest, which was about the average amount for the last ten days. My regiment was on picket, and as our line was formed about midnight in the thickest darkness, I was not aware of the fact that we were encamped just under the southern crest of a hill upon whose northern slope was the whole Rebel army; and I have learned since, that *then* was in session, within gunshot of our line, the last Confederate council of war. There were present General Lee, General Gordon, commanding the infantry, General Pendleton, chief of artillery, and General Fitzhugh Lee, as head of the cavalry. Longstreet was too busy to attend. Surrender seemed inevitable, but they decided to make one last heroic effort to break through our lines, and to General Gordon was assigned the leading of the forlorn hope.

But we were all unconscious of this, and at the very first rays of dawn were startled from our slumbers by a shower of shells that for half an hour poured down upon us, and made us execute some lively manoeuvres if only to save our legs. I found that, though it was Sunday and I was a clergyman, it was hardly wise to refuse those pressing invitations to dance. I was standing with Col. Caspar Crowninshield **(Note 14)** and Lieut. Col. William H. Forbes **(Note 15)** as these shells plunged into the earth or skipped about on the surface, and we were all thoroughly spattered with dirt. Sheridan felt that this shelling was only meant to strike terror into our ranks, and to make an easier path for the advance of the Confederate infantry which would speedily follow. So he threw out our advance cavalry, dismounted, as skirmishers, and awaited the onset, meanwhile sending couriers, as he had frequently through the night, to hurry up our advancing infantry.

It was a beautiful Sunday morning, fair dawn of a fairer day. The country was white and pink with the beautiful blossoms of the plum, the peach, and the pear; but we had little time then to enjoy this pleasant outlook, nor to think of the church bells that would soon be chiming over the hills of home their call to come to the service of the Prince of Peace. Still were we not in the same service, though following the track of grim-visaged War? And were we not to behold that morning the gladdest coming of Peace that mortal eyes had ever witnessed? Only *then* we did not know it, and we were beset with ominous portents and filled with apprehensive fears. For as soon as the artillery on the crest of the hill before us ceased its fury, the Confederate infantry came striding down the slope with that swinging gait which had so often sent terror to as many of us as did not care to be shot. We received them with as destructive fire as we could command, and held to our ground as *long* as we could, and then slowly and sullenly gave way inch by inch, as indeed we must before their longer-range weapons and their heavier lines of advance. Our stand was so tenaciously held, however, that General Gordon reported to Lee that he did not know whether he was fighting infantry or dismounted cavalry. Still we gradually gave way, until, to our great joy and the Confederates' utter dismay, there appeared on the crest of the hill behind us the headquarters flag of General Ord, and soon there blazed up a bristling line of the bayonets of his infantry. Then we knew that all was well; and our bugles sounded "Forward!" and our cavalrymen now in turn pressed back the disheartened Confederates, till we received orders to remount, and dash across the slope of the hill to get in on the enemy's left flank, leaving his centre to be met by the infantry, who were now formed in line of battle with the Fifth Corps on the right and the Army of the James on the left. Crook and McKenzie with their divisions of cavalry completed the line of defence to the left. Sheridan joined Merritt on the right of the line, with Devin's and Custer's divisions, and at once ordered us to advance in the face of a heavy fire of artillery towards some higher ground from which we could have a clear sweep for a charge upon Gordon's left flank. We soon reached the crest which overlooked a wide open valley in which lay the proud Army of Northern Virginia completely at bay. They presented a spectacle sorry enough — a thin line of battle made up of Gordon's troops in front facing Ord and Sheridan, another scant line in the rear facing Meade, in all about eight thousand fighting men, and between these two lines of battle the disorganized debris of the artillery and wagon trains and the gaunt figures of nearly twenty thousand unarmed stragglers too weak to carry their muskets. Sheridan had just made his dispositions to charge, when we caught sight of a rider from out the enemy's lines bearing a flag of truce. Custer dashed forward to meet the messenger, and taking the flag galloped back and along our lines as a signal to stop our advance.

This famous flag of truce was really a towel which Maj. R. M. Simms drew from his haversack to protect himself from our fire as he galloped into our lines to request a cessation of hostilities. General Custer, who received it, was willing to stop our advance temporarily, but left it to Generals Sheridan and Gordon to order a little later a temporary truce which held till Grant and Lee arranged the terms of surrender and ended the war. It was of this temporary truce that General Gordon gives this story, and it reveals the utter destitution of his command. He says: "I called Major Hunter of my staff and told him to carry forward a flag of truce. He replied, 'General, I *have* no flag of truce.' I told him to get one. He replied, 'General, we have no flag of truce in our command.' I said, 'Then take a handkerchief, put it on a stick and go forward.' 'I have no handkerchief. General.' 'Then borrow one and go forward with it.' He tried, and reported that not one of the staff had a handkerchief, and it was useless to seek for one among the men. 'Then, Major, use your shirt.' 'You see. General, we all wear flannel shirts.' At last, however, we found a man who had a white shirt. He gave it to us, and I tore off the back and tail, and rigging this on a stick. Major Hunter bore it aloft towards the enemy's lines."

The immediate effect of this cessation of hostilities was — as maybe imagined — very different with the different armies. General Gordon says of his men: "The poor fellows broke utterly down. The men cried like children. Strange indeed that they should have wept at surrendering in so unequal a fight, at being taken out of this constant carnage and storm, at being sent back to their families, at having their starved and wasted forms snatched from the hungry jaws of death! Yet they sobbed aloud, and wrung their hands in an agony of grief. As General Lee rode down the lines and saw the men crying, he said in a broken voice, 'Oh, if it had only been my lot to have fallen in one of our battles!'" "In a few hours" — General Gordon continues — "in a few hours that army was scattered, and the men went back to their ruined and dismantled homes, many of them walking all the way to the Carolinas and the Gulf, all of them penniless, worn out and well-nigh heartbroken."

Contrast with this sad picture our joy that knew no bounds. We all dismounted, and such a scene of handshaking and embracing I have never elsewhere witnessed. Some tossed their hats and cheered; some rolled on the ground, yelling like Indians; some sobbed like children, only with exuberance of happiness. It was the very madness of joy. I would confess — if it were not so undignified — that on that Sunday morning a certain overjoyed Chaplain might have been seen standing wrong end up, his hands on the ground and his feet in the air, as if he had actually bidden farewell to his understandings. The wild cheers that ran along the line told the story from rank to rank, and an audible wave of joy swept through the whole army. The long and anxious war was over. Our country was saved. Home was near. Our lives, which a moment before did not seem worth the tossing of a die, now seemed priceless with the hopes of peace.

The terms of capitulation were soon arranged. They were liberal and magnanimous, as befitted the occasion. General Lee afterwards declared: "I wish to do simple justice to General Grant when I say that his treatment of the Army of Northern Virginia at its surrender by me is without a parallel in the history of the civilized world. When my poor soldiers had nothing to eat, he issued the humane order that forty thousand rations should be immediately furnished them. [General Grant says, "I authorized General Lee to send his own commissary and quartermaster to Appomattox station, where he could have, out of the trains we had stopped, all the provisions wanted."] When I was directing one of my staff to make out a list of things to be surrendered, and named the horses. Grant said, *No! No! General Lee, not a horse; the men will need them for the spring ploughing.' I told Grant there was nothing he could have done to accomplish more good for them or for the government. When Grant said that my officers might retain their side-arms, I was again thankful; but when he disclaimed any desire to make a parade of surrender, I was indeed overjoyed and felt that *that* was a touch of magnanimity that bespoke a great soul."

Grant says, "I felt like anything rather than rejoicing at the downfall of a foe who had fought so long and valiantly and had suffered so much, and when our artillery began to fire a salute of a hundred guns to celebrate the victory, I ordered it stopped; the Confederates were now our prisoners and I did not want to exult over them."

And our whole army responded to our leader's magnanimity, and would do nothing to humiliate those whose terrible sufferings and agonizing mortifications were calculated to draw pity even from hearts of stone. We respected in them a devotion that had stood the final proof. Both sides had fought with heroic bravery, and each had brilliant victories or successfully contested fields as the crown of its valor. If the victors at Appomattox could recall a Malvern Hill, an Antietam, a Gettysburg, a Five Forks, the vanquished could recall a Manassas, a Fredericksburg, a Chancellorsville, a Cold Harbor. On that 9th of April the soldiers shook hands over the bloody chasm, and woe to him who shall ever seek to unlock that brotherly embrace!

As soon as the articles of capitulation were signed, the two commanding generals came out of the house, and each went his way, but how different in appearance and feeling! Lee was tall and stately, dressed in a fresh suit of Confederate gray with all the insignia of his rank, upon his head a high gray felt hat with gold cord, in his hands long buckskin gauntlets, and at his side the splendid dress-sword that had been given him by the State of Virginia. As he looked into the valley towards his army, he smote his hands together in an absent sort of way, and seemed to see nothing till his horse was led in front of him. Then he mounted; and a sadder man I have not seen as he rode silently away bearing the ignominy of the "lost cause" back to his dispirited followers, his disrupted State, and his dismantled home.

Grant was rather short and thick-set, and was dressed in his campaign clothes, which were all spattered over with mud from his ride of thirty-seven miles that morning. He had on the 8th been following Meade in Lee's rear. He wore a sugar-loaf hat, a frock coat unbuttoned, a dark vest, dark blue pants tucked into top-boots, and no sword. He had felt very sick for twenty-four hours, and had used the most heroic remedies in vain. But when he got word at noon that day that Lee was ready to surrender, "on the instant," he says, "I was cured." Yet three hours later, when all was over, I could read in his impassive face no emotion as he, like Lee, also rode silently away, though he was to send off a despatch that should electrify the North, and set all the church bells ringing with joyous peals at this new coming of the Prince of Peace with glad tidings of great joy that shall yet be to all people **(Note 16).**

As soon as I could get pen and paper — which was when the Cavalry stopped on April 14th at Nottoway Court House to rest and refit — I wrote my resignation, being desirous to begin at once my chosen lifework — the ministry. Talking about it with Sheridan, I asked him what he was going to turn his hands to now. He replied, "I know nothing but war, and I suppose I shall follow army life." But most of us were out of our element there, and hastened to get back to civil life. All of us, however, were unaware of the terrible tragedy that was then enacting in Washington.

When on April 9th Lincoln received the news of the surrender his heart bounded with joy, and, with his usual reference of all things to Providence, he ordered to be placed on the Capitol this Scripture: "Thanks be to God who giveth us the victory." The next morning — April 10th — Lincoln spoke his joy from the balcony of the White House to the multitudes gathered in front, and among them was one who said to his fellow-conspirator, "That will be the last speech he will make." And so it was

"That when the morn of peace broke through
  The battle's cloud and din
He hailed with joy the promised land
  He might not enter in."

Alas! the Savior of the Nation was to be its great Martyr. Only four days later — April 14th — was fired the fatal shot. If the deed must be done, there could be chosen no more fitting day than Good Friday, that had witnessed the crucifixion of the great Saviour of men.

The news of the terrible tragedy in Washington did not reach our camp till Saturday, when I was making my preparations for a Sunday service of farewell to my regiment, and I almost felt that I must withdraw my resignation, as it seemed on first thought that the war must continue. But the calmer second thought brought the assurance that the hands of the assassin could not turn back the floods of joy that were already lifting the hearts of victors and vanquished to a new sense of love for a common country. And this I said to the men in the final service on Sunday, April 16th, at Dress Parade, and told them that what seemed then the darkest of tragedies would prove to be the brightest of transfigurations, and that Abraham Lincoln would at once be lifted among the immortals. The greatness of his character had hitherto been hidden under the homely simplicity of his bearing and his childlike willingness to follow rather than to lead. But this humble waiting on events — which so many had thought his greatest weakness — would now be seen to have been his greatest strength, because it was really waiting on God, and when he saw clearly which way God and Duty pointed, then nothing could keep him from instant action. He waited two years before he freed the slaves. But when he heard the clock strike the Providential hour he signed without trembling the Proclamation of Emancipation — the most momentous individual act of modern times.

I count it one of the most precious privileges of my life that I once took in mine the hand of Abraham Lincoln — the *brotherly* hand that at the first Inaugural held out to the threatening South this olive-branch: "We are not enemies, but friends. We must not be enemies. Though passion may have strained, it must not break our bonds of affection. The mystic chords of memory stretching from every battlefield and patriot grave to every living heart and hearthstone all ever this broad land will yet swell the chorus of the Union when again touched, as surely they will be, by the better angels of our nature." And I rejoice to have held in mine the *firm* hand that kept true the rudder of the Ship of State through all the storms of war; the *kindly* hand that heartened the soldiers in the field and in the hospital, wrote letters for the sick, and smoothed the pillow of the dying; the *tender* hand that wrote the Gettysburg address, and the Second Inaugural with its "malice toward none" and its "charity for all." But more even than for all these I am proud to have clasped the *strong* hand that struck the fetters from millions of slaves and laid firm and forever in freedom the foundations of our nationality.

Notes

***Note 1,** page* 8. — These simple Services of Ordination at the Harvard Divinity School, July 14, 1863, reveal the deep meanings of the struggle of 1861 to 1865. In their essence they are very like the ideals of our now-united Nation in the present world-conflict.

Ordination
Of Mr. Charles A. Humphreys

To the Editor of the Christian Inquirer: —

In that little Divinity Hall Chapel you undoubtedly well remember and love, were gathered on the morning of the recent "Visitation Day" — while "the rain descended and the floods came" without — a few interested friends to ordain a Chaplain of the Second Massachusetts Cavalry Regiment, Mr. Charles A. Humphreys of the graduating class.

The exercises consisted of Prayer and Selections from Scripture by Mr. Chaney of Hollis-street; Ordaining Prayer by Dr. Noyes; Charge by J. F. W. Ware; Right Hand by Edward H. Hall, Chaplain 44th M. V., a closing hymn, and benediction by the new chaplain. It was somewhat amusing, as the audience broke up, to hear their expressions of surprise at having got through an ordination in less than forty-five minutes. I have been asked to send you the accompanying parts.

Charge

My Young Friend and Brother, — This occasion is new to our ecclesiastical annals, and there can be no one here who does not feel its peculiar interest and solemnity. The consecration of a young man to the service of God in the Church always impresses; but the service you now choose is not in the Church. What she has to offer of peace, of honor, of struggle, you turn from. It is not the Church that calls you to-day, but the country; and you stand at the altar, set apart by our prayers, as before by your own, to that service she asks of you. And yet, in serving your country, in taking your part in the lot of the day, are you not serving the Church? God, who has guided your young steps into this way of duty, keep you in it, and bless you!

The work of the army chaplain has never been satisfactorily limited or defined. I suppose that it cannot be. It is for each man to make of it all that he can, and the kind of man he is will determine the chaplain he shall be. Take, therefore, no counsel of those going before you, but go to make your own place, watching for opportunity, and doing your utmost everywhere. At home, where conventions and customs enclose, a man must yield to them somewhat, if he do not get overlaid by them. Your occasions, your duties, are not, cannot be limited for you. You enter a broad and largely untrodden field. You must make your own work. No man may do more than a chaplain — few have done less than some.

As preacher, your occasions will not be many. In the stir and uncertainty of active campaigning, there is little opportunity, perhaps less inclination, for the stated services of religion. A brief exhortation, with brief prayer, will be all you can ever wisely attempt. Speak earnestly out of your own life to the lives about you. Forget books, and theologies, and all nicety of language — the mere training of schools — and speak straight on, and simply the things which shall lead men out of themselves unto God. Exhort, instruct, rebuke, and have faith that no word uttered can return to you void.

I have heard it said of one of our brethren, "Oh! he was no chaplain at all. He never once said we were sinners." Do not be anxious to call men that word. It does little good. It satisfies the demand of some sects; it has a seeming of piety; but it never helps men to be better. They want broad, wholesome, indisputable truths and principles to stand upon, to build from. Give them these, and your work will be with power and success.

Your great work will be in your daily intercourse with officers and men. You are to teach from your life more than from your lips. I say *officers* and men. Do not overlook the former. Many chaplains find their position with the officers exceedingly unpleasant. They are barely endured as an uncomfortable necessity, and they become untrue in this branch of duty for the sake of their peace, and have sometimes terribly lapsed in their dignity and character. The officers are a part of your charge. You are not merely chaplain over the rank and file, but what will try your manhood more, what is of quite equal importance to the service and the country, to the men and the homes, you are chaplain over the officers. Though they may not feel it, or wish to, though you may be tempted to forget it, they are a part of your charge; and it is the emphatic word of one who has preceded you, that if the officers are not what is right, the chaplain can make them so — while it was the equally emphatic assertion of one high in regimental command to me lately, that where the officers were right, the moral tone of the soldier returning from service would be found to be higher than when he left home. I need not tell you, then, what a duty it is that devolves on you here. If I were you, I would know something about every man in my regiment — not his character only, but his history — what are his home-ties, his previous occupation, and what his future purpose; and then I would keep strictly, not a mere note-book, but a somewhat fuller diary for present reference, and for after use. I would find somehow to get at every man — in some way get and keep an influence over him. I think this can be done by a constant watchfulness and a little tact. The opportunities are little and many. In camp, in hospital, on the march, on the field, find out some *way* to do something. Great occasions, trying occasions, will *come*. You can *make little* ones — and you know what mighty things little things are. That is the way with men's hearts. Where you can be of any use, do any good, do not hesitate. Let position, and dignity, and convention, and etiquette go. They are small chaff where a soul may be helped. Take your manhood and apply it to their manhood. The soldier is singularly receptive, not of words only, but of influence. A very little thing will give you a warm place in his regard — a great control over him. In earnest himself, he sees clean through a sham; he despises all cant; he does not want to be stooped to; but to any hearty, honest manliness he gives a prompt and hearty return. He is singularly childlike. He will seek you in your tent; and lean on your word as he never would do at home. I have been surprised to find the man, brave, self-reliant on duty, in danger, coming to me as a little child, and as he never would at home; and it is the general testimony that those who have always been a law to themselves — never were led — in the life of the camp, when not in the line and pressure of duty, become singularly dependent; and the man who was at home always cheerful, in service is liable to depressions. His absence from home, the tone of public remark, the fatigue and harassing of the march, the discomfort of bivouac and picket, the tedium of guard duty, the monotony, or scantiness of rations, the thousand annoyances and privations of his condition, tend to depress him. The *morale* of a regiment may depend upon you. You must always be cheerful. Never let them catch you down-hearted or timid. Have a kind, hearty, genial word for all, always. Have you a good, clear, ringing, honest laugh? Use it. It is God's gift to you. It is contagious. It is better than a dram to a fainting spirit. Wherever you are, and whatever the strain of despondency about you, feel that it is your duty to keep a good heart, and you will find yourself the support of many.

My friend and brother! take these imperfect words — not the technical words of a charge, for I feel myself too young yet to assume such a task, especially in this place, where hallowed lips, long dumb, strove to show me the way into my work — as an assurance of the interest with which I shall follow you into a field from whose duties I have myself, it may be unwisely, shrunk. No man I so to-day envy as the man who goes out to this duty you have chosen. I am sure that you go to it from no impulse, no self-seeking, with no low hopes or aims, but out of a deep conviction, and a feeling, earnest heart. God will lead you, day by day. Day by day, your duties will unfold before you, and fresh opportunities arise. In your quiet, every-day intercourse and life, is to be your success. You will soon be known. Men will talk of you by the camp-fire, and in the tent. Without looking for any marked, startling results, be sure that your honest labor will not be in vain. It will bless others, and redound in blessing to yourself.

Right Hand of Fellowship

It is my pleasant duty, my brother, to bid you welcome to your new and untried work. I can do it very sincerely. It is a rare initiation into the Christian ministry that lies before you. I congratulate you that your entrance upon your calling falls in times and amid scenes like these; and that you are inclined to push forward at once to the front, where the truth you are to defend is receiving and dealing its heaviest blows.

It is with no common interest that Christianity looks upon this bloody strife. Indeed, she is deeply and mainly responsible for it. It is those stubborn, inexorable truths which she utters; those immutable laws which she proclaims; those seductive ideas at which she hints; justice, freedom, the sanctity of man, which lie at the bottom of the contest, and thrust themselves forward in every new battle-field. These are the mischievous cause of all our woes. But for them, the country might be slumbering still in her selfish materialism, undisturbed by any appeal from outraged justice or offended humanity. Having brought on the struggle, therefore — having rendered it inevitable — Christianity is bound to attend it to its close. Having guarded her sacred principles through all their hidden conflicts, it would be base recreancy to desert them when they enter on an open strife, and the battle-field is shifted to a stage where the world can see it.

It is with a purpose, therefore, that Christianity sends her representatives to the front to-day. Nor can she honorably do otherwise. And happy are they to whom this service is assigned.

You will go, my brother, where the old conflict of ideas has taken on itself a visible and palpable form. While others view it from afar, you will step into its very presence, and see it face to face. While others are speaking vaguely of the high inspirations of the hour, dimly conscious that such there are, you will place yourself in actual contact with them, *feel* their mighty power, and carry off their richest teachings. You will go, too, for a short season — never again perhaps, in this earthly life — where the musings and speculations of our religious faith become vivid and intense realities. For all this I congratulate you, my brother. Have I not a cause?

But I congratulate you as well, that you have chosen to consecrate your calling, at its outset, to the practical wants and living demands of the hour, to show how competent is the faith which you hold to deal with man's daily necessities, to interest itself in his common concerns, to appreciate his human needs, to go hand in hand with him, even into life's struggles and perils, and if suffering comes, to bind up the bleeding wound, and pour in the oil of manly sympathy and tender, loving charity. So religion wins its holiest triumphs.

Shall I not congratulate you, too, Christian minister as you are, that you are to enter on the practice of your faith where it will receive its severest and most pitiless tests? where none but a masculine, sinewy faith will do? where religion must strip itself of all its pretences, and abide by its simple realities? must forget its exclusiveness and lend itself to the largest, most comprehensive charity? where eyes, quickened to clearest insight, penetrate through every disguise in which mock-piety loves to wrap itself? where earnest souls sicken at all hypocrisies, yet yield themselves so unresistingly to the power of pure and lofty truth?

Capt. J. Sewall Reed, 1st Tenor   Capt. Josiah S. Baldwin, 1st Tenor

Major William H. Forbes, 2d Tenor
Chaplain Charles A. Humphreys, 1st Bass Capt.
Goodwin A. Stone, 2d Bass

CAMP QUARTETTE

And, when all else is said, I congratulate you, as a man and a citizen of this republic, that you are to have a hand in the mighty struggle in which *human freedom,* insulted and imperiled so long, is vindicating its majesty, and crushing its life-long foes to the earth. Great will be your joy, as the years pass by, that you have been an actor in the historic strife; and that you hallowed your calling by connecting it so intimately with the endangered cause of human progress.

Accept, then, my brother, this Hand of Christian Fellowship. There are greetings in store for you, I know, from camp and hospital and field, which will put these poor words of mine to shame. But in friendly sympathy I offer them.

In the name of the little brotherhood whose circle you now enter — in the name of that larger Church, broader than all party-lines, which, in these trial-hours, is gathering in its converts by thousands — in the name, higher and holier still, of that humanity to whose sacred cause you consecrate your fresh strength to-day — I bid you welcome to your labors. May God's blessing rest upon them, and your best hopes be amply fulfilled!

Note 2, page 8. — Photograph of Camp of Second Massachusetts Cavalry at Vienna, Va. Field and Staff Officers' Tents. Chaplain, Major Forbes. Colonel Crowninshield. Adjutant Kinne. Surgeon. Line Officers' Tents. Company Tents.

Note 3, page 8. — In the Harvard Glee Club I had sung first bass, and in our extemporized quartette in camp I took the same part, with Capt. Goodwin A. Stone, H. C. 1862, as second bass, Maj. William H. Forbes, H. C. 1861, as second tenor, and Capt. J. Sewall Reed as first tenor till he was killed at Drainesville, February 22, 1864, when Lieut. J. S. Baldwin took his place.

Note 4, page 8. — The books sent by my dear friend Rev. Henry Wilder Foote of King's Chapel were about two hundred volumes, some of them elegantly bound. They were in response to his appeal to his parishioners, who also contributed as many magazines. The books were not only well bound, but of a distinctly high order. I could furnish to my men the works of the poets — Hood, Wordsworth, Tennyson, Longfellow, Whittier, Holmes, and Lowell, and in dramatic poetry, Shakespeare. In history I had Gibbon and Macaulay, Sparks and Bancroft. In fiction I had Dickens and Scott and Thackeray and Bulwer and Bronte and Irving and a host of others.

Note 5, page 12. — My young friend, and neighbor on Humphreys Street, Dorchester, Samuel Groom, son of Thomas Groom, the well-remembered stationer of State Street, sent me in a single large box — twelve sets of Magic Divination Cards, four wood puzzles, three boxes of jackstraws, ten wire puzzles, twelve Solitaire boards made by his own hands with the help of his younger brother John, twelve boxes of marbles for use on the Solitaire boards, six boxes of wooden dominoes, three games of Authors, twelve Chinese puzzles, twelve checkerboards made of pasteboard, twelve boxes of counters, two wooden checker-boards and two boxes of checkers, twenty jew's-harps, one set of chessmen, eleven boxes of card dominoes, an abundance of pencils and pens and notepaper and envelopes, and some books and magazines — withal a splendid contribution to the entertainment of the soldiers.

Note 6, *page 12.* — It was in the yearning of Governor Andrew's great heart towards a race in bondage that he found a brave coadjutor in my college classmate Robert Gould Shaw, a boy of twenty-three, born in Boston and brought up in a family that for many years had been devoted to efforts for the emancipation of the blacks. So his mind was clear, and his heart was aglow, as to his duty to assist in every possible way to redeem a race of slaves. His only hesitancy was his youth and inexperience. He had enlisted as a private in the New York Seventh Regiment on the day of the first bloodshed in Baltimore. He was soon commissioned Second Lieutenant in the Second Massachusetts Infantry Volunteers, and rose to a captaincy within a year, having shared in all the battles in which this regiment was engaged. Early in 1863, Governor Andrew offered him the colonelcy of the first colored regiment to be raised in Massachusetts. He at first declined, in the modest consciousness of inability for so important a post. But soon after, he accepted the appointment, and said: "What I shall have to do is to prove that the negro can be a good soldier. I shall not be frightened out of it by its unpopularity." "If the raising of the colored troops prove such a benefit to the country and to the blacks as I pray and hope, I shall thank God a thousand times that I was led to take my share in it." We all felt that in thus accepting the leadership of a colored regiment, Shaw not only championed an unpopular cause at the *North* but made himself an outlaw with the *Confederate* authorities. And indeed they passed an act in their Congress declaring that any white officer captured while in command of negroes should be executed as a felon. I well remember the day, May 28, 1863, that Shaw led his regiment from Boston; how proud I was of his heroic bearing; how sad I was at his probable fate. And it came full soon. Leading his men in the charge against Fort Wagner, he fell with them just at the entrance of the fortress.

> "Right in the van
> On the red rampart's slippery swell,
> With heart that beat a charge, he fell
> *Forward* as fits a man." [James Russell Lowell.]

> "He and his dusky braves one moment stood, and then
> Drave through that cloud of purple steel and flame
> Which wrapt him, held him, gave him not again,
> But in its trampled ashes left to Fame

An everlasting name." [T. B. Aldrich.]

He was ignominiously buried in the trench "with his niggers," as the Rebels scornfully declared. But this ignominy of the trench was, like the ignominy of the cross, transformed into immortal glory, and now he stands out as an ideal knight, the champion of a race redeemed.

Note 7, page 18. — Herman Melville was born in New York City August 1, 1819, went to sea in 1837, and after many adventures in the islands of the Pacific returned to Boston in 1844. He published "Typee" in 1846 and "Omoo" in 1847. In 1847 he married Elizabeth, daughter of Chief Justice Shaw. In 1851 he published "Moby Dick," a classic among whaling stories, and in later years nearly a dozen others. He died in New York, September 28, 1891. His widow died in Boston, July 31, 1906.

Note 8, page 31. — This is the picture of Bartlett that I sent to Sculptor French, and which he acknowledged thus: —

Glendale, Mass.
July 30, 1902.

Dear Mr. Humphreys, — The photograph came safely and is a very valuable addition to the material I have to work from in moulding the statue of General Bartlett. Thank you very much not only for sending this to me, but for the kindly interest you have always taken in my doings.

With much regard I remain
Faithfully yours,
Daniel C. French.

This was Whittier's most worthy tribute to Bartlett: —

WILLIAM FRANCIS BARTLETT
Born June 6, 1840.

As Galahad pure, as Merlin sage,
   What worthier knight was found
To grace in Arthur's golden age
   The fabled Table Round?

A voice, the battle's trumpet-note,
   To welcome and restore;
A hand, that all unwilling smote,
   To heel and build once more!

A soul of fire, a tender heart
   Too warm for hate, he knew
The generous victor's graceful part
   To sheathe the sword he drew.

Brevet Maj. Gen. William F. Bartlett

Note 9, page 43. — An address given in the First Church, Dorchester, June 19, 1864, commemorative of Walter Humphreys, by Rev. Nathaniel Hall: —

On the soil of Virginia, near one of the fields recently swept by the storm of battle, is a freshly-made grave, bearing on its head-board this inscription:— "Private Walter Humphreys, Co. A, 13th Mass. Volunteers." [This head-board soon disappeared and the grave is "unknown."] We gather, in heart, this afternoon, around that distant grave. We come to pay a tribute of honoring affection to the memory of him whom that inscription designates; to recall the more recent incidents of his brief career; to depict the leading features of his character and life; to speak of him in words of simplicity and truth, — less to honor him than to benefit ourselves. It is fitting we should do this. Born and reared among us; until war sounded its clarion trump — sounded it, as he felt, for him — hardly leaving his native village; here presented, in infancy, for baptism; these walls the witness, from childhood up, of his listening presence; the Sunday-school enrolling him, early and late, among its cherished members, — it is fitting he should be thus remembered by us, were there not the added and appealing claim that he has given his life in our behalf, that he sleeps in a patriot's grave. Had his body returned to us for burial, we should have yielded above it public tribute — as we have over those of our brothers and sons who fell before him, in the same holy cause. Why withhold such tribute because his body rests afar." Nay, we will *not* withhold it. His relations to our country's conflict, to our church, to ourselves — above all, his private worth and his Christian example, urge to its bestowal.

Walter Humphreys was born on the 4th of July, 1842 — auspicious day on which to begin a life that was to be laid down, in the flower and beauty of it, for the cause of freedom and the rights of man. Little thought we, at that time of national prosperity and peace, that ere that cradled babe should have reached his majority, his arm would be needed, with a million more, to strike in defence of the nation's imperilled liberties and life. His childhood and youth were unmarked by extraordinary incident. Home and school, work and play, express the main diversifications of those swiftly, but calmly, speeding years. Nor was there anything remarkable in the gradual developments of his inner life; save that, beyond most, there was in him, and more and more noticeable, as characteristic traits, a singleness of mind, a sincerity of heart, an honesty of purpose, truthfulness, docility, sobriety, a sense of responsibleness, a conscientious fidelity. "He was the most conscientious," says his father, "of all my children"; the full worth of which eulogy they only can estimate who have known those on whom the comparison is based. How far these qualities were referable to implanted tendencies of nature, and how far to influences of education, He alone knows who sees, with omniscient eye, those subtlest of all workings which attach to the formative period of moral character; — though, doubtless, the ancestral head-stream whence flowed his life had much to do in giving it its puritanic type of excellence, as had the domestic and social influences into which he was born, in nurturing and shaping it.

He became early interested, and more and more as mind and heart unfolded, in questions of moral reform, and took such active part as a youth may, but as few comparatively do, in their advocacy and promotion. He exhibited in himself a worthy specimen of that product of distinctive New England culture and training, which consists in an intelligent apprehension of great public movements, and an earnest interest in them, long before the time of constitutional citizenship. With nothing of an unbecoming forwardness — at the farthest remove from this — he did not shrink from committing himself, among his associates, to any cause his convictions led to the approval of, nor to any course with reference to it which seemed right and obligatory. The remark has especial application to his connection with the Temperance Reform, in whose organized and active ranks heart and conscience led him to an early enlistment, and his fidelity to which no after "enlistment" served to lessen. His convictions of its importance, his sense of responsibility, and ever-wakeful conscientiousness, constrained him to work for it, whenever he saw, or thought he saw, a rightfully available opportunity, or a possibly impressible subject. He was not content, as too many are, with what the mere *example* of abstinence may effect, in this cause. The example, indeed, is much. Argument and appeal go but for little where it is wanting. But better both, — the persuasion of life and lip, of deed and word; life and deed yielding authority and emphasis to lip and word. It is not for me to speak of the comparative worth of organized action, in this Reform, and that which is private and personal; but I am moved to say that where the object is the rescue of the individual, private and personal and unofficial action, in a spirit of friendliness and sympathy, must, beyond all other, be effective to its end. Such, I understand, was one of the ways in which the conscientiousness of our young brother showed itself, in relation to this particular Reform. And it seems to me worthy an especial mention, as being so rarely found, in

Private Walter Humphreys

young or old. We do not enough consider, any of us, our responsibility for the use of opportunities given in the ordinary relations and passing intercourses of life, for such word of counsel, warning, encouragement, as we may be competent to speak. Conventionalisms, timidity, distrustfulness, restrain and bind us.

The war found him a youth of eighteen, engaged in a regular occupation. Its call came to him too loudly, at last, too personally, to be resisted. He heard in it the call of country, of freedom, of justice, of humanity. The voice within said, "Go." That voice, ever imperative with him, he of course obeyed. Considerations of a personal nature would have held him back. Natural tendencies and dispositions — tastes, temperament — said, "Stay." The sense of duty was too strong for them. Patriotism, humanity, pleaded too persuasively in the recesses of his heart. I think I am not saying too much when I say that none have gone forth to our great conflict with purer or more disinterested motives. Nothing, I am sure, would have taken him from the peaceful conditions, so consonant with his nature, in which his lot was cast, to enter upon the arena of military life, to assume the bearing, to endure the notoriety, to follow the pursuits of the soldier, — nothing less would have done it than the stern urgency of principle, than the divine persuasives of sentiment. With many who enlist, as we know, a natural susceptibleness to martial attractions, a love of change, of adventure, of distinction, of approbation, mingles with higher motives, even where higher motives are predominant. I think that with him they mingled not at all.

He went. He bade "good-bye" to home and friends, and turned, with manly heart, to meet the unknown fate awaiting him in the then hotly-waging contest. What a magnet — how potent — the war has been, to attract into conscious and manifest life the latent heroism of our homes! From beneath how many a lowly roof, and stately too, have issued youthful forms, clad and armed for camp and field — forms that had never known privation, hardship, sacrifice, — ready, hastening, to encounter them; — encountering them with unflinching and uncomplaining heart; passing, as by a bound, from the softness of youth into the gristle of moral manhood; surprising us into the knowledge that our boys are heroes! What a school for individual unfolding has the war afforded! What a training-ground, in other than the military sense! What instances have gleamed, through its smoke and dust, upon our half-believing vision, of intellectual and moral development and growth, — what revelations of character, power, nobility, enforced by its incentives, opportunities, appeals! "Are not such instances exceptions?" Doubtless, and rare ones, too. But they exist. Many a heart, watching from far-off homes, can point to them; their earlier solicitudes brightening into hopes, their fears ending in thankfulness. The war did, I judge, for our brother — its incentives, opportunities, appeals — what years of ordinary experience would have failed to do, in bringing out and maturing faculty and trait, and lifting him towards the height of a true manhood.

Enlisting, as a private, in the 13th Mass., then in the field, in active service, he left home, in the August of '62, to join it. It was with much difficulty, and after days of fatiguing travel, that he found his regiment; pressing forward, as it was, with the rest of the army of the Potomac, under Gen. Pope, in his attempt against Richmond. He came up with it to find its advance changed to a retreat, in rapid and excited movement, before the enemy; necessitating for him, in addition to what he had previously endured, seven days of still more wearing and intense fatigue. The result was physical exhaustion to a degree disabling him from duty, and sending him into a hospital, in Philadelphia. After being there for some time as patient, he was made Ward Master within it, and for many months served in that capacity; his impaired health excluding him from camp and field, but enabling him to much humble usefulness. So feeble was he for a time that it was proposed to him to obtain a discharge and return home; but he preferred to remain at his providentially assigned post, in hope of being able to rejoin his regiment; which at last he did. His stay at the hospital was made useful above and beyond the discharge of prescribed duty. In how many ways and to what extent we know not; but we know that his conscientiousness led him, there, as every where, to make use of all available opportunities for doing good, while his example of genuine and unpretending goodness told upon all who were brought in contact with him. He exhibited, while a patient, the strength and radicalness of his temperance principles, in refusing to take spirits, though prescribed by his surgeon; as also, afterwards, his benevolent interest in the cause, by originating and organizing a total abstinence society among the inmates of the hospital, of which he was one of the leading officers.

He left the hospital in December, and went into camp, at the winter-quarters of his regiment, in Virginia; and towards the last of April started with it, on the great campaign, yet in progress, under Gen. Grant. In a letter to his brother, dated May 3d, he speaks of the momentous character of the campaign they were commencing, in its possible issues and certain dangers, and adds, "If it should so happen that I should not again write, that I should offer myself up on my country's altar, believe that I was faithful, and that I faltered not in danger. Don't allow the folks to take an undue amount of anxiety in regard to my welfare, and if it should so happen that I fall, try to make them consider how honorable the death. I am very cheerful and contented." They were pencilled and hurried lines, written at night, in the expectation of starting at daybreak. He ends them thus, "May God crown our efforts with success." May 11th, he writes to his father, from a just contested field, "I am still safe. A great battle has been raging for six days. I have been in the midst of it, have been engaged in several charges, but have not been wounded. Terrible was the storm of cannon and musketry yesterday. I was not engaged with a musket, but was detailed to carry ammunition, in the midst of shot and shell. A great many have been killed and wounded." May 15th, he writes to his brother from Spottsylvania, giving a brief account of what had transpired in the last few days, and expressing himself in terms of tender endearment toward those at home. The day was Sunday, and he says, "Tell them, that though I am not sitting with them at church to-day, I am sitting in the broad Church of Nature, where I can commune with myself about heavenly things." A week after, May 22d, he again writes, reporting an advance from Spottsylvania to Guiney's Station, and speaking of his good physical condition, with the exception of foot-soreness, from incessant marches. "Our Lieut. General," he says, "does not rest after one day's engagement with the enemy, but still presses him before us." "We proceeded yesterday," he writes, "for some distance on the Fredericksburg and Richmond railroad. I assure you it was cheering to think, as I stepped from sleeper to sleeper, that I was on the direct road to Richmond." This was the last letter received from him. June 1st, eight days from the date of it, while moving forward, with his brigade, under fire of the enemy's sharpshooters, to establish a new line of breastworks, he received a wound in the abdomen, and was borne, by a loved comrade, to the field hospital, where, on the evening of the next day, he died.

"I saw him several times," — writes the chaplain of the 39th Mass., to whom he was before a stranger — "and had the sad pleasure of administering to his wants. He received intelligence of the probable fatal result of his wound with great calmness. He did not seem to suffer much, and retained his senses clearly. When asked if he had any messages for his friends, he said, 'Send them my love, and say good-bye to them.' He placed his Testament in my hands, saying that they might prize it as a keepsake. He was buried this morning, in a piece of woods, on the road to Cold Harbor." "He sustained an excellent character, used no intoxicating beverages, no profane language. From his conversation I judged him to be a Christian and prepared for death." "The fairest and best are taken [concludes the writer, whose letter does credit to his own heart, as well as to the subject of it] the fairest and best are taken — the sacrifice is great — but the reward is sure." To this testimony from one to whom he was a stranger, I will add that of a young fellow-soldier and friend, who during this campaign had fought and slept by his side, though not able to be with him at the last: "I have always respected him," he writes, "for his Christian attributes, but more lately, by association with him, discovered he had true bravery. From the commencement of this campaign he has always been in his place. His physical strength and my own I judge to have been nearly the same, and thus I am enabled to appreciate his self-denials. We had a week of tedious marches, by day and night; had much fatigue duty, often after marching by day throwing up breastworks at night; had rain upon rain, in which he was wet to the skin, and lay down with nothing under or over him; was under fire more or less every day, — and yet he showed nothing of ill humor; I did not hear from him one word of complaint; he asked for nothing but 'good news,' and when that came was happy." The writer speaks especially of one time, when bullets and shells were coming thick and fast around him, how he preserved a perfect calmness; and at intervals, when unoccupied with the work for which he was especially detailed and waiting orders to resume it, how, instead of resting himself, he found employment in assisting, with thoughtful kindness, the wounded soldiers, coming at the time in crowds from the front, about a quarter of a mile distant. In another letter, to his own family, this young comrade writes, — "Humphreys never shirked a duty."

Testimony like this, from friend and stranger, is of priceless worth; though we looked for no other. We who knew him at home, and knew the spirit in which he went from us, could not have believed otherwise than that he would stand firm and faithful in the time of trial and danger, and do well the part assigned him, wherever and whatever it might be. And yet, it was a mighty trial, it was an appalling danger; and no wonder if, momentarily, he had quailed before it. He did not quail, the testimony is, even momentarily, but bore himself, at once and through all, with a calmness and courage which must have drawn its inspiration from a higher than mortal source. We are accustomed to hear of the practical worth of religious principle in other spheres and connections; these times have led us to know its value on the battle-field; how it endues a man with an unfearing and persistent and unconquerable bravery, as far superior in effect as it is in source to the reckless dash and fevered impulses of the mere fighter for vengeance or a name. Walter Humphreys was a hero. It needed not that he should become a soldier to assure us of it. For common and daily life has its calls for heroism; and they are answered there. They were so by him, — in his stern fidelity to a sense of duty and of right. Nor was he less a hero because his place was in the ranks; because his name, as inscribed above his sleeping dust, has no prefix save that of *"Private."* Praise to those who lead on to victory; praise no less to those who follow, and achieve it!

Another is added to our youthful dead. We had hoped to welcome him home, when the cause which demanded him should have won its final triumph — his patriotic self-devotion would hardly have permitted it before. It cannot be. Vainly among those who may then return to us, shall we search for him. His voice shall have no part in the ascending psalm of a people's thanksgiving over a redeemed and peace-encircled land. It is well. He has done what he could to help forward that glorious consummation. He has died nobly, for noblest ends. He has left a fair and stainless record. He has bequeathed a memory which it will do us good to cherish.

In the words, just received from his distant post, of a brother, who, in a kindred spirit, is serving the same blessed cause, — "He loved great principles, labored for them, fought for them, died for them. Into his short life was compressed more of real lifeexperience than commonly enters into the longest lives. His struggles to find out the path of duty, his courage in following it as soon as discovered — these developed in him a very strong character." "He left us when his soul was firm in its aspirations after good, when he rejoiced in the freshness of its strength." "You cannot know how thankful I am that Walter was not found wanting in the terrible trial of his faith and courage. I was confident it would be so, when he enlisted. Let us who are left emulate his goodness and faithfulness."

Touching tribute, from an elder to a younger brother! Beautiful "farewell," to be breathed from the home of earth — to be borne to the Home of Heaven! Blessed the homes that have such to give to country and to God! Blessed the country that has such enrolled among the hosts of her defenders!

Note 10, page 53. — The address delivered by Rev. Charles A. Humphreys, Chaplain of the Second Massachusetts Cavalry, at the funeral of Capt. Thos. B. Fox, Jr., in Dorchester, July 28, 1863, was as follows: —

Another hero has fallen. Another lover of his country has sealed his devotion with his life. Let us not weep. The sacrifice was willing. The object was worthy. "The Country" has a more sacred meaning now to many hearts. The life that was, still is; but broader, purer, nobler. Let us not weep for our own loss. He has only exchanged this transient life in mortal flesh, for an eternal life in immortal memories and undying affections. His shrine is now in our own hearts. His fitting monument is his remembered life. Let us not weep for him. He fought for his country. Who could leave a brighter record? He died for his country. Who could wish a better epitaph?

Capt. Thomas B. Fox

The record of his life is simple, but it is the simplicity of purity and nobleness. He needs no written memorial, for his life wrote itself. It was known and read by all who met him. A more open nature I have not known. A casual acquaintance did not, however, see his best qualities. He was so frank that he would not conceal his worst side, and so strong in his conscious integrity that he cared not to put forward his best side. His generosity of spirit, his purity of soul, his devotedness of purpose and his exalted aims; these were not known to all.

His school life is known to most of you his townsmen. He was always upon the stage in public-school exercises; and you well remember his flashing eye and rich full voice as he caught the spirit of his theme, or declaimed some thrilling passage from the orators that he loved. His college career was brilliant and honorable. As a scholar he took very high rank, one year standing second in a class of a hundred. As a "society man" he had few if any equals. As a debater he was masterly, showing a peculiar fitness for the profession of his choice. As a speaker he was convincing and impressive. He received the highest honor in the gift of his class; being chosen their orator. His classmates of 1860 will miss a genial companion and warm friend, and will mourn the loss of him who has been one of their brightest honors. Yet they cannot but rejoice in the honor of his death as of his life. Captain Fox is the seventh martyr that they have already given to their country. Four have fallen from one regiment — the noble Second Massachusetts Infantry — whose record will be none the less brilliant, that its officers have in so large a measure been taken from those who had been trained only in professional pursuits. Harvard shall have no brighter honor than the devotion of her sons to their country's cause, and shall rear no nobler monument than to those who fell in her service.

But, friends, we do not come to-day to mourn for private griefs or to speak of private honors. The honor and the grief are for us all. Even those who looked on our friend as son and brother do not to-day mourn their private loss. They gave him to his country in the bright promise of his early manhood. He fought bravely in her service. And now that he lies cold and dead, they would have the last sad rites devoted to the same blessed cause. And how fitting! for he, too, would have it so. On earth as we walked together, ofttimes he would unlock to me his deepest soul. But those lips never spoke more persuasively than now, and I seem to see deeper into his spirit than when I grasped his warm hand and gazed into his friendly eyes. Let me give voice to his spirit, as it speaks to me to-day of the duty of loyalty and the beauty of sacrifice. Ah! how thrilling the call to patriotic devotion that comes from the poor dumb mouths of our country's martyrs! With what a terrible force the lesson comes to us from lonely firesides and deserted homes! The voice of our brothers' blood cries to us from the ground to learn this lesson quickly, and to learn it well. As a people we have not felt, and do not feel, enough respect and reverence for established authority, and the American pulpit has been remiss in failing to urge this respect and reverence on the ground of moral duty and religious principle. But our soldiers, by their words as well as by their acts, are teaching us more effectively the duty of loyalty.

I have been with those who left home and friends, the cultivation of literature and the pursuits of peace, to follow in the path of grim-visaged War; who left us with our blessings on their heads; but who through the long months of weary toil and impending peril have been turning their faces homeward for sympathy and encouragement only to see the flush of patriotism paling in our cheeks and to hear our words of complaint and faintheartedness; I have been with those who have learned in the face of death to see things as they are; who dealing with stern realities have caught the power to distinguish sharply the true from the false, and have learned to value that which is founded in the eternal realities; who in the illumination of pure and noble desires to serve their country have seen with clearest vision what that country needs; and these have told me that the great want of this country is loyalty, loyalty founded on a religious conviction of duty. The voice of our country should be to us as the voice of God; and it *is* to all true souls.

Some feared that after the first thrill of patriotic devotion, when pain and sacrifice should be seen to be inseparably connected with devotion to principle, patriotism would then die out. Of course there are craven spirits everywhere and at all times; but the cold form before us starts into life to hurl back the insinuation that patriotism can die out in noble hearts. He left for the war in the midst of disaster to our cause, after the battle of Cedar Mountain, in which his own regiment lost many officers. The last thing he did before leaving was to attend the funeral of Captain Abbott of the Second, his college classmate and friend. But he was cheerful, and only gathered fresh courage from the costly sacrifice. Let us to-day catch some of his spirit. Let us renew our vows of devotion to our country's cause, and if the name of *Fatherland* cannot move us to patriotic feeling, let the silent eloquence of this wasted life stir us to our duty.

Wasted life did I say? No! His spirit speaks to me again of the eternal beauty of sacrifice. Nothing worthy is gained but through sacrifice. The world was saved by sacrifice; and our country, baptized in the blood of her noblest sons, shall work out for herself a new salvation and take the path to a higher destiny. I hear him say, —

"O do not falter, peace must come by pain,
  Heaven is not found, but won;
Hold the dark angel till he moulds again
  The peace he hath undone."

No, brother, we will not falter; while the memory of thy life holds a place in our breasts, we will be true to our country; and inspired by thy noble sacrifice, we too shall dare to die in her defence. But do thou, brother, —

"Go to thy home, at noon, from labor cease;
  Rest on thy sheaves, thy harvest work is done;
Come from the heat of battle, and in peace,
  Soldier, go home; with thee the field is won."

Note 11, page 67. — Lieutenant Amory, paroled in Charleston, September 23, 1864, so far recovered his strength as to return to his regiment at Winchester December 27, 1865, and remained till the end of the war, and passed before Lincoln and Grant in the Grand Review in Washington, and reached his home July 12, 1865, supremely thankful that, spite of his sufferings and disabilities, he could see the war through to its end, and feel that he had some share in its glorious consummation. But the price he had to pay was a lifelong martyrdom of ill health. Yet like a true soldier he never complained, and did what he could, managing large business interests, and from his ample resources helping quietly all good causes. He passed away November 5, 1913, leaving behind him a blessed memory and an honored name.

Note 12, page 85. — In regard to undertaking this labor, the sculptor, Daniel Chester French, wrote me, October 9, 1884, "I am very anxious to do my best in this very important work and on so inspiring a subject as General Lowell and want to do it when I have plenty of time and under the best conditions." When the bust was finished and placed in Memorial Hall he wrote me, March 8, 1886, "I am happily disappointed in the effect of the bust, since it is in position. It looks better than I expected, and is one of the few things of mine upon which I can look without more regret than pleasure." I myself was not greatly surprised at this confession of the sculptor's frequent disappointments, for I knew that his ideals were always far ahead of the possibility of their full expression in the cold marble. Nor was I greatly surprised at his marvellous *success* when I considered his conscientious and patient fidelity, of which I had seen many evidences.

Lieut. C. W. Amory

One of these he revealed in a letter to me, November 6, 1884, in which he said, "In modelling the bust everything in the shape of a photograph will be valuable, even those taken in childhood sometimes furnishing a proof of some doubtful form." But the best proof that I found of the sculptor's success was the satisfaction of Mrs. Charles Russell Lowell. It had been quite difficult for me to get her permission to have the work done. Of course she saw in her husband a thousand things that no marble could express. But she wrote me February 23, 1885, "It is wonderful that Mr. French should have been able to get so much character into the bust, and I am perfectly satisfied to have it remain as a likeness of Colonel Lowell."

Framingham, March 10, 1886.

To the President and Fellows of Harvard College:

Gentlemen, — In behalf of his fellow-officers of the Second Massachusetts Cavalry Volunteers and other friends of the late Gen. Charles Russell Lowell I have the honor to present to you his portrait-bust, sculptured by Daniel C. French of Concord in Italian marble and now set up in Memorial Hall in the niche kindly assigned by you October 20, 1884.

Yours respectfully,
Charles A. Humphreys.

The "other friends" spoken of in this formal presentation were John M. Forbes, William Amory, J. Huntington Wolcott, Charles E. Perkins, and Edward W. Emerson.

A pleasant incident in connection with the photographs of the bust of Lowell was this: I sent one to Col. Robert H. Renshaw, a classmate of Lowell, H. C. 1854, and I directed it to him at the island of Teneriffe, where in 1879 I had last seen him. I was voyaging through those summer isles — Fayal, Madeira, and Teneriffe — in search of health, and on the latter island in the valley of Orotava I found Renshaw and he invited me to come to his house and, as he said, "take pot luck" with him. His "pot luck" was dispensed in a banquet of ten most elegant courses, and his hospitality was unbounded. And yet the last time we were near each other he was living on one onion — as I have told on page 277 — because Sheridan, with whom

Gen. Charles R. Lowell

I then was, had stolen his Uncle Robert's supply-trains. Renshaw married a niece of Gen. Robert E. Lee and was Quartermaster on his staff, and when the war was over his mortification led him to abandon his native land and take refuge in Teneriffe. His delight now in recalling the old college days before the war was most manifest, and I could tell him of the buried animosities and the more strongly cemented Union. At any rate we had a great time clasping hands over the bloody chasm, and when I had photographs taken of the Lowell bust, I decided to send one to Colonel Renshaw at Teneriffe. What was my surprise and gratification when I received from him the following letter!

Richmond, Virginia,

27th April, 1885.

Dear Mr. Humphreys, — I cannot tell you how much gratified I was last night to receive your kind letter of 4th March enclosing a photograph of the Bust of my old friend Chas. R. Lowell, for which I beg you to accept my most cordial thanks. Your letter was forwarded to me from Teneriffe. I left the Islands in 1882 and have since been residing in Virginia where I hope one of these days to have the pleasure of meeting you and showing that 2½ year old Charlie of whom you so kindly speak. Reciprocating your kind wishes and with most cordial regards, Believe me.

Very Sincerely Yours,
Robert H. Renshaw,

Note 13, page 107. — This photograph of Lieut. Huntington Frothingham Wolcott is copied from a portrait of him by William M. Hunt. His younger brother was our honored Governor Roger Wolcott, who thus speaks of the soldier boy: —

Commonwealth of Massachusetts, Executive Department,

Boston, Jan. 12th, 1898.
Rev. Charles A. Humphreys,
Randolph, Mass.

My dear Mr. Humphreys, — I returned to you yesterday the paper on the battles of Dinwiddie Court House and Five Forks, which you were kind enough to send to me. I read it aloud on Sunday evening to my Mother and our children, and we all found it deeply interesting. It is a most graphic account of those days so full of destiny to the country. They were the times that made men heroes at an age when we should now consider them hard-

Lieut. Huntington Frothingham Wolcott

ly more than boys.

Please accept my thanks, and believe me

Very truly yours,
Roger Wolcott.

Lines in memory of Lieut. Huntington F. Wolcott by Chaplain Charles A. Humphreys: —

Not All Is Lost

The look of love, the gentle modest ways
That charmed you through his happy childhood's days;
Youth's larger hopes, yet self-contained and true,
Eager to gird himself life's work to do,
    These are not lost.

The manly spirit, and the loyal soul.
The daily record writ on honor's scroll.
The honest heart on faithfulness intent.
The wholesome life in ways of virtue spent,
    These are not lost.

The reverent listening to his country's call,
The cheerful giving of his strength, his all,
The brave farewell to native home and state,
The fortitude to meet a soldier's fate.
    These are not lost.

Not one is lost. In memory's vista bright,
Transfigured all shall rise to clearer light,
And things, deep hidden in the day's fierce glow.
The night of death shall clear, and you shall know
    They are not lost.

[Dedicated to Mr. and Mrs. J. Huntington Wolcott.]

Note 14, page 123. — Caspar Crowninshield was born in Boston, October 23, 1837, received his early education in Boston schools, and finished his preparation for college under Rev. William C. Tenney of Northfield, where tales of his magnificent physique and athletic prowess were often repeated with admiration.

Entering the class of 1860 at Harvard, he became at once its athletic champion, and on "Bloody Monday," September 1, 1856, led us Freshmen to victory over the Sophomores, he himself forming the head of a living wedge that clove our confident opponents asunder, and made a way for the ball to be pushed to its goal. This was only the third Freshman victory in the whole history of the college. When I say that in this encounter Caspar Crowninshield was easily the first, it should be noted that of the seventy who lined up behind him, sixty-one had the pluck, five years later, to fight for their country, fifty-one of them as commissioned officers, and on the more bloody fields of war twelve of them laid down their lives, and among them was the hero of Fort Wagner.

Through our college life, Caspar Crowninshield was stroke oar in a crew that never knew defeat, and on Class Day he was our Chief Marshal. He had been chosen without a question, and bore the honor without a peer.

After graduation he gave himself to business, till the war broke out, when he at once put himself into training for military service, and accepted a commission as captain in the Twentieth Massachusetts Infantry. Going to the front in September, the very next month finds him heroically leading a forlorn hope, after the defeat at Ball's Bluff, where, after sending by boat across the river his men who could not swim, he strips off his outer clothing, takes his watch in his mouth and his blanket on his shoulders, and swims across amid a shower of death-dealing bullets. C. B. Brown of the Nineteenth Massachusetts Infantry writes: "About four o'clock in the morning, Caspar Crowninshield turned up, in shirt and drawers, with a blanket over his shoulders, after a cold swim across the river. All unite in praising his gallant conduct on the field of battle."

In another month he followed his special aptitude and his personal inclination, and joined the cavalry, accepting a captaincy in the First Massachusetts, and doing distinguished service with it in South Carolina and Virginia, till January 30, 1863, when Col. Charles Russell Lowell drew him into the Second Massachusetts Cavalry, with the offer of the senior majority, and all his subsequent military career was with this regiment, of which he took command as soon as it reached the field, since Colo-

Lieut. Col. Caspar Crowninshield

nel Lowell was at once put in command of a brigade, and Lieut. Col. H. S. Russell was on other duty.

In a career that was always brave and resourceful, it is difficult to pick out special achievements. I have spoken of Ball's Bluff; I will allude to only two others.

When General Early, in his advance upon Washington, in July, 1864, reached its outer defences, and, to his surprise, found them well guarded, he sought at once to save himself by retreat. As it happened, the Second Massachusetts Cavalry was then the only regiment available for pursuit, and it started immediately to harass the enemy. Our advance battalion, led by Colonel Crowninshield, came upon Early's extreme rear guard — composed of Jackson's cavalry brigade — just beyond Rockville, and charged upon them gallantly. Gen. B. T. Johnson writes: "The Second Massachusetts Cavalry hung upon our rear and made it very uncomfortable for us generally." The flying Confederates were annoyed into many a counter charge, all of which were stoutly repelled.

The other occasion I would specify was his successful charge at Cedar Creek, after his commander, Lowell, had been mortally wounded in two unsuccessful charges. Crowninshield said: "I never expected to succeed or to get out alive. The enemy's fire was terrific. Compared with it, Ball's Bluff was child's play. But I saw the infantry charging on the right, and I charged and said, 'God, just take my soul!'"

General Crowninshield was never wounded, though often under fire. Twice he saved himself by swimming, once at Ball's Bluff and once at the North Anna River. On this latter occasion he showed his quickness to meet an emergency. Following Sheridan in his raid round Richmond, in March, 1865, we came to the river after dark, being ourselves near the end of a column that was ten miles long. All before had passed over in safety. But in the darkness we missed the ford, as we were only guided by the horses in front of us, and they had gradually been pushed down stream by the force of the current, and when we came to cross we struck deep water and our horses had to swim. In the confusion many a horse and rider went down to his death, I was pushed from my horse and trodden down to the bottom of the river. Managing to wriggle away from the struggling mass, I shouted, as soon as I rose to the surface, "Where is Colonel Crowninshield?" thinking he had, perhaps, met a worse fate than myself. But there was no reply. I soon, however, discovered that, in order to save the others from a watery grave, he swam to the shore and found the ford, and set lights to guide the rest of the column. Strange that no one else had thought of that necessity for their safety. If my Colonel was never wounded, I know he was spattered with mud by a shell that, fortunately, refused to burst, for I was standing with him, on the morning of Lee's surrender, when the last shell that was ever fired from a Rebel battery fell harmless at our feet.

I do not trust myself to speak of the proud admiration and affectionate regard I felt for my classmate and my Colonel. He was one of the most lovable of men, simple as a child, but brave as a hero. Sheridan said of him: "He is very near to me in feeling and sympathy. I like him very much. He has a noble nature and a true patriotism."

He was "one of those whose faith and truth on war's red touchstone rang true metal." One of those loyal souls who felt

> "'Tis man's perdition to be safe
> When for the truth he ought to die."

Faithful soldier, we bid you welcome to your well-earned rest.

Brevet Brig. Gen. Caspar Crowninshield died in Boston, January lo, 1897.

Note 15, page 123. — William Hathaway Forbes was born in Milton, Mass., November 1, 1840; Second Lieutenant, First Massachusetts Cavalry, December 26, 1861; First Lieutenant, July 27, 1862; Captain, Second Massachusetts Cavalry, January 14, 1863; Major, May 12, 1863; taken prisoner at Aldie, Va., July 6, 1864; Lieutenant Colonel, October 21, 1864; mustered out, May 15, 1865; died October 11, 1897.

This is the skeleton-record which I would like to clothe in flesh and blood, and make to live again. But how can I picture that manly form with its distinguished bearing, that fair face with its lofty look, that elastic step quick on errands of service, that winning presence that drew all hearts? And when I would look within at the pure spirit and the generous soul, I am prevented by the thought of his modesty from saying all I would like of his worth, and he was so close to me through the most trying scenes that I dare not trust myself to speak my love for him. I can only utter a few simple words of happy remembrance of his youth's patriotic devotion.

He was an unspoiled favorite of fortune; and, outwardly, had everything to lose by going to the war. But his spirit of knightly chivalry had not been smothered under the love of pleasure and power that wealth frequently fosters. He saw, beyond the fields where men delve for greed and gold, the heights of heroism where men die for country and honor, and "what he dared to dream of, he dared to do."

> "When I remember with what buoyant heart,
>   Midst war's alarms and woes of civil strife,
> In youthful eagerness thou didst depart
>   At peril of thy safety, peace, and life,
> Ne'er from thyself by Fortune fair beguiled,
> I name thee to the world — Stern Duty's Faithful Child."

He was one of these heroic men who, in the trial of battle, was ready to lay bare against the hostile bayonet his own fearless breast. At Aldie, when his command was scattered and the day was lost, he would not yield the field, but charged alone against the on-rushing line of the enemy, pierced with his sabre one at least of the Rebel officers, and would not surrender till he was pinned to the ground under his own fallen horse.

> "To front a lie in arms, and not to yield,
> This shows, methinks, God's plan
> And measure of a stalwart man,
> Limbed like the old heroic breeds.
> Fed from within with all the strength he needs."

He was, indeed, "fed from within."

> "His strength was as the strength of ten
> Because his heart was pure."

"All the ends he aimed at, were his country's, his God's, and truth's."

> "He followed Truth, and found her
> With danger's sweetness round her.
> And he, our brother, fought for her,
> At life's dear peril wrought for her,
> So loved her he would die for her."

How near he often came to death on the field by the chance of the unseen bullet, no one can say; but I know of the fierce intent of the barely escaped sabre-thrust, and of the almost unendurable tortures of hope-deferred amid the exposures and starvation of southern prisons. Twice he was taken out and told that he would be exchanged, and twice he was brought back to what seemed a living death. Yet he kept up good courage, even after both his messmates were released before him, and patiently endured unto the end, sustained by invisible trusts. Seldom did he close his eyes to try to sleep on the floor of the work-house or the earth of the prison-pen, without leading us in singing that sweet song, from *Der Freischütz*, whose adapted words are not only a hymn of trust, but also a prayer of faith: —

> "When o'er the western hills the sunset tints blending
> Show us how quickly fades all that on earth is bright,
> Then to unfading realms our prayer is ascending —
> God of the fatherless, guide us, guard us to-night."

Of him Emerson's words seem most fitting: —

> "There is no record left on earth,
> Save in tablets of the heart,
> Of the rich inherent worth,
> Of the grace that on him shone,
> Of eloquent lips, of joyful wit;
> He could not frame a word unfit,
> An act unworthy to be done.
> Honor prompted every glance;
> Honor came and sat beside him."

If we call them heroes who fell on the field, amid all the sustaining inspirations of glorious war, how much more heroic is he, who, having passed bravely through the perils of the fight, bears uncomplainingly, month after month, the unspeakable horrors of Confederate prisons, and then, year after year, the hardly-concealed marks of their blighting touch. Not all the heroes died in battle. A finer heroism may still live on in those who, through weary decades, have borne about with enfeebled strength the dread entail of war's exposures.

Yes, thou true and noble soul, we honor equally the courage with which you went out to fight, and the fortitude with which you came home to endure.

"Hail! and farewell! thine earthly work doth cease;
  Rest on thy sheaves, thy harvest toil is done;
Come from life's well-fought battle, and in peace.
  Soldier, go home, for thee the field is won."

Our lessening ranks bring us together closer, shoulder to shoulder, and make more precious the remembered heroisms of a life like that of Forbes. God make us all as noble, and keep us all as true.

"O beautiful! my Country!
Among the nations bright beyond compare,
  What were our lives without thee?
  What all our lives to save thee?
  We reck not what we gave thee;
  We will not dare to doubt thee.
But ask whatever else, and we will dare."

The father of William Hathaway Forbes was John Murray Forbes, and we called him "The Father of our Regiment," because he did so much for us. So I will add here a short sketch of his patriotic labors.

John Murray Forbes died at Milton October twelfth, eighteen hundred ninety-eight, in the eighty-sixth year of his age.

Of this long life, filled as it was with honorable labors, I may speak of those only that concerned the country's welfare in the Civil War. But merely to name them would fill volumes. I can mention only a few, as illustrations of numberless patriotic labors to which he gave his strong intellect and his sympathetic heart.

Before the war he did what he could to avert the strife, and became one of the Peace Commissioners, seeking to bring about a reconciliation. Failing in that, he gave himself with utter devotion to the suppression of rebellion. He planned with General Scott for the saving of Fort Sumter, but their efforts came to naught through the treachery of high officials. Not discouraged, he gave himself to any unpaid and unofficial service that promised relief to the country in its dire distress. Was the path of Abraham Lincoln to the White House beset with Rebel plots, Forbes is foremost in making futile their snares. Was the path of Governor Andrew, in his preparations for war, beset with innumerable difficulties, Forbes removed the heaviest of them by assuming responsibility in untried situations, and pledging support where state funds were lacking. Did the war find us without a navy, Forbes planned the equipment of the merchant marine into an effective arm for striking strong blows at rebellion. Did English sympathy with the South imperil the foreign operations of the national treasury, Forbes must be sent abroad to check Rebel plans, and sustain our government's credit. Did the heart of Massachusetts agonize at the slow recognition of the manhood of the negro and the opportunity for his soldierly succor, Forbes must be sent to Washington to put more conscience and common sense into military plans. Did the heart of the North bleed for the sufferings of her soldiers in Rebel prisons, Forbes pours streams of gold into the hands of the Commissioners of Exchange in the hope that some of it would filter through the hands of the prison-keepers to their starving victims. When I was released at Fort Sumter, in 1864, I found unlimited gold awaiting me to be used to relieve my messmates left behind. When I reached my home nearly exhausted with prison exposures and starvation, that paradise of Naushon with its warmer than English hospitality was thrown wide open to me to recruit in, and the generous hearts that had welcomed there the artist Hunt and the poet Whittier, Holmes the wit and Emerson the philosopher, thought nothing too good for even the humblest soldier. No day passed in that island home without some work for the army. The waysides were stripped of the floss of the milkweed to make pads and pillows to ease the wounds of the soldiers in the hospitals, and nimble needles plied day and night to knit warm coverings for the exposed pickets. I wonder that there was a horse left in the stalls; for Mr. Forbes, besides supplying many of us cavalrymen with an outfit, insisted on supplying our losses in the field, and our Colonel had thirteen horses shot under him in a campaign of two months.

I cannot stop to speak of the inspiration of his personal visits to our camp, nor of the immeasurable beneficence of his charities, that did not cease with the close of the war, but have through thirty years and more smoothed the weary path of many a disabled veteran.

I would like to tell of Mr. Forbes in other relations than as the friend of the soldier, — of his keen foresight in business, the balanced wisdom of his practical counsels, his forceful championship of political purity, and of the numberless streams of his benevolence, only exceeded in beauty by the modesty with which they were poured forth. It would be a delight to draw aside, for a moment, the veil of his lovely home-life; but I must be satisfied here with celebrating in my honored friend his supreme fidelity to that strenuous strain of loyalty in his ancestral traditions drawn from generations of Highland chiefs, that gave to us a patriotism broader and finer than the devotion of any Scottish clan, and a helpfulness larger and richer than any Old-World beneficence.

Of Mr. Forbes I may say as Milton did of Lycidas: —

"His fame grows not on merely mortal soil.
 Nor in the glistering foil
 Set off to the world, nor in broad rumor lies;
 But lives and spreads aloft by those pure eyes
 And perfect witness of all-judging Jove
 As he pronounces lastly on each deed —
 Of so much fame in heaven expect thy meed."

Note 16, page 126. — In Memoriam Ulysses S. Grant: A Discourse preached at First Parish Church, Framingham, Mass., Sunday, August 9, 1885, by Rev. Charles A. Humphreys: —
 "He that humbleth himself shall be exalted." — Luke xiv. 11.

As I recall that marvellous career which yesterday ended in a march of triumph to the tomb, the one characteristic that rises most frequently upon the attention and the one key that offers a solution of its marvel is humility.

"Nearest the throne of God must be
 The footstool of humility,"

and the highest *earthly* throne that this age has seen reared in the sight of the world was reached by the humblest of men, by a man who was willing to take the second place, — indeed, to lose himself in a cause, to *sink* his own aspirations in loyalty to his country's need. The minds of the people are now filled with the exaltation that he attained, — with the honors that have been so heaped upon him in these later years that a National Museum has been found their only fitting depository; with that triumphal journey round the world, a journey such as no other man, be he king or conqueror, ever made, all the greatest of earth's potentates receiving him as a peer and all the peoples pouring adulation at his feet; and now with that last journey that draws the whole nation into uncovered ranks of silent grief to line the lifeless body's pathway to the grave, and wakes a universal requiem whose mournful cadence sweeps, not only through every city and village of this land, but whose far-away echoes are heard in England's ancient Abbey, nor will they cease till they circle with sad but admiring remembrance the circumference of the globe. But let me lead your thoughts away from this unparalleled exaltation to a humility as peerless, and find the key to this marvellous fame in a no less marvellous simplicity. For this man, who in 1880 strode "the earth like a colossus," in 1860 found "none so poor to do him reverence." The man who in 1865 let fall his mailed hand, like the hammer of Thor, and with one blow crushed the giant, Rebellion, in 1861 could not get even a hearing for his request to serve in any lowest position. For five years previous to 1860 Grant's life was a seeming failure. He had put his hand to the plough, but failed to wring a satisfactory subsistence from the earth. He had put his mind to business with as little success; and, when the war broke out, he was sweeping out a leather store, and running on errands, or making a poor attempt at a bargain behind the counter. Who could have imagined in this leather-seller of Galena the making of the greatest captain of the age? Yet the elements were all there, and chief among them was humility. For had he not already a record of which he might be proud? Had he not, a youth of twenty-four, thrown himself into the deadly breach at Palo Alto, and been promoted twice for gallantry at Molino del Rey and Chapultepec, and mentioned in all the dispatches for distinguished conduct at the capture of the City of Mexico? In this last action, Grant exhibited some of his, afterward *famed,* characteristics. In the advance upon the city, the vanguard came upon a parapet that obstructed the way, and, finding themselves exposed to its raking fire, all sought such shelter as they could find, except Lieutenant Grant, who, regardless of danger, personally reconnoitred the position, and soon returned and called out, "Captain, I've found a way to flank the enemy," and the captain replied, "Well, go on, we'll follow." And the work was carried. From this first flank movement, with a handful of men, to those masterly marchings by the left flank that pushed Lee and his sixty thousand Confederates from the Rapidan to Richmond, and that last flank movement that drew Lee out of Richmond into the open country to be cut up piecemeal by Sheridan's cavalry and to be utterly blocked at Appomattox, Grant's strategy was ever the same, — a bold front and, at the same time, a move for a better position.

And, in this advance upon the City of Mexico, Grant showed his fertility of resource at critical moments. To guard the approach to one of the strongest gates, a parapet had been thrown forward and a cannon mounted upon it. There was no possible way to flank it; but Grant instantly conceived, and speedily carried out, the extraordinary plan of seizing a neighboring church and mounting a howitzer in the belfry, and his own hand trained the gun that drove the enemy from the parapet, and in a few hours opened the way for the entrance of our victorious arms.

But, spite of these signal achievements and these brilliant openings into military glory, the young captain left the army, and seemed just as content with obscurity as with acting before the eyes of the nation. All truly great men are willing to bide their time, for they are humble before the majestic and inscrutable march of destiny; and most great men have had years of ripening in obscurity before they entered into the full fruitage of grand achievement. So Grant had his seven years of growth in secret; and, because he was humble, it became a natural and vigorous growth. In these years, he laid deep and secure the foundations of his after success. His seeming failures knit the fibres of his patience till they became withes of steel. His lack of friendly help taught him self-reliance, and his poverty, to be content with a little. A humble man can learn of calamity, while a proud man will be wearing himself away against the bosses of the Almighty's shield. Grant's character deepened and broadened in his unhonored obscurity. Amid "the slings and arrows of outrageous fortune," he was as cool and patient as under the leaden rain of the hostile musketry. If he did not succeed in one effort, he calmly set about another. If he could not push forward in a given line of labor, he turned to another without losing heart or hope. By reason of his quietness of manner and modesty of assumption, those about him could not suspect his abilities. He did not suspect them himself, for his time was not yet come.

Upon this humble leather-seller of Galena, now thirty-nine years of age, one April morning flashed the glare of Sumter's beleaguered guns. It lit in his heart, as in so many others, a fresh flame of loyalty; and, like so many others, he threw himself for all he was worth into the scale of the country's salvation. What that worth was he little knew, although he might even now have been justified in holding it at a high valuation. But his genuine modesty kept his own estimate well within the circle of sure accomplishment, and he offered his services to the government in any lowest capacity; but, while waiting for the answer that never came, he wasted not one moment, but turned, as was his nature, to do what he could, and that was to drill a company. Thus began that humble service which, step by step, in rapid but sure upward progress, led him to the loftiest power. In May, he commanded a company; in June, a regiment; in July, a brigade; in August, a division; and in less than nine months he was a Major General, had command of the largest military division in the country, and had won at Fort Donelson the first substantial victory for the Union arms. And yet every step of this promotion was unsought, — was, indeed, thrust upon him by the necessities of the situation. By the upward gravitation of his personal achievement, he reached such heights of power as he was best fitted to command. No career was ever less controlled by luck. He moved like a fate to his destined end, and with the least possible friction; for, if his humility kept him from grasping at power, it also made him willing to take a responsibility that he knew how to fill. Thus, the truest humility nourishes the noblest self-reliance and the strongest self-assertion. Though you would not press *yourself* forward, you can dare anything for duty. Though you would not lift a finger to defend *yourself,* you would stand like a rock for your country. So Grant modestly took such responsibilities as he found he could fulfil, and never stopped in his pursuit of enemies to take any of the prizes of honor held out by his friends. Thus, after Vicksburg capitulated on the 4th of July, 1863, making the largest surrender of men and material that modern warfare had seen. Grant did not set about having, as well he might, a 4th of July glorification, but at once prepared to use the new confidence of victory in pushing the enemy with fresh vigor. So, when Richmond fell, it did not occur to him, as it would have to most commanders, to make a grand parade of entrance into the city; but he at once moved to the left to capture the retreating Confederates. And, at the surrender of Appomattox, — when, after four years of Herculean effort and untold sacrifices on the part of the North, the giant form of rebellion lay prostrate at his feet, — Grant would not make any parade of surrender, would not cast upon the conquered one shadow of humiliation, but, with a generosity akin to the divine pity, at once spread a table before him in the presence of his enemies, and said. Arise, and eat! Well has it been said, —

> "His sword's bright conquests pale beneath
> Its mercy, when it sought its sheath."

I think none of you will suspect me of vindictiveness, and yet I will confess to a momentary sense of disappointment, shared indeed by nearly all the Union troops, when the order came for us to turn homeward without any of the dramatic formalities of surrender. I had not forgotten the picture in the school history that had fired my boyish imagination by its portrayal of the surrender of Lord Cornwallis, and it seemed to me that this was a grander occasion and a more famous victory. But our thought was unworthy, and our vision was short-sighted. Grant, however, with a marvellous greatness of soul that took in the broad perspective of the years, said: "No! They are once more our countrymen." And, as he rode through our lines and the artillery began to pour forth their salutations in his honor, he ordered the salvos to cease, lest they should wound the feelings of the prisoners, — thus not only exhibiting his own magnanimity, but laying the foundation for that reconstruction of the relations between the North and the South which has obliterated all sectional feeling, and to-day shows us one country, from Maine to the Gulf and from ocean to ocean, mourning alike our hero dead.

It may be well to recall here General Lee's own impression of what I will call the sublimest act of Grant's military life. He said: "I wish to do simple justice to General Grant, when I say that his treatment of the Army of Northern Virginia at its surrender is without a parallel in the history of the civilized world. When my poor soldiers had nothing to eat, he issued the humane order that forty thousand rations should be immediately furnished them. When I was directing one of my staff to make out a list of things to be surrendered, and named 'the horses,' Grant said: 'No, no. General Lee, not a horse! the men will need them for the spring ploughing.' When Grant said that my officers might retain their side arms, again I was thankful; but, when he disclaimed any desire to make a parade of surrender, I was indeed *overjoyed,* and felt that *that* was a touch of magnanimity that bespoke a great soul." Great soul, indeed! How, in the perspective of the years and before the levelling of death, thy act of generous humility stands out in surpassing grandeur beyond any possible glory of victorious triumph!

It is worth remembering, to the supreme credit of Grant, that he persisted in maintaining these generous terms, even against the determined efforts of his superior, Secretary Stanton; and that, when Charles Sumner led a committee of the Senate in asking him to allow his picture to be painted in a proposed historical portrayal of the surrender, Grant, with a fine sense of propriety and a truer humility, again said: "No: they are our brothers. Let us not perpetuate their humiliation!" And he kept to the end this generous magnanimity; and even in that last fearful fight with malignant disease, when every moment was torture, and every effort was, as he said, one more nail in his coffin, he took pains to write this message, "It has been an inestimable blessing to me that my life has been prolonged till I have seen for myself the happy harmony between those who but a few short years ago were engaged in mortal conflict." And he made this his farewell message, which, like Washington's farewell address, went straight to the hearts of the people, "Let every man look henceforth to the prosperity of a united country."

No wonder the Southern heart responded with peculiar earnestness. As one of their journals beautifully says: "Those on whose downfall the temple of his fame was builded will sow no thorns on his grave to prick the violets planted there."

But besides this generous magnanimity to his country's foes, this self-forgetting devotion to his country's good, Grant's humility nourished also the noblest self-reliance and the strongest self-assertion; and let us now turn to see how he exhibited these his most famous qualities. I know of nothing in military annals to compare with Grant's pertinacity of purpose, his iron determination, his immovable confidence of success. The old Scottish clan which claims General Grant as its most noted descendant had for its war-cry, "Stand fast, Craig Ellachie." It seems as if a happy genius had at every great crisis of Grant's career whispered to his silent soul the same old cry, "Stand fast, thou crag." And he stood fast. When, on reaching the field at Fort Donelson, he found that his right flank had been crushed, he said at once to his generals, "Gentlemen, this position must be retaken." And when that was done, and his troops came face to face with the frowning parapets behind which was a force stronger than his own, he thought not of the possibility of failure, and said to General Buckner, who asked his terms: "I have no terms but unconditional surrender. I propose to move at once upon your works." At Shiloh, when his troops had been defeated and driven back to the river, and General Buell said to him: "What preparations have you made for retreat? These transports will not take ten thousand men across the river, and we have thirty thousand," Grant replied, "I have not despaired of whipping them yet; and, if they whip me and I have to cross the river, ten thousand is all I shall need transports for." And he gave orders to assume the offensive in the morning. So it was in many a fight. When both sides seemed exhausted, Grant would go at it again, and win the advantage.

After Shiloh, Grant passed through the severest and most depressing period of his fortunes. But it only brought out into stronger relief the sublime patience of his resolve to serve his country to the uttermost, whether he himself rose or fell. When Sherman wrote him, "You have richly earned promotion," Grant replied, "I care nothing for rank, so long as our arms are successful." A very short time before Vicksburg, it seemed as if the jealousy of one of his superiors in rank, and the distrust of many of his subordinates, and the despondency of the whole country would make Grant the scapegoat of their envy and despair, and drive him from his command. But he was saved to the country by Lincoln's sturdy sense, which detected the staying quality of the General's determination; and, when he was urged to depose Grant, he said, in his homely but meaningful way, "I rather like the man: I think we'll try him a little longer." That *little longer* gave us Vicksburg, and satisfied the country that to this silent General it could anchor as to a rock. "Stand fast, thou crag," the country then replied. Thus, Grant came to the throne of his power by the simple logic of necessity. It was the time when war had ceased to be a play of politicians at Washington or a masterly inactivity of generals at the front; when the farce of a holiday parade had been enacted, and the first scenes of the fearful tragedy had already begun, and the people were ready for the boundless sacrifice. Then there was need of a leader like Grant, who, at his very first battle at Belmont, on being surrounded, burned his camps behind him, and said, "I guess we can cut our way out as we cut our way in"; and who, at Vicksburg, cut himself away from his base of supplies, and, leaving in his rear a larger army of the enemy than his own, turned with a sublime effrontery to strike the army that was coming to relieve Vicksburg, and then turned back and accomplished the surrender. In battles where Southern desperation was likely to weigh equally at least with Northern loyalty, Grant's personal qualities determined largely the successful result. He had a force of will that could turn obstacles into helps. He moved with the assurance of destiny to the accomplishment of his purposes. After he had, at Vicksburg, opened the mighty Mississippi till it "rolled unvexed to the sea," he took command of all the Western armies, and rolled them toward Chattanooga in resistless tide, till they surged up even to the clouds, and on Missionary Ridge and Lookout Mountain overwhelmed rebellion. Then, coming East, how he stood before Washington like the "shadow of a great rock in a weary land," giving us the confidence that the uttermost would be done to crush the country's foes! With what tremendous energy he started on that fearful campaign which in a month disabled fifty thousand of his men, and left its gory track from the Wilderness to Cold Harbor! To the people of the North, he seemed like a grim viking ordering each day a fresh skull of blood for his butcher's feast. And he was called a butcher. But we who followed him knew that he was as tender as a woman, and that he regretted every drop of heroic sacrifice. There was no way but this. Lee was too skilful himself to be conquered by brilliant manoeuvres. What was needed was hard blows and constant wearing away of the armies of the rebellion. To this. Grant bent the whole force of his giant energies. After the Wilderness, when everybody else was discouraged and feared to uncover the way to Washington, Grant said: "If Lee is in my rear, I am in his." "I propose to fight it out on this line, if it takes all summer," and, having made his dispositions, for the morrow, "went to his tent and slept soundly till morning." All through these thirty days of battle, with their appalling spectacles of suffering and their terrible losses, he never wavered nor thought of retiring. When Burnside reported, in the fearful struggle at Spottsylvania, that he had lost connection with Hancock, Grant sent this response, "Push the enemy: that is the best way to connect." When General Lee was told, after the repulse of the Union troops at Cold Harbor, that Grant was in retreat, he replied: "That cannot be true. Grant never retreats." And it was so. While giving these crippling blows to the Confederate Army, Grant, by his daily movements to the left, got into the position he desired for turning the flank of all the armies defending Richmond; and, at Petersburg, he planted himself like a mighty rock beetling toward the raging rebel sea, and saying, "Thus far and no farther, and here shall thy proud waves be stayed." And they *were* stayed. And so this mighty man of war conquered an enduring peace; and, when he took off his mailed glove, his hand was as soft as a child's. "His strength was as the strength of ten, because his heart was pure." Because he humbled himself, he subdued, not only the rebel arms, but the rebel hearts; and, because he was willing to become at once a simple citizen, the people lifted him upon a throne of highest exaltation, — not with the Caesars and Napoleons, who have waded through blood to empire, but with the Washingtons, who have taken the sword reluctantly and sheathed it gladly, who in danger have borne calmly upon their shoulders the destinies of mighty States, who have loved to serve their country more than their own advancement.

I cannot stop to recount Grant's victories of peace, no less renowned than those of war: his defence of the financial integrity of the government, not less heroic, amid the sophistries and temptations of the hour and against the oppositions of good men, than his supreme assumption of responsibility amid the repulses and perils of the Wilderness campaign; nor that other grander victory which signalized his civil administration, the treaty of Washington, which will some time lead the world to the arbitraments of peace. Nor can I stop to recall that grander victory still, — that serene mastery of himself in disease and death that has fitly crowned his earthly triumphs: —

> "Life's closing scenes without a stain,
> His death-march trod through fiery pain,
> With heart unmoved: how these unroll
> Heroic grandeurs of the soul
> In victories whose lessons stand
> A light and promise to the land!"

Thus, I have traced the grand and imposing qualities that blaze out before the world's admiring gaze to their silent, secret source in humility of spirit. No self-love blurred Grant's intuitions of duty. No worldly considerations ever rose up to block the path of his loyal devotion. When General Sherman wrote to Grant in 1864, congratulating him on his appointment as Lieutenant General, he spoke thus, with the spirit of a true prophet: "You are now Washington's legitimate successor, and occupy a position of almost dangerous elevation. But, if you can continue as heretofore to be yourself, simple, honest, and unpretending, you will enjoy through life the respect and love of friends, and the homage of millions of your countrymen." That prophecy has been more than fulfilled. Grant did keep his simplicity to the very height of his power. When he commanded a million men in arms, he did not lift himself above the humblest in the ranks. On the occasion of a journey from Culpeper to Washington, just before he was to set in motion the colossal enginery of war, a special car was assigned to him and his staff; but, when he saw the guard keeping out the common soldiers who, with their leaves of absence, were pressing for a chance to ride to Washington, he said, "I occupy but one seat in this car, let as many as can come in." And he shared his seat with a private all the way to Alexandria.

Grant had also that finest quality of greatness which appreciates greatness in others. He said, "I never flattered myself that I was entitled to the first place: the men whom I selected for lieutenants could, I believe, often have filled my place better than I did."

Friends, am I not right in making humility the finest aroma of that most famous life? We read in the Old Testament that when Huldah, the prophetess, came to King Josiah, whose merciful and popular reign had revived Jewish loyalty and reestablished the ancient glory of the Hebrew state, she said, "Thus saith Jehovah, Because thine heart was tender, and thou hast humbled thyself before the Lord, therefore thou shalt be gathered to thy grave in peace." Again has that prophecy been fulfilled, and the greatest soldier has become the truest messenger of peace.

Last evening, as the slant rays of the declining sun threw their sheen over the Hudson and up the bluff by the Riverside, a soldier's bugle sounded over the great Captain's grave the call to sleep. To-day, in the proud hearts of a nation saved, he rises to live again and forever.

> "His battles fought, his duties done,
> His country's life by valor won.
> That call was but a reveille
> To wake to immortality."

In Honor of the Citizen Soldiers of Dorchester Who Fell in the War of the Rebellion, 1861-1865

Tributes

I - Oration

At the Dedication of the Soldiers' Monument in Dorchester, September 17, 1867, by Rev. Charles A. Humphreys.

Friends and Fellow-citizens: —

As we stand under the shadow of this monument which we dedicate today, its silent pointing to the heavens, its voiceless record of noble names, remind us that our theme is beyond the power of words to portray, and that silence is here the most fitting eloquence. All great things are silent, — the eternal hills, the ocean in its depths. They have no speech nor language; yet their peaceful stillness is more eloquent than the roar of tempests at the surface, or the blast of winds at their summit. So this silent orator tells more eloquently of the grand achievements and the glorious deeds of our heroes than any spoken eulogy that mortal lips can frame. How impressive is its simple silence! It bears no record of the valor of our soldiers; it lavishes no praise on their patriotic devotion; it does not even name the bloody fields where one and another laid down their precious lives; but so long as this shaft shall stand, so long as its stony finger shall point to the open heavens, — so long shall it tell the story of their sacrifice, and point the passers-by to those lofty and divine principles of liberty from which they drew their courage and their strength.

It is a high and sacred duty that we this day fulfil. It is not only our martyr brothers that we honor by this memorial, but also ourselves. By it, we pledge ourselves to a like devotion. If we honor them because they died that the nation might live, let us show our sincerity by so living that the nation may have more abundant life. Let us not excuse ourselves by saying that we cannot of ourselves do much. It was not with such faint-heartedness that they girt on their armor. Our little band of martyrs could not save the nation; yet they gave what they could, and all they could, to the common cause, and so are equal sharers of the common triumph. It is the noble distinction of our country not only that the people can rule it. but that they alone can save it. Imperial Rome could not live without her Caesar: Alexander yielded to his successors the empire of half the world; but without him, it could not keep its integrity. All the ancient dynasties crumbled with the ashes of their leaders. The supremacy of modern European nations depends chiefly on the diplomacy of a few. Bismarck builds a mighty kingdom on the ruins of the German Confederation, while France loses caste with the duplicity of Napoleon, and England comes to a standstill with the obstinate selfishness of her ministry: but our nation can decline only with the decline of public virtue, and can live only in the life of the people. Our hundred martyrs are only a handful compared with the hundreds of thousands of victims offered on the altar of the country; yet each of them fought for the nation and not for any leader, and in each one's sacrifice the nation found salvation. It is not presumption then, but the very spirit of our institutions to raise an enduring memorial of each and every martyr of liberty, and to give a national significance to each hero's devotion.

Will any one say that, because ours was a civil war, memorials of its victims must of necessity perpetuate sectional bitterness? I repel the insinuation. Not one of those whose devotion we celebrate to-day fought for a section or a party, but for the whole country. Not one of them lifted his arm against the South, but against treason wherever it might rear its horrid front. They were not the victims of passion, but the martyrs of principle. We celebrate not the triumph of a section, but the saving of a nation. The names which we with pious care have cut in the enduring stone were long before claimed by the Genius of Liberty, and set with more enduring lustre among the brightest pearls in her diadem. Need we then hesitate to reveal our memorial to the world? Will any true son of liberty ever turn with averted face from its brilliant record? When our nation is again united in a common devotion to the principles of freedom, which are the very life of the republic, shall we then be ashamed to recall the names of those who died in her defence?

But even if our monument, besides celebrating the virtues of our heroes, should also recall the crimes of the Rebels, and revive the long-smothered indignation against the plotters of treason in the South, still let it stand. We may forgive, but we cannot forget, — we must not forget. We owe it to our brothers not to forget their sacrifices. Upon their wasted lives we are rearing the structure of a nobler civilization. Their blood has nourished the seeds of liberty, their names will ever be its truest inspiration. Shall we reap the fruits of their devotion and refuse to honor their memories? It was the painful necessity of their position to fight against their own flesh and blood. Shall we therefore conceal the record of their fidelity? Shall we not rather hold in more abundant honor those who left houses and lands and kindred for the sake of a noble principle? How often friend met friend in bloody fray, brother lifting the sword against brother! They felt that love of country was a holier tie than love of kindred; for the happiness of millions was involved in the nation's salvation. Let us not forget, then, their self-denying devotion. We owe it to our country not to forget her defenders. The nation lives only in the devotion of the people; and we must, by every appreciative celebration and every enduring memorial, perpetuate the remembrance of those who gave everything for her salvation. The national character is moulded by the traditions of its own experience. The masses of men do not look abroad for their teachings of wisdom and their illustrations of heroism, but to their own ancestry and their own community. The strongest communities or peoples are those that are richest in these traditions of heroism and devotion.

It is not in the decline of national power, but at its height, that the memorials of greatness are reared. The neglect of them is the sure sign of national weakness and decay. When Greece forgot the heroes of Marathon, she forgot also her own glory. When Rome forgot Brutus and his compatriots at Philippi, she forgot also her own liberties. When England forgot Cromwell, or remembered him only to disgrace his ashes, she disgraced herself, and forgot her supremacy in the glittering attractions of a luxurious court. When our country shall forget to honor her defenders, shall neglect the memorials of their heroism, she will have forgotten also her own true dignity, and have neglected the fountains of her truest life. No, we will not forget our fallen heroes. As long as freedom has a name to be honored and loved, her martyrs shall be remembered; and if ever we are tempted to be false to liberty, their blood will cry to us from the ground, and their spirits will still rule us from their urns. To the people of France, for long years after his death, the ashes of Napoleon were a more potent spell than the flash of a hundred thousand bayonets. They cringed before the ghost of the tyrant quicker than to the sword of his tools. No such horrid nightmare haunts the graves of our heroes; yet the spell of their names shall be as powerful. For long years to come, yes, forever in the history of our land, the grave of a martyr of liberty shall be stronger than the throne of a tyrant, and the ashes of her patriot defenders shall overcome the legions of treason though they advance terrible as an army with banners.

In the war through which we have just passed, the traditions of the Revolution were as inspiring as the immediate demands of the crisis. We believed that as God had been with our fathers He would also be with us. We trusted that a like devotion to liberty would meet a like reward. We read and we repeated to others the story of their sacrifices. Lexington and Bunker Hill were our rallying cries. The blood-stained snows of Valley Forge nerved our endurance. The triumph of Yorktown inspired our faith. The Charter of Independence became the certificate of the national life. The South threatened to violate the sacred memories of the Revolution by calling the roll of her slaves under the shadow of Bunker Hill. But from beneath her hallowed sod there came such inspiration that a million freemen sprang to arms and defied the impious threat. The Rebels fought not alone against Northern steel, but against their own and the country's history, against their own and the country's life. God and nature were against them. The stars in their courses fought against rebellion. The result was not doubtful. *In decisive battles, truth always musters the heaviest battalions.* So to-day those who under the specious pretext of a restored Union are plotting for a re-established system of oppression, are plotting against the national life, and will surely fail. Our country has not vanquished her open enemies only to fall by the thrusts of her pretended friends. She is stronger than ever before in the faith of the people. She stands not now as in the Revolution, the hopeful field whereon freedom and high civilization might achieve new triumphs for man. Our country holds to-day a grander position and a nobler fame. She stands before the world as the arena whereon Freedom and Slavery have closed in fierce death-grapple, and Freedom stands triumphant. If our fathers and brothers died for a glorious hope, shall we not live for a grand fruition.^ Our fathers feared that the stripes of their dear-loved banner might come to symbolize the exactions of a foreign tyranny, and our brothers died with only the hope that its stars might not go out in disastrous night. But to us the stripes are crimson with the blood of a hundred thousand heroes whose ebbing life was the flood tide on which our liberties rose for a vantage-ground of eternal security, and its stars stand firm as the stars in heaven, not only undiminished, but ever increasing in number and in lustre.

What an inheritance has thus been transmitted to us as the inspiration and the pledge of our fidelity! We need not now search the annals of ancient history for illustrations of heroism and patriotic devotion. We need go no more to Marathon and Thermopylae. We need not appeal to Leonidas to inspire our courage, nor suffer the trophies of Miltiades to break our sleep. We need not even go back to Lexington and Bunker Hill, to Prescott and Warren. We have in our own times as bright a galaxy of noble names, as grand a pile of trophies. Where are the fields that shall dim the lustre of Antietam and Gettysburg, of Winchester and Cedar Creek, of Vicksburg and Port Hudson, of Murfreesborough and Lookout Mountain? Where in military annals are the movements that compare in rapidity with the raids of Sheridan, in grandeur with the march of Sherman, in persistency with the advance of Grant? Where in history are the generals who can cast a shade upon the names of Lyon and Sedgwick and Kearney and Macpherson? Where are the commanders braver than Rogers and Winslow and Farragut and Foote? What nation or people has such an illustrious roll of young heroes — Ellsworth, Winthrop, Baker, Shaw, Putnam, Lowell? And if we come nearer home, what private memorial ever bore nobler names than ours? Do you speak of courage? At Gettysburg, they moved not one step backward before the fiercest onset of the desperate foe. [1] Do you speak of gallant daring? Their advance at Kenesaw Mountain was not checked till their poor bodies were riddled with bullets. [2] Do you speak of endurance? In the Wilderness for thirty days they marched and fought and intrenched, and marched and fought and intrenched, every day nearer the Rebel capitol, and in the last grand effort at Cold Harbor met defeat only with death. [3] Do you speak of fortitude and patience? Do you not know that eleven of those whose names are here surrounded with an enduring wreath of glory met without a murmur a most inglorious death, away from friends, without one tear of sympathy, wasting away inch by inch in the loathsome confinement of the Rebel prisons? I will not multiply horrors in order to magnify their virtues. But, tell me, is there a brighter page in history than that which we have stereotyped to-day with these familiar names? To-day we give them to history; but not alone to her cold and voiceless record. We have also inscribed their names upon the tablets of our hearts, and there they shall live in a bright immortality of grateful remembrance.

I have spoken of the value of our traditions to patriotic devotion, now so multiplied that almost every fireside has its own heroic tale.

But their value depends chiefly on connecting them with the traditions of the national life. We must not repeat the story of the glorious deeds of our heroes without recalling also the sacred principles for which they risked their precious lives. They fought first and foremost for the national integrity; but for the national integrity chiefly because it was the synonym of universal liberty. God in his all-wise providence had planted the vine of liberty in this western world at the foot of the tree of our national life, and had so entwined their rapid growths that the axe could not cleave them apart without destroying both, nor could the propitious rains water the roots of liberty without nourishing also the national life. As in the Revolution, the colonists did not in the beginning fight for independence but for justice, yet were soon taught by providential experience that justice could not be reached except through independence, so, in the late war, our people did not in the beginning fight for freedom, but for the national life; yet were soon taught by providential events that the nation could not be saved except through liberty. And as at the birth of religious liberty in Judea, God had prepared a grand empire under one head, its subjects obeying the same laws, familiar with the same language, sharers of a common civilization, and all from the gates of Hercules to the farthest Ind bearing the common dignity of a Roman citizen, and this unity of laws and language invited Christianity to the easier conquest of the world, so at the birth of civil liberty in the "Mayflower," God opened a wide continent, and raised up a great people, and gave them liberty for their inheritance, and freedom for their possession, and bade them scatter these blessings throughout the world. For the security of these priceless treasures, we first won our independence through the devotion of our fathers, and now by the fidelity of our brothers have established our nationality on the basis of universal liberty. It only remains that we still be faithful; that we now and forever link our traditions of patriotic devotion, so full and fresh to-day, with the traditions of liberty which God has entwined so closely about our national life; then we shall enter upon such a career of glory as we can scarcely now foresee.

Our most immediate duty is to secure the fruits of our triumph, and lay the foundation of a lasting peace. Oh for a Hampden or a Washington, who, having caught the spirit of a great struggle and brought it to a successful close, can also, by wisdom and moderation, restrain the excesses of victory and soothe the anger of defeat! Alas! our village Hampden, our second Washington is gone I gone with those who in camp and field and hospital laid their rich gifts of life upon the altar of the country! gone to his boys whose bright and gleaming ranks beyond the river of death opened to welcome what we could so hardly losel Still we will not repine. Our salvation does not depend upon one man or set of men, but upon the people, and the lessons of this war have been too deeply burned into their hearts for them now to prove untrue. Let the people see to it that treason is made odious and rebellion fully crushed; that loyalty is encouraged and disloyalty rebuked; that liberty is made the inalienable possession of every inhabitant of our land, and that all within our borders, of whatever race, sex, or condition, are allowed free scope for the development of all their powers, and are intrusted with all the duties of citizenship for which they may be fitted by their intelligence, their capacities, or their natural position. What a glorious career will then open to our nation! Fearing no enemies within or without, she will attain a dignity she has not yet assumed; she will be a leader among the nations, too great to excite their envy, too magnanimous to stir their hate. Her freedom will be the inspiration of every struggling people, and her tranquility the rebuke of every trembling tyranny.

Yet not in laws alone shall she lead the nations, but in literatures and every field of knowledge. We have not only broken the fetters of the slave, but we have begun to break the fetters of the mind. As the common mind goes forth to mingle in strife or sympathy with the minds of millions, and sees open before it all the opportunities and privileges that the greatest can possess, and feels that it participates in the dignity and glory of the mighty mass, and sustains an equal share in its protection and support, it cannot but expand with the expanding thought, and must rise above all mean conceptions and narrow views, and image forth in its own development the grand unfolding of the national life. Great nations beget great thoughts; and it is only with great struggles that great literatures are born. The relentless plough of war has broken the surface of the popular mind, and brought up the rich sub-soil of deep convictions and broader aims, and it now lies furrowed and fallow for the sowing of whatever thoughts befit a great nation and a free people.

Would that some Homer or Virgil or Dante might arise to catch the spirit of the age and mould the aspirations of the people into a worthy epic that would be a priceless legacy to all coming time! Or rather, would that there might arise one greater than they all! For the struggle through which we have passed developed more of daring adventure and thrilling romance, more of calm endurance and heroic devotion than Virgil ever saw, or Homer ever sung; and its terrible earnestness and fearful sacrifices would furnish the theme of a "divine tragedy" that would need a greater than Dante to portray. The age must make its own interpreter. Meanwhile we can all do something to establish and perpetuate the principles for which our brothers died. Let us see to it that the rich seeds of precious lives that have been sown broadcast over the land bear living fruit in a purified government and a regenerated people. Let us catch the spirit of the age, and press on in the path of the nation's destiny. The time is ripe for grand attempts and grander results. Freedom is daily achieving victories for which but lately we scarce dared to hope; and the spirit of Republicanism is rising in such a flood that its refluent waves are engulfing the thrones and tyrannies of the old world, and lifting the oppressed people into liberty and manhood.

Is not this place also inspiring? Old Dorchester bears a noble record of public virtue and devoted patriotism. In 1630, her founders, led hither by their love of Christian liberty, having first by a fair equivalent obtained a release of the land from the Indian chief, used great efforts to civilize the neighboring tribes and convert them to Christianity, thus laying the foundations of her civil polity in enlightened justice and earnest religious faith. In 1652, by public vote, a general collection was taken up in the town for the maintenance of Harvard College. In 1664, the town drew up a petition for civil and religious liberty; and in general took such a stand in those early colonial days that, in all civil assemblies and military musters she was allowed the precedence in honorable position. Nor did she discredit her reputation in after time. Years before the Revolution, the town voted to encourage domestic manufactures, and lessen the use of foreign luxuries. She especially prohibited the use of tea except in cases of sickness; and in 1774 voted to pay her province tax into the treasury of the "Sons of Liberty," instead of to the treasurer of the Crown, declaring that the attempt of Parliament to impose upon the colonies laws without their consent was a tyrannical usurpation. In the Revolution, having early voted to sustain the Continental Congress if they should see fit to declare an independency with Great Britain, Dorchester gave to the army one-third of her men over sixteen years of age, and in the late war for our national existence, with a population of only ten thousand, she furnished one thousand two hundred and seventy-seven men, which was one hundred and twenty-three in excess of all calls; and of these, one hundred and twenty-seven became martyrs of liberty, ninety-seven of them our own townsmen.

Theirs are the holy rites of commemoration that we celebrate to-day. About their names we here intwine an imperishable wreath of glory. To their memories we consecrate this monumental shaft. We have placed it under the shadow of the church, for theirs was a sacred cause. It stands in view of the sounding ocean whose ceaseless beat and roar shall not outlast their fame. We will also enshrine them in our heart of hearts; and, inspired by their devotion to the country, we will here consecrate ourselves anew to her service.

"The patriot spirit has not fled;
   It walks in noon's broad light,
And it watches the bed of the glorious dead
   With the holy stars by night.
It watches the bed of the brave who have bled,
   And shall guard this rock-bound shore.
Till the waves of the bay, in their mystic play,
   Shall break and foam no more."

[1] Thos. B. Fox, Jr., Captain, Second Regiment Massachusetts Infantry Volunteers, died July 25, 1863, of wounds received at Gettysburg, Pa.
[2] Henry W. Hall, Adjutant, Fifty-first Regiment Illinois Infantry Volunteers, fell June 27, 1864, pierced with eleven bullets, in the charge upon the Rebel intrenchments at Kenesaw Mountain.
[3] Walter Humphreys, Company A, Thirteenth Regiment Massachusetts Infantry Volunteers, fell at Cold Harbor, June 2, 1864.

II - Memorial Day, 1894

Address in Town Hall at Randolph, Mass., by Rev. Charles A. Humphreys.

Friends: —

It is a pathetic picture that is presented to-day of the swiftly lessening ranks of the living marching to cover with the flowers of grateful remembrance the swiftly multiplying ranks of the dead. At the close of the war, of the two and one-half millions of soldiers who had been mustered in defence of the Union, more than two millions survived, one-seventh having paid with their lives the precious cost of freedom. But the full price had not yet been given, nor even now is it all discharged. Each year sends an increasing number of our comrades to join the silent dead. The ranks to which there can come no new recruits are daily depleted by fast increasing disabilities. The youngest soldier of the Union must now be long past the median line of life, and of the great leaders of the war, only General Sherman reached the scriptural span of threescore years and ten, and it has been noted that by those who endured the exposures of service in the field, the line of threescore years is seldom passed. So we cannot help seeing that the coming years will make still wider gaps in our ranks. Although only two years ago the army of living soldiers and the army of the dead were exactly balanced, to-day the dead who receive our tributes outnumber the living by a quarter of a million, and the time is not far distant when the last survivor will totter to the tomb. But doubtless grateful hearts and full hands will still scatter flowers for many years to come. The remembrance of these heroes will inspire all with nobler aims and finer devotions. The tendrils of grateful memory stretching from all hearts to every soldier's grave will bind the living to a glad rivalry in loyal service. So, comrades, as to-day we leave them in their flower-besprinkled graves, let us go forth to life's common cares with a higher purpose.

It is often harder to live truly than to die nobly. I sometimes feel like envying those who gave up their lives on the field of glorious war and thus wrote their names high on the scroll of fame among the world's immortals. Happy lot! One short hour of glorious life is worth an age without a name. Yes! Harder than to give up life in one outburst of enthusiastic devotion is to give up health and drag through long and weary years an enfeebled body, seeing the prizes of life grasped by stronger hands, forced to yield every race for honors to swifter feet, cherishing still a soldier's eagerness for the front of battle, but disabled and left lonely and useless in the rear. This indeed is the harder sacrifice. Yet let us make it cheerfully. Let others outrun us in the race for wealth and power. We will press towards the mark for the prize of a higher calling, and as we once offered our lives for our country's defence, we will still dedicate them to its advancement. And when we consider the grand march of our people in population, in prosperity and in power, when we see the new industrial vigor of the Southern States which were so crippled in the Rebellion, when we behold them cherishing an equal patriotism with ourselves, when we recognize that each year adds so much to the value of the Union, should we not be thankful that our lives have been spared, and that we have been permitted to see not alone the triumph on the field of glorious war, of the armies to which it is our increasing pride to have belonged, but a grander triumph of reconciliation in the green pastures and by the still waters of a prosperous peace?

How like a vanishing vision seem the hardships and exposures of the war through the dim distance of thirty years! How its agonizing losses have been transformed into glorious gains! Memorial Day has now less of sadness than gladness — gladness in the possession of such heroic memories. I think it is a mistake, after nearly a generation has passed, to half-mast our flags. They should rather be lifted to the peak and flung to the breeze in joyous exultation over those heroes,

"Who died that we might claim a soil unstained,
A realm unsevered, and a race unchained."

We now recall without pain but with a happy pride the sacrifices they made. We do not now think of them as dead.

"They really live in history's deathless page
  High on the slow-wrought pedestals of fame,
Ranged with the heroes of remoter age;
    They could not die who left their nation free,
    Firm as the rock, unfettered as the sea,
  Its heaven unshadowed by the cloud of shame."

Comrades, though we are only the dwindling rear guard of the grand procession of the soldiers of the Union the larger part of which has crossed the flood, and nearly all of whose leaders are now awaiting us in the silent halls of death, we will be proud to have once been their companions. What a thrill their names still excite: dashing Hooker fighting in the clouds at Lookout Mountain; splendid Hancock charging with many a forlorn hope, and achieving what seemed impossibilities to less courageous hearts; heroic McPherson falling before the splendor of his abilities was fully appreciated; undoubting Thomas firm as a rock against the whelming waves of disaster at Chickamauga and a sure salvation for imperilled Nashville; faithful Meade leading the patient Army of the Potomac to its hardly won triumph; fiery Sheridan snatching victory from defeat at Cedar Creek, and striking the death-blow of the Army of Northern Virginia at Five Forks; resourceful Sherman cutting the Confederacy in twain by his march to the sea; and above all, outshining all in his full-orbed glory, persistent Grant pushing all our armies slowly but surely to triumph! What an array of magnificent commanders! But whatever the grandeur of their position, they did not exceed in devotion the common soldier whose name is unremembered but who gave all he had to his country. All to-day are in equal honor.

"They fell devoted but undying;
The very gale their praise seems sighing,
The waters murmur of their name,
The woods are peopled with their fame,
The meanest rill, the mightiest river.
Rolls mingling with their fame forever."

III - Dedication of Flags

At First Parish Church on Meeting House Hill, October 15, 1916.

Address by Rev. Charles A. Humphreys

Dear Friends: —

I am asked to speak to you on "Our Flag and the Spirit of its Defenders."

At its best and as I generally saw it in the Civil War that spirit was an utter devotion with no thought of anything but duty, with no fear of anything but dishonor. People wonder how a soldier can dare the dangers of battle. He dares them because he forgets himself and is thinking only of duty and service. He follows the flag because it symbolizes his country's safety and humanity's salvation. He hears above the thunder of artillery and the hiss of bullets the voice of God calling him to risk his life for truth and right. He sees beyond the flaming mouths of the enemy's musketry the hands that would dishonor his flag and destroy his country. So of course he dares everything and counts not his life dear to himself if he can give it in defence of that flag's honor and that country's imperilled life.

I could not trust myself to begin to speak of the transcendent worth of the few who were nearest to me, who grew up with me in our church school, and who were nourished with me under the fostering inspiration of Rev. Nathaniel Hall. What words would suffice to tell of him who was the closest companion of my school and college days — Thomas Bailey Fox, my college chum, the chosen orator of our Class of 1860, a born advocate, who had before him the largest promise of public usefulness, whose manly heart panted after the championship of *noble* causes, but who laid aside all these high hopes to throw himself into the "imminent deadly breach" at Gettysburg, —

> "And for guerdon of his toil,
> And pouring out his life's best oil,
> Tasted the raptured fleetness
> Of Truth's divine completeness."

Or how could I speak of that highly gifted, generous-hearted schoolmate (son of our devoted pastor), Henry Ware Hall — who challenged the admiration even of his foes when he fell, pierced by eleven bullets, as he led a storming column up the heights of Kenesaw Mountain, —

> "And in warm life-blood wrote a nobler verse"
> Than poets sing or tuneful lips rehearse;
> "Lived battle-odes whose lines were steel and fire
> And shaped in squadron strophes his desire."

Nor can I speak as I would of that younger hero — Walter Humphreys, a brother dearly beloved — who gave the rich promise of his opening life to his country's service, and, a private in the ranks, followed his regiment's bullet-pierced colors from the Wilderness to Cold Harbor and somewhere on that fatal field sleeps in an unknown grave.

> "Oh for the touch of a vanished hand,
> And the sound of a voice that is still!"

Ye sad waters of the Chickahominy, flow gently where he lies! Thou sacred soil of Virginia, — how sacred now! — weave above his head a chaplet of perennial green! Ye pines that strike your eager roots into that holy dust, wave your tops in ceaseless worship for the glory of a soul that leaped transfigured out of the gloom of your shadowing tent! He knew when he lifted the banner of his country that it was also the banner of the Cross, and when Death glared upon him from behind the glistening bayonets of the foe, he did not fear. I hold as sacred a scrap of paper upon which he wrote this last message to his old home, — "I must say I am ready for the coming contest." Dear Brother, we will weep no more! Your sacrifice was willing. Soldier, go home; for you the field is won!

> "I with uncovered head
>   Salute these sacred dead.
> Blow trumpets, all your exultations blow!
> For never shall their aureoled presence lack;
> I see them muster in a gleaming row
> With ever youthful brows that nobler show;
> We find in our dull road their shining track,
>   In every nobler mood.
> We feel the orient of their spirit glow.
> Part of our life's unalterable good.
> Of all our saintlier aspiration;
>   They come transfigured back
> Secure from change in their high-hearted ways.
> Beautiful evermore, and with the rays
> Of morn on their white Shields of Expectation."

Dear Friends: —

After this tale of some of the sacrifices that our Civil War demanded more than half a century ago, and after witnessing for two years the greater sacrifices demanded by the worst and wickedest of all wars, in which a military caste has attempted to set *might* on the throne where *justice* should be omnipotent, I rejoice to have lived to see the founding, and to become a member, of a world League to *Enforce* Peace. For that way lies the hope of humanity,

> "[When] war-drum[s] [shall beat] no longer,
>   And [all] battle-flags [be] furled
> In the Parliament of man,
>   The Federation of the world."

Then shall our national and state flags be more loved than ever, as they will be the symbol of finer loyalties than war invokes and become the inspiration of the more beneficent victories of peace. And to-day as they are lifted before our eyes here, let them hearten us to fight fearlessly and confidently for *freedom* and the *truth,* because we know that behind them are the succoring legions of the whole Christian army, and thy right hand, O God, and thy holy arm that assure us of victory.

Appendix

More intimate glimpses of a Chaplain's life as revealed in his diary and home letters — 1863-65.

April 4, '63. Harvard Divinity School. My classmate Harry Russell, Lieutenant Colonel Second Massachusetts Cavalry Volunteers, having asked me to be the Chaplain of his regiment, I walked into Boston, where he is recruiting the men, and told him that I would accept if the other officers also wanted me.

April 20, '63. I went out to Readville, where the Second Massachusetts Cavalry is in training, and Col. Charles Russell Lowell told me that the officers would no doubt want me to go as chaplain.

May 22, '63. Had a letter from Col. N. P. Hallowell of the Fifty-fifth Massachusetts Regiment (colored), asking me to Induce John Chadwick, who was here in the Divinity School, to accept a commission as Chaplain in his regiment; but I did not succeed.

July 4, '63. Gov. John A. Andrew to-day signed my commission as Chaplain of the Second Massachusetts Cavalry Volunteers.

July 14, '63. Divinity Hall, Cambridge. I was ordained in the chapel here this morning, George L. Chaney, John F. W. Ware, Edward H. Hall, and Dr. Noyes taking part in the service.

July 19, '63. Sunday. I preached in my home church, giving my pastor — Rev. Nathaniel Hall — a labor of love.

At the end of the service he made an ordaining prayer — making up thus for his enforced absence at my Cambridge ordination.

July 28, '63. Sad to tell, my first public service after my full ordination as chaplain was to join to-day with Chaplain Quint of the Second Massachusetts Infantry and Rev. Nathaniel Hall in the funeral service for my college-chum Capt. Thomas B. Fox, Jr., of the Second Massachusetts Infantry, who received his mortal wound at Gettysburg. (See Note 10.)

August 19, '63. Bade good-bye to all at home — joy shining through my tears, the joy of going to serve my country. Took the 5.30 steamboat train for New York.

August 20, '63. Going through Philadelphia, I called to see my classmate William Eliot Furness, but found that he had gone to the war in a colored regiment. Still I had a very pleasant call on his father. I was much surprised to have him tell me that he had recommended me to his brother. Rev. William H. Furness, as a colleague. That may perhaps be considered when the country is safe. Now the soldiers in the field shall have my best and my only labor.

Washington, D.C., August 21, '63. Was mustered into the "service of the United States for three years, unless sooner discharged." Called at Armory Hospital on Miss Anna Lowell, sister of Colonel Lowell, and on Miss Mary Felton, daughter of President Felton — old Cambridge friends. At noon I took the boat for Alexandria and then carried my luggage on my shoulders three-quarters of a mile across the city to the cars for Fairfax station. It was pretty tough work under a hot sun. I arrived at Fairfax at 3.30. I would have walked to my regiment six miles away but that the country here is infested with guerrillas. I telegraphed to Colonel Crowninshield and he sent an ambulance and a cavalry escort and I reached camp at 9 P.M.

August 22, '63. Cavalry Camp near Centreville. I breakfasted on hardbread, fried pork, and water, with Colonel Lowell, Majors Crowninshield and Forbes, and Lieut. Goodwin Stone.

Sunday, August 23, '63. Had a ten-minute service in each of the three wards of the brigade hospital, and at dress parade of my regiment. Sung in the evening in Major Forbes' tent, where my quarters now are.

August 24, '63. Mosby has captured a hundred horses that were coming to this regiment, and Colonel Lowell has started after him, and the camp seems deserted.

August 27, '63. At ten o'clock I conducted a funeral service over John McCarthy of Company A, who was killed in the skirmish with Mosby. Not only his company, called the California Hundred, led by Capt. J. Sewall Reed, but also all the field and staff officers, led by Colonel Lowell, attended the service. This recognition of valor always tells for good with the men and makes them more brave in danger and more faithful in every duty.

Alexandria, August 28, '63. I have just partaken of the hospitality of the Sanitary Commission at the "Soldiers' Rest." My napkin was marked, "U. S. Sanitary Commission, Boston Branch." It pleased me very much to share in Boston's generosity in a Southern city. I came here with disabled Captain De Merritt of my regiment. I am taking him to Seminary Hospital in Georgetown. The journey though only eighteen miles is quite difficult. At camp the Captain — with a wandering brain and a broken leg — was put into an ambulance and I went in by his side and was driven under guard of six cavalrymen to Fairfax station, six miles away. There I had to wait one and a half hours for the train. Then I put the Captain into a baggage-car and sat down beside him and rode for two hours to Alexandria. Here, with the help of another man, I carried the Captain on my shoulders quite a distance to the Soldiers' Rest. Then after two hours I put the Captain into another baggage-car and reached Washington at 5 P.M., having started from camp at 9 a.m. There was yet an hour of waiting till I could get an order to take the Captain to the hospital, and then another ride with him in an ambulance to Georgetown finished for me the trying day's labor, except that in the evening I wrote to the Captain's wife in Sacramento, Cal., and to his mother and sister in Durham, N.H., telling of the Captain's condition.

August 29, '63. By invitation of Rev. James Richardson — Harvard College 1837, Harvard Divinity School 1845 — I spent the night at his elegant mansion formerly owned by Banker Corcoran. He and his wife accompanied me to Alexandria, and I reached camp by way of the steam train to Fairfax and then by our wagon train to Centreville. Mr. Richardson is General Agent of the United States Sanitary Commission, and he invited me to make his house my home whenever I was in Washington.

September 3, '63. I spent a good part of the day copying muster-rolls so that I can have in alphabetical order a full list of the men of my regiment and the company to which each belongs for reference, especially in distributing the mail. I have already recorded about six companies and the address of the nearest relative of each soldier,

September 6, '63. Sunday. When I called this morning for singers for the Regimental Service in the barn, nineteen soldiers responded, much to my gratification. The band — with its twelve brass instruments — can accompany the singing, as I have obtained from Ditson's many of the scores of music for hymns.

September 11, '63. The Second Massachusetts Infantry on its way to the front stopped for a noon rest near our camp, and my classmate Billy Perkins and my fellow-townsman John A. Fox dined with me.

September 12, '63. I was especially interested to-day in one of the patients in the hospital, a Frenchman who had very early followed his taste for art, and moulded busts and painted portraits. He showed me photographs of his folks in Paris, and they seemed very genteel and cultivated. He left home at nineteen, and lived two years in Switzerland, and travelled in Germany and Italy. Coming to this country he enlisted in the Second Massachusetts Cavalry only three weeks after his arrival in Boston. He took a great interest in the photographs that I carried in my pocket. Looking at my Divinity School classmate D. H. Montgomery, he exclaimed, pointing to his own forehead, "Plenty of brains!" And his observation was correct. Looking at the sisters of my Divinity School classmate W. W. Newell, he threw up his hands in admiration — as a Frenchman knows how — and shouted, "Beautiful! Beautiful!" And I thought so myself. Coming to my college classmate Will Gannett, he said: "He is solemn. Strong character," and no one ever doubted *that*. Coming to another college classmate, Harry Scott, he said, "I have seen him." Here I thought I had caught him napping, and I replied, "I guess not." But he was quite positive, and soon recalled his name. He had seen him only once, and that at Gloucester Point, where I knew that he was accustomed to visit. I thought this showed a peculiar power of distinguishing faces and characters. In my pocket collection I had a photograph of Edwin Booth — my great admiration on the stage — and. the little Frenchman said at once, "He is an actor," though he had never seen him nor heard of him before. Of the group of Longfellow children he said, "That is copied from a painting," and it was. I could easily believe it when he told that when he was a boy he used to frequently ride in the street-cars of Paris just to study faces and characters.

September 15, '63. I was taken with a fever last night and severe headache. It was my tribute to the climate here and perhaps the drinking-water which we have to get from a brook one-quarter of a mile away. Adjutant Baldwin took care of the mail while I should be sick.

September 17, '63. Visited the hospital to-day. Almost well. Headache all gone. I have invited the men to visit me freely at my tent. I can accommodate eight on a pinch — three or four on the bed, three on the bench, and one in the easy-chair.

September 18, '63. Heavy rain. A tempest of wind is beating down a great many tents of officers and men. I put on my rubber suit and went to work sinking the pins of my tent. All men fit for service left at 2 p.m. to chase after Mosby. I superintended the putting up of Major Forbes' tent, which is next to mine.

September 23, '63. I picked out to-day, from a lot of one hundred and fifty, a roan-colored horse and paid the Government one hundred and eighty-four dollars for him.

October 1, '63. In Washington to-day I went to the Sanitary Commission, and without money and without price got seventy-five woolen shirts for my hospital patients. This Commission is a very great blessing to the sick soldiers.

October 2, '63. Returning from Washington by train to Fairfax station, I found my horse ready for mc. My servant Gabriel had ridden him down with the wagon train. As it was raining very hard, I did not like to wait for the return of the wagons, so I took two men from the wagon train guard for an escort and started at once on a six-mile gallop through the mud, which was from four to six inches deep. It was a glorious ride spite of the drenching of my best suit and the filling of my boots with water.

October 12, '63. Last night we were awakened by shots on the picket line, and it was not a minute before the Headquarters Bugler sounded the call to arms, which was immediately repeated by the buglers of the three regiments of the brigade. I was up and dressed with the first call. In ten minutes all the men were in line, facing the direction from which the shots were heard. Thus they remained for half an hour, till the orderlies who had been sent out to find the cause of the firing returned and reported a false alarm. Then the men were dismissed, with orders to lie on their arms for the rest of the night.

October 14, '63. Cannonading at the front all day. Orders to be ready to move at a moment's notice. Meade's army has fallen back to Centreville, only a short distance from us.

October 16, '63. Have not unpacked yet. We may have to move at any time. We are now at Vienna, Va.

October 18, '63. Great excitement in camp; everybody under arms, and horses saddled. One of Mosby's men has been brought in. It is Sunday, but I could have no service and cannot reach the hospital, which is now at Fairfax. Last Sunday I went to the hospital there, and took letters to the patients, and spent several hours with them. Until I came here, Sunday was like every other day. Now there is a little change for the better. I cannot hope to do much, but I shall try to do my best.

October 22, '63. Just now a sergeant came to my tent and said hesitatingly, "I want to ask of you a favor." "I shall be most happy to do anything," I replied. Says he: "I am somewhat acquainted with the book business. When I enlisted I was in Crosby & Nichols' store. I would like to borrow a book, if you please." I told him I would delight to lend him any he liked in my list, and he picked out "The Minister's Wooing" and one of Shakespeare's plays.

Sunday, November 1, '63. No regimental service today, as no meeting-place was available. I went as usual to the hospital. Hon. Seth Washburne from Red Wing, Minn., was there. His son, Corp. Luman P. Washburne of Company L, had been wounded October 9th and I had notified his father of an unfavorable turn in the Corporal's condition, and he had started two hours after receiving my letter.

November 2, '63. I carried some games to the hospital to-day, and the patients were delighted. I brought also a valise full of books, and all were taken.

November 3, '63. The men for some time have come freely to my tent, and I began to-night to call on them. I began with Company A.

November 7, '63. At the request of my colored servant — Caesar S. Harris — I to-day drew up a Will for him, to be signed to-morrow with his mark in presence of Maj. William H. Forbes and Capt. J. Sewall Reed. He has three thousand dollars in gold hidden in the earth under a board (plank No. 4) of the floor of his tent. He has also the jaundice and thinks he may die. He flatters himself that the secret of his wealth is safe with me, but I have made no promises. The first item in the Will was — "I give and bequeath to Captain J. Sewall Reed, as a mark of my appreciation of his repeated kindnesses to me — $500.00 in gold." I hope that the widow of Captain Reed, who at the date of this writing — February 26, 1918 — is still living, will not be puffed up with hopes of a fortune from this item of my black Caesar's Will, but she should be pleased with its unsought tribute to the husband of her younger life. I have kept this Will these fifty-four years and more as a curiosity, and now smile at its legal phraseology, as it reads: "Know all men by these presents that I, Caesar S. Harris, being of sound mind, though infirm body, do, on this 8th day of Nov. 1863, declare this to be my last Will and Testament — to wit!" It sounds as if the Chaplain was a full-fledged graduate of a law school.

November 8, '63. Colonel Lowell brought his wife to camp to-day. She was Josephine Shaw, a sister of my classmate Bob Shaw, of whom I have already made mention in Note 6.

November 9, '63. I put up my chapel tent with the help of six men.

Sunday, November 15, '63. Could have no service, as the ground in my chapel tent was one puddle of mud after last night's heavy rain. Went to the hospital as usual.

November 17, '63. I rode to Washington under escort of Sergeant Armstrong and three of his men. I had letters for some of my regiment who were in hospitals there. To find out where they were I went to the rooms of the Sanitary Commission, whose books give the arrival and departure of every soldier to and from every hospital in and about Washington. Rev. Frederic M. Knapp, Secretary of the Sanitary Commission, invited me to be his guest for the night, I slept in the room that President John Quincy Adams used to occupy.

November 18, '63. Met my classmate Charley Whittier at Willards. He is a major on General Sedgwick's staff. I rode back to camp by way of Falls Church with our letter carrier — McLean. The camp seems quite homelike with Mrs. Lowell here, and Mr. John M. Forbes of Milton spending a few days.

Sunday, November 22, '63. My chapel tent is thirty miles away. I am at Aldie under the shadow of Mount Zion Church, but not for worship. It is in the enemy's country, and I have been with Colonel Lowell on a scout to Middleburg, and we are now taking our captured prisoners to our camp at Vienna.

November 23, '63. Visited all the wards of the hospital. Told the patients of my experiences yesterday and of the success of our expedition. They were interested and delighted.

November 24, '63. My colored servant — Caesar — has recovered from the jaundice, and my dreams of wealth, from the care of his fortune that he intrusted to me by his Will, have vanished in thin air. Had a short but very pleasant ride with Capt. Francis Washburn. He is a brother of Mrs. George M. Bartol of Lancaster, Mass., and of Hon. John D. Washburn of Worcester, Mass., who later became our Minister to Switzerland. I have told elsewhere of Francis Washburn's promotion to be Colonel of the Fourth Massachusetts Cavalry, after the resignation of Col. Arnold A. Rand, and of his marvellous daring on April 5 and 6, 1865, at High Bridge, where he received his mortal wound and was brevetted Brigadier General by special recommendation of General Grant, forwarded to Washington immediately after the battle, and when his wound was not thought to be mortal. He lived to reach his brother's home in Worcester, where he died April 22, 1865, amid universal tributes of praise.

> "When faith is strong, and conscience clear.
> And words of peace the spirit cheer,
> And visioned glories half appear,
>   'Tis joy, 'tis triumph, then, to die."

November 25, '63. Had a delightful ride to Washington alongside Colonel and Mrs. Lowell. It took us four hours.

November 26, '63. Day of New England Thanksgiving. This has been mine. Before breakfast I arranged the mail, directing letters sent here by mistake, and franking those without stamps. After breakfast I went to the hospital, carrying books and papers. I bought yesterday in Washington a Catholic Prayerbook and a Methodist Hymn-book and I gave them to two patients of the Sixteenth New York Cavalry, which with the Thirteenth New York Cavalry and my regiment make Colonel Lowell's brigade. I had the latest edition of the Boston *Journal* for a man who used to be a reporter for that paper. I had also for another Edward Everett's Oration at the Consecration of the Cemetery at Gettysburg. The patients in one ward had been trying the game of solitaire; some had tried it a hundred times, they said; but not one had succeeded in jumping out all the marbles and leaving the last in the centre of the board. I helped them along a little by doing it once very fast so that they could catch a little idea of it without making it too easy for them to get the whole. In another ward I wrote a letter for a New York soldier sick with typhoid fever, and the convalescent patients I started on the game of tivoli, much to their delight. In another ward I talked half an hour with a New York patient — a Frenchman of cultivation, who had been a teacher of French, Latin, and Greek in a New York seminary. The conversation was instructive to me and entertaining to him. In another ward I left Holmes' last book of poems, and in the last ward I left "Ida May" and "Hiawatha," and talked half an hour on the war, three patients from the Second Massachusetts Cavalry taking part in the conversation. Nearly all the patients were in good spirits, as the day was delightful, and all who could take it were expecting turkey for dinner. So I spent three hours in the hospital and lost my own chance for dinner. For as I returned to camp I found the officers and men — all who could be spared — starting out for a holiday sport in testing the speed of their horses. Each company picked out its best horse and set him against the rest. Colonel Lowell and wife went out to witness the race, and also all the officers of the Second Massachusetts who could be spared from camp. So, though I had had no dinner and knew that I could have none later, I joined the cavalcade and rode about two miles to Lewinsville, where the race was held. Of the Company horses A Company beat. Of the officers' horses Major Forbes' blood mare beat. The weather was perfectly splendid — bright, sunny, warm, and clear.

November 27, '63. Took tea and spent the evening with Colonel and Mrs. Lowell and his visitors — Mr. John M. Forbes of Milton with his son Malcolm. His older son, our Major, William H. Forbes, of course was there. Had a fine time.

Sunday, November 29, '63. At 9.45 the bugler sounded the first call for church. At 10.30 our Regimental Band led by Henry Fries — brother of Wulf Fries, the noted violoncellist of Boston — played a quickstep, and all the men who chose fell into line and marched to the bam behind Colonel Lowell's headquarters. About seventy-five were present. I preached a Thanksgiving sermon from the text, "Thanks be to God, who giveth us the victory." After this service of about forty minutes, I conducted three shorter services in the wards of the hospital.

December 2, '63. I rode alone to Washington to call on our Captain DeMerritt at St. Elizabeth's Hospital. Dr. Nichols told me that he was cured and had just left. I traced him to the Ebbitt House, and was delighted to find that he was about to rejoin the regiment. He seemed perfectly well. I had taken him to Washington, August 28th, a wreck in mind and body. He said he did not know how he could ever repay me for my kind attentions. I told him I was sufficiently repaid by his recovery, and that I had done nothing beyond what, as chaplain, I was bound to do. I met here Bill Lamb — Harvard College 1859. He was the basso-profundo of our Harvard Glee Club, and I had a very pleasant chat with him. Then I went to the Carver Hospital and found four of our men and told them about their companions in the regiment and took a good many messages back to them in the camp. I met a private of the Sixteenth Massachusetts Infantry, who said that his chaplain was Rev. Arthur B. Fuller, and that he was splendid, and that any of his men would have died for him. That was a good thing to hear of an elder brother in the Unitarian ministry whom I had seen many times before he left for the front in 1861 and who died in the service at Fredericksburg, December 11. 1862. "While in Washington I bought for my camp library some of the best of Scott's and Dickens' novels, and then left at 3.30 p.m. for my lonely ride through the guerrilla country-, but fortunately was not chased as I had been several times before.

December 7, '63. I have received already from home four boxes of books and they are all in constant demand by officers and men. Since payday I have sent a good deal of money by Adams Express home for the men, and have kept a record of each package of currency. I have distributed many games in the hospital — checkers, tivoli, solitaire, fox-and-geese, backgammon, and puzzles. It has been so cold lately that with the help of Dearborn of Company A — a carpenter from Maine — I have boarded up the sides of my wall-tent, and on the back side made a large old-fashioned fireplace with a chimney of clayey mud and sticks. Except for a downward draft in some directions of the wind, my fireplace is quite cozy and comfortable.

December 8, '63. Yesterday, the regiment began regular drills, and to-day I joined them in the mounted dress parade and made a prayer.

Sunday, December 13, '63. At the morning service in the barn Colonel and Mrs. Lowell and officers from the Second Massachusetts and Thirteenth New York Cavalry were present besides about forty of the men. I had two services in the hospital. In the evening I had a good many callers at my tent, among them Capt. Louis Cabot and Lieut. J. A. Baldwin.

December 15, '63. I began to-day to make a catalogue of my books so as to check them when loaned. At 5 p.m. I conducted funeral services over two New York cavalry men. In the evening Maj. William H. Forbes, Capt. J. Sewall Reed, Lieut. Goodwin Stone, and I sung in my tent for half an hour, when Dr. Oscar C. DeWolfe came in and we had some hot chocolate together.

December 19, '63. All who could be spared from camp are out on a chase after Stuart. I could not go because of a funeral service for Sergeant Bishop. I am the only officer left of the Field and Staff. I spent the evening with Mrs. Lowell.

December 24, '63. I went out to-day a mile and a half beyond our picket line to marry two Rebs at the bride's house. Last Thursday a young man, born in New York, but a year's resident of Virginia, came to my tent and made the request. I feared it might be a trap to let the guerrillas catch me. So I asked Colonel Lowell if it was safe. He said, "Perfectly," but that I might have an escort if I wished. So I promised to go. I set to work at once to prepare a service, as I had never performed the ceremony. I had among my books the King's Chapel service, and with that as a model I prepared a very solemn service that would make the parties hesitate to take the vows if there was any infidelity in the matter. This I thought especially necessary, as I did not know them and there were no courts here to receive promises of marriage. I started at 3.30 p.m. with a guard of three mounted men of my regiment with their sabres, pistols, and carbines. A pleasant ride of two miles brought us to the home of the bride — an old-fashioned two-story house, for long years undisturbed by paint, and seriously crippled by age. I stationed my guard on two sides of the house, with orders to give the alarm on the approach of any guerrillas, and, if they came in large numbers, not to regard me but by all means to save my horse. A young man, some relative of the family I suppose, met me at the gate and invited me in. Having got me inside the door, he seemed to think that his part of the programme was finished, for he seated himself without introducing me to any of the family. So I bowed reverently to an old man in the corner, and dutifully to an old lady at his side, whom I took to be his wife, and familiarly to the young bridegroom, whom I had seen at camp, and as gracefully as I knew how to a young lady at his side, whom I took to be the bride. Some of them may have responded to my salutation, but there was no evidence of it, as I heard nothing and none of them rose. It seemed as if they were all pinned to their chairs. Then, without any invitation, I sat down in the only vacant chair, and asked sundry questions about the family, which were answered in the briefest possible way, generally by a yes or a no or a nod. Then I rose and, with a please, asked the bride and bridegroom to stand. When I came in the ceremony to say to the bridegroom, "Wilt thou," *et cetera,* he shook his head, but whether up and down or sideways I would scarcely dare to swear in a court of law. So I told him to say, "I will." The bride was more ready to respond, and said "I will" as if she meant it. I thought it out of the question to ask if they would signify their union by giving and receiving a ring. I saw no jewelry of any kind, and I did not wish to embarrass them. Even during the prayer none of the company arose, nor when I pronounced the benediction. After this I approached the bride to salute her and went more than half-way, but as she did not move, nor seemed very accessible, I only gave her my congratulations with a shake of the hand, and likewise my good wishes to the bridegroom, and then found my way out without any showing, and mounted my horse and galloped back to camp. A quieter wedding could hardly be imagined. It marked the impoverishment of the country, that there were no neighbors to join in the celebration, no flowers to adorn the bride, no ring to pledge in marriage, no cake to give the guests. Yet the family was respectable and would have been well-off but for the war. Virginia is paying a terrible price for her secession.

December 25, '63. Christmas Day — Friday. In token of the festival I got the band to play for the patients in the hospital. Dr. DeWolfe invited Colonel Lowell and myself to dine with him. A half-dozen callers filled up my evening.

December 27, '63, Sunday. I preached a sermon appropriate to the Christmas season, and held three shorter services in the hospital. In the evening, in my tent, I opened my Christmas box from home, with the help of Major Forbes and Lieutenant Dabney.

January 1, '64. I visited the hospital and wished all a Happy New Year.

January 3, '64, Sunday. This is the coldest day known here for seven years. It nearly froze me in my bed last night and came nearer freezing some of our men on picket. The church call sounded as usual, but only eight men came. The band could not play because of sore lips. I read a few verses from Scripture and offered prayer. Then we sung a hymn and I gave the benediction. I went down to the hospital to hold services, but the patients detained me so long in talking with them individually that I had no time for a formal address. I think I did them more good by my sympathy than I could have done by my exhortations.

January 8, '64. The Chaplain's quarterly report on conditions in the Regiment: —

Cavalry Camp
Vienna Va. Jan. 8th '64

To C. Crowninshield
Major Commanding 2d Mass. Cav.

I have the honor to submit the following report of the moral and religious condition of the regiment as observed in the quarter ending Jan. 1st, '64, and further in accordance with "Revised Regulations," I respectfully offer certain suggestions for the social happiness and moral improvement of the troops.

As to the religious condition of the regiment, I cannot speak with any certainty. True religion is never demonstrative, and it would need an acquaintance of years to know to what extent each man recognized his relations to God, and his obligations to obey God's laws. These things constitute religion, and they cannot be measured by words or tabulated by figures. Still while I cannot speak with certainty of whatever true religious feeling and principle there may be in the regiment, it is easy to expose habits and practices that must inevitably, if unchecked, undermine all religious feeling and weaken all religious principle. Most prominent among these is the habit of profanity, by which I mean only the taking of the name of God lightly and thoughtlessly upon the lips. This thoughtless familiarity with the name of the Deity is sure to breed contempt for his rightful authority over the actions of men.

Those who take his name lightly upon their lips cannot have his law an abiding influence in their lives, and those who habitually take his name in vain, will surely, though perhaps insensibly, lose all reverence for his sacred character, and his solemn commands; and this reverence for God's character and law is the foundation of all religion, and the only sure guide to a true life. For these reasons I can suggest nothing that will more conduce to the religious improvement of the regiment, than absolutely to forbid all open profanity, and to charge all commissioned and non-commissioned officers with the execution of the order, for all profanity is an infringement of military rule, as well as a violation of the laws of God. The extent to which profanity has become a habit both among officers and men is really appalling. I cannot pass down any company street without hearing the name of God either taken lightly in sport or irreverently in a curse. I cannot even sit long in my tent without hearing loudly shouted some imprecation with the name of God thoughtlessly added. Men imprecate curses upon their horses in the name of God, and so loudly that all in the neighborhood can hear, and yet I have never but in one instance seen it rebuked. Officers in the same way imprecate curses on their servants, and sometimes upon their men. Oftenest, however, the name of God is taken lightly in a sportive jest. I do not speak of these things in any way because they grate harshly on my own ear, but wholly because of their influence upon those who practice them. Regard or respect for my office — I gladly give this tribute — restrain profanity in my presence; I would that regard for God would restrain it everywhere. But as this cannot be relied upon as a sufficient restraint, it seems necessary to enforce strict military rule to that effect.

Besides the profanity of trifling with God's name, there is also the profanity of trifling with God's judgments by curses and execrations. This habit is as open and common as the other. Men call down the wrath of heaven and imprecate the pains of hell upon their horses or upon one another as thoughtlessly as they would say "Good morning!" To curse in jest is sacrilege, to curse in earnest is blasphemy. Both are violations of military as well as divine law, and officers should be charged with their suppression. While we believe in God's approval of our cause, and pray for his help, let us not trifle with his judgments, not take his name in vain.

Another obstacle to the moral and religious improvement of the regiment is the slight attendance upon church service. I speak of this with great diffidence as I am conscious of great weakness in conducting public religious service. I have not years to give authority to my instructions, nor experience to give weight to my teachings, nor eloquence to make them attractive. Still I do my best, and such service is almost the only means I have to call the attention of the officers and men to their religious obligations and sacred duties. The men have attended as regularly and in as large numbers as could be expected while their duties were heavy, and their officers gave them little encouragement by their example. The former cause is a necessity of the service, the latter is in contravention of the direct recommendation of the Articles of War. I did not wish to accept your offer to require attendance upon church service, but would be glad if you would strongly recommend such attendance by officers and men.

As to the moral condition of the regiment, it is good while the temptations to immorality are withdrawn. Men cannot gamble after they have exhausted their own money, and that of those who are cajoled into lending to them, nor will they get intoxicated when the whiskey is out of their reach. Still there is more gambling and intoxication than there should be or need be. I respectfully suggest that you advise Company commanders to recommend to their men as they have opportunity to send their money home or put it on deposit. This to restrain gambling. I also suggest — as a preventive of intoxication — that you recommend to officers never to give an order for whiskey, unless they feel sure that it will not be abused. I am sorry to have to report in this connection that I have seen even one officer intoxicated in camp, and have heard in ways that compelled me to believe the truth of the statement, that another officer has been intoxicated when on duty. While I am proud of the general character and bearing of the officers, it is sad to record even a single instance of such loss of self-respect.

In conclusion I beg leave to report in general that there seems to be a better tone of feeling in the regiment now than in the early part of the quarter. Many who then tried to get into some other organization have since confessed that it was a most foolish movement, while the rest have settled down into a resigned content. There is less complaint of duty and discipline, though I suppose that neither of them has been relaxed. The sharing together of dangers and service is daily giving more harmony and unity to the regiment. While we are in winter quarters the men need not find time lie heavily on their hands, as I can supply all that wish it with entertaining reading. The hospital is in very good condition, and our sick and wounded are in general cheerful and contented.

I close with the hope that in another quarter I may be more faithful to my duties and more successful in my work, and that the regiment may go on improving morally and spiritually till we all become true soldiers "without fear and without reproach."

All of which is respectfully submitted

C. A. Humphreys
Chaplain 2d Mass. Cav.

January 13, '64. I distributed to-day five knit caps among the officers and forty pairs of cavalry mittens among the men.

January 14, '64. While taking my usual exercise this afternoon riding horseback, I met — as frequently of late — Colonel and Mrs. Lowell, out for the same purpose, and I joined them for the rest of the ride.

January 20, '64. I rode with Mrs. Lowell this morning to witness the brigade drill. It was an imposing sight.

January 23, '64. The band played this evening before Colonel Lowell's headquarters, and on their return volunteered one tune before my tent.

January 30, '64. At the hospital, by the death-bed of a New York cavalryman, Mrs. Colonel Lowell and I held a little service, helping to make less lonely for him the passing over. This month has seen many changes in our officers. We had as good a set as ever led a regiment, and that is the reason they are leaving for promotion. We have given six lieutenants, two captains, two majors and one surgeon to the Fifth Massachusetts Cavalry (colored), besides supplying it with a colonel — Harry Russell, who was chiefly instrumental in putting me here. We have also given a lieutenant colonel — Francis Washburn — and senior major — Louis Cabot — to the Fourth Massachusetts Cavalry. We also supplied one captain to the Twenty-fifth New York Cavalry. Their places are supplied by promotions from the ranks.

February 4, '64. One of the patients at the hospital, who fought so furiously in an engagement, and with his sabre pierced his Rebel adversary three times and then received a shot himself, is now well and returned to duty to-day. Another patient, who was shot through the breast by a guerrilla, has recovered, and is now walking round. It is strange to see men recover after such dreadful wounds.

February 6, '64. A deserter from E Company was brought in to-day. He had left us only two weeks before and was caught in the act of charging upon our men with a body of guerrillas whom he was leading. But they deserted him as soon as they saw that our party was nearly as large as theirs, and then he tried to escape. A sergeant of his own company pursued him, and the deserter turned in his saddle and fired several shots at the sergeant. A ditch happened to be in the way of the deserter's flight, and in the attempt to jump it his horse came short and fell into it. The deserter then tried to run away, but the sergeant was too quick for him, and, though he had exhausted all his shots, he held his empty pistol to the face of the deserter and made him surrender. He had on a Rebel uniform and had filed at his former Sergeant every charge that he had in his pistol. His weapons were all taken away, his arms tied behind his back, and his feet tied to the saddle girth, and thus he was brought in, reaching camp about 3 p.m. A drumhead court-martial was at once ordered, Lieutenant Dabney acted as judge advocate, and at the request of the deserter I acted as his counsel. After sitting about two hours the court sealed its judgment and adjourned. I did not know the sentence till after breakfast Sunday morning. Then Colonel Lowell sent for me and told the deserter's doom. I went immediately to the guard-house and the deserter requested to see me alone. So the guard stationed themselves outside. His first question was, "Well, Chaplain, what are they going to do with me?" I said, "They are going to shoot you at eleven o'clock." He was thankful, he said, that they did not sentence him to be hanged. (The execution of the sentence is described in the main text of this book, pages 19-22.)

Sunday, February 14, '64. I offered prayer at dress parade this morning and appeared at inspection. Had three services in the hospital about noon. Had regimental service at 2.30 p.m.

February 17, '64. Miss Nellie Shaw came to camp to visit her sister, Mrs. Colonel Lowell. She brought some Jew's-harps for the men in the hospital and they were much appreciated.

February 19, '64. Took tea at Colonel and Mrs. Lowell's with Miss Nellie Shaw. She is charming.

February 21, '64. Sunday. Church call as usual at 10.30. Although four companies were away or on duty, a larger audience than usual gathered at the barn, among them Colonel and Mrs. Lowell and Miss Shaw.

February 22, '64. To celebrate Washington's Birthday and at the same time give pleasure to the patients in the hospital I had the band play for them this morning, and I went through the wards as usual. In the afternoon the regiment had some field sports till 5 p.m. At 5.30 news came that Capt. J. Sewall Reed's scouting detachment of one hundred and twenty-five men had been ambushed and badly cut up by Mosby. In twenty minutes we started to their relief with two hundred men. We went two miles beyond Drainesville and found that Captain Reed and eight men had been killed, and eight lay wounded on the field, while Capt. George A. Manning and Lieut. William C. Manning and fifty-five men were taken prisoners. To the surgeon and myself was left the care of the wounded and the dead. The latter we placed in a large open wagon, and the wounded in such other vehicles as we could find in the vicinity. We dared not take two who seemed to be dying but who might possibly revive if unmoved. We worked hard all night. Some of the wounded had broken legs, and screamed with agony as we lifted them into the wagons. These farm wagons were without springs, and as we wended our way home over the rough roads the cries of the wounded were excruciating. One of them died before we arrived in camp, which was about ten o'clock in the morning. I came in a little ahead of the column to break the news of Captain Reed's death to his wife, who had come to visit him. She knew better than I did that he was a man without reproach, but I could tell her that he was a soldier without fear, and faithful to every duty, and much loved by his men. Later in the day I took the body to Washington, to be prepared for its long joiirney to Massachusetts, and the next day, after celebrating, in presence of the whole regiment, the funeral rites due to the others whom we brought in from Drainesville, I accompanied Mrs. Reed to her home in Dorchester, where the funeral of her husband was held. Captain Reed had been one of our camp quartette, and it was more than a month before we had the heart to sing again. Then one of his best friends — Lieut. Josiah A. Baldwin — took his place with us, and camp began to assume again something of an aspect of cheerfulness. Meanwhile the music of the band had been a comfort, as it played every night at sunset and sometimes later in the evening. The disaster at Drainesville brought not only to the whole camp this long month of depression in spirit, but to me a marked depression also of vitality. Its three days and nights of exhausting labors took away from me ten of the fifteen pounds of added weight which I had gained in the three previous months after I had become acclimated to camp life. While I was in Dorchester a lady from Watertown came to me and inquired very anxiously about her son, who was in my regiment. I told her that when I left camp he was perfectly well. At that moment he was very sick in the camp hospital, and when I returned he was dead and buried. I appreciated what a terrible blow that would be to his mother; so I sought out every comforting thought and every pleasant reminiscence, and arranged to have the body sent home, and then wrote to her as best I could. At such times one learns to be thankful for his faith in the care and love of the Father in Heaven.

Sunday morning, April 10, '64. Captain Phillips of our regiment brought in ten prisoners. He had been out less than twenty-four hours, and yet had gone twenty-five miles to Aldie and taken these Confederates from their beds. Some of them had been engaged in the fight at Drainesville. Their capture caused us a good deal of satisfaction. This was the New England Fast Day, and I made my service appropriate to the occasion, taking my text from Isaiah lviii. 6, "Is not this the fast that I have chosen?" I chose as the voluntary, the Prayer from "Der Freischutz," which was beautifully rendered by the band. My prayer followed, taking its suggestion from the sweet harmony of the great composer, and expressing the deep desire of the soul to be in harmony with God. In my address I spoke first of the duties we owe to ourselves of self-examination and spiritual improvement, and second of the duties we owe to humanity in this crisis of the nation's history. Nearly all the officers were present, with Colonel and Mrs. Lowell, and many of the men. After the service I went down to the hospital and went through the wards, speaking a word to each patient, and then held a service in Ward 2. I delighted two men that day at least. One was a Frenchman, the other an Italian; and I gave each a Testament in his own language, as neither of them could read English. I had sent to New York for these books.

April 11, '64. At 11 A.M. I married C. Mason Kinne and Lizzie K. D'Arcey. Kinne is our Adjutant, as popular a man as there is in the whole brigade. So the interest was very great. He had heard through another of our officers of an attractive young lady — a friend of that officer's wife — and had started a correspondence with her about three months ago. About six weeks ago the wife and her friend came to Washington and then to camp, and have been here since; and the Adjutant has seen no reason to regret his chance correspondence, and asked me to marry them. So last Saturday I went to see the young lady and made her acquainted with the form of marriage that I should use. She said she had a very strong sense of the ludicrous, and she was afraid that some little accident of word, or some humorous aspect of the unusual surroundings, would make her laugh. I assured her that there was no reason for her to fear, and that the solemnity of the service and the deep significance of the vows would overbalance all inclination to lightness. They were married in a house just outside the camp, and all the officers of the regiment were present who could be spared from duty. *They* little thought of the sacred nature of the occasion, and were quite merry before the couple appeared. I first addressed the gathered friends, declaring that matrimony was "an honorable estate instituted by God and approved by what is highest and best in man, and forasmuch as it should not be entered into lightly or unadvisedly, but reverently, discreetly, and soberly," I charged them, if any one knew "cause or just impediment why these two persons should not be united in matrimony," he should then declare it. No one protesting the banns, I then addressed the couple, and adjured them by every solemn obligation to confess if they knew any reason why they might not lawfully be joined in marriage. The bride had by this time forgotten all thoughts of the ludicrous, and the deep solemnity of the situation started the fountains of her tears. Then I put to them the usual questions answered by "I will," and said, "You will now declare your plighted love by giving and receiving a ring," and while he held it on her finger he repeated after me, "With this ring I thee wed, and to thee only do I promise to keep myself so long as we both shall live." Then she repeated after me, "This ring I take in pledge, and to thee only do I promise to keep myself so long as we both shall live." Then I declared them "husband and wife," and offered prayer, and called down upon them the benediction of heaven. The service thus closed, I congratulated them and wished them all possible happiness. Till this moment the bridegroom had kept a firm countenance, but now he too burst into tears, and even among the officers looking on there was scarcely a dry eye. Still, solemnity is not inconsistent with joy. The tears of the bridal couple were the overbrimming of their cup of happiness, and the officers wept in happy sympathy, and wondered if such joy would ever be their own. Military etiquette holds even at weddings, and Colonel Crowninshield was the first of the officers to step up and congratulate the couple, and he saluted the bride in such a brave, blunt way that everybody smiled, and the other officers took courage and felt that they could do as the Colonel did. It was a soldier's freedom, and several who had never spoken to her took the liberty of a kiss. All agreed that this was the nicest wedding they had ever seen. The Adjutant has a pass for two or three days to make a bridal tour to Washington — rather a strange one, in box cars along with prisoners and contrabands, but it will do for wartimes, and it made little difference to the newly wedded in their happy absorption in each other. As I am copying this description of the wedding from a home letter written in the afternoon of the day of the ceremony, April 11, 1864, and this is March 7, 1918, I will now add that this marriage proved to be one of the happiest that I ever knew. The bride of that day, four years ago made a widow, found the chief comfort of these later years in the happy memories of her wedded life. She sent me from the home of her daughter in Berkeley, Cal., a card of Christmas remembrance, December 25, 1917, and on January 7, 1918, passed on herself, leaving behind her two daughters and six grandchildren.

April 13, '64. I rode to Washington and carried a pistol for the first time to defend myself from guerrillas. Saw Miss Anna Lowell at Amory Square Hospital in Ward K and arranged for her to receive my Camp Library, as the spring campaign is soon to open, and I must be ready to move at the shortest notice. After receiving the box she sent me this response: —

My dear Mr. Humphreys, — The box of books was very welcome, and I wish you could have seen the eagerness with which my men took them out when the box was opened. I never happened to have any of the games you sent, and the Jackstraws especially have been greatly enjoyed. I wonder that I never thought of them before.

I hope when you are in Washington you will not pass our hospital without coming in, for I shall always be glad to see you.

Yours truly,

Anna Lowell.

April 25, '64. Went to Washington to send home for my men in the regiment nineteen hundred dollars of their last pay-day receipts. As I dined at Willard's, General and Mrs. Burnside were at the next table. His corps passed through Washington, and President Lincoln watched them from a balcony at Willard's, and he was rousingly cheered by the soldiers as they passed. In the evening I recreated by going to see Davenport in Othello.

Sunday, May 1, '64. No regimental service to-day. The whole brigade is out, as the spring campaign is opening at the front. I spent several hours of the morning at the hospital. In the afternoon I went out maying with Mrs. Lowell. We picked pansies and violets in profusion, as they grew wild in the woods. On our way back we caught sight, in the distance, of our brigade scouting party led by Colonel Lowell, and the way Mrs. Lowell walked to welcome her husband was a delight to see, but I could hardly keep up with her. For myself, I had at once to be busy with the care of the wounded and the dead. A sergeant — a fine soldier — had been killed, and Captain De Merritt had been wounded, with two of his men. Twenty-four Confederate prisoners were captured and sent on to Washington. Colonel Mosby's commission and many of his private papers were found, among them a vote of thanks by the assembly at Richmond for his boldness and skill in capturing General Stoughton at Fairfax. [Two months later he was to try his "skill" on me at Aldie, but without success, as revealed in the story of my capture the next day, after his chasing me, and while I was caring for the wounded and burying the dead at Aldie. I may as well copy here a letter I received from him forty-two years later when I invited him to dine with me: —

The Brunswick,
Copley Square, Boston, Mass.,
April 27th, 1906.

My dear Sir, — On my return to-day from Maiden where I spent last night I received your kind letter. I regret that I cannot accept your polite invitation. This evening I am engaged with the Middlesex Club. Tomorrow evening I leave for Washington.

Very truly,

Jno. S. Mosby.

Sunday, May 15, '64. Colonel Lowell's mother from Cambridge was at my service to-day.

May 20, '64. We are very anxious to get to the front. I have no love for a fight, but I want to be with those who — like my younger brother — are in The Wilderness bearing the burden and heat of the conflict. I wrote to my Divinity School classmate W. W. Newell the other day, advising him to leave the White Mountains and come out here and do something for the war. His next letter was directed from Washington, and now he is in Fredericksburg tending to the sick and wounded. A week ago I was in the Sanitary Commission offices in Washington and heard them order four thousand crutches. That is only one small item of their immense expenses. I visited one only of the hospitals, and saw several thousand wounded soldiers — all cheerful sufferers. How glorious it is that men will risk everything for what they hold dear!

May 21, '64. As the First Battalion of our regiment, composed of Companies C, F, G, and I, are stationed at Muddy Branch to guard the fords of the Potomac in that section, I feel that I must make them a visit. So I started to-day for Washington alone on my roan horse Jaques, with my saddle-bags and my india-rubbercoat; and as it was a very warm day I rode leisurely, taking three hours for the trip. I dined at the Ebbitt House, where I had agreed to meet Capt. Charles E. Rice and Lieut. John T. Richards, who were returning to their battalion in Maryland. They soon made their appearance, and we started at 6.30 for a ride of twenty-three miles to Muddy Branch. It was a very pleasant ride in the cool of the evening. We reached camp at 10.30, and I have seldom seen a prettier sight than as it appeared then in the moonlight. I could only think of Aladdin's Palace or a spectral encampment. Every one but the guards was asleep, and in the officers' quarters each bed was occupied except the one reserved for me. Rice and Richards crawled in with some other officers.

Sunday, May 22, '64. Six of us officers went to church in a neighboring village, and we heard a Presbyterian preacher, and I stopped for the Communion, as the pastor's invitation specially gave a welcome to members of the church in all denominations, I was a little chagrined, however, when the minister addressed us who communed as "saved" and the rest who looked on as "lost." I had been a member of my home church for eight years, but had never learned that there was any safety for the soul but eternal vigilance, and I surely did not think that my fellow-officers who remained in the back seats of the church were any worse than myself. The preacher said that unless they joined the company of the communicants they were "as oxen or asses driven to the eternal slaughter-house." I would not partake of the elements of Communion after that false and insulting description of my companions.

We had ridden about four miles to church, and on the way back we escorted a young and charming governess home to the house of an old Southern planter who as a suspected Rebel had been confined for a time in Fort Lafayette. But he was very hospitable to us and invited us to stop to dinner and to come to his house at any time. However, we stopped only to rest and refresh ourselves for a few minutes. That evening, at my request, a dress parade was held, and after it I held a service and addressed the men as they sat down on the grass. Then we spent the rest of the evening singing in the open air.

The next day Captain Rice and Lieutenant Richards escorted me on a cool and beautiful ride of about twelve miles up the river, on the towpath of the canal, and we inspected the log houses where our men are stationed to guard the fords of the Potomac. At Edward's Ferry we stopped and dined with a planter who looked of the type of Legree in "Uncle Tom's Cabin." Nearly all his slaves had left him. None remained but old women and children, and these were at work out of doors on the hay and corn. He treated us very kindly, and would take nothing for our fare.

After resting about two hours we jogged on through a very rich and fertile country that has become historic through the war. I saw the place where General Banks' division was stationed in 1861, and the ford where General Hooker crossed with his whole army on the way to Gettysburg. At about six o'clock we stopped for the night in the fine mansion of a rich citizen who was a Union man when the Union armies were about and a Confederate when the Confederates were near. All the servants were slaves, but very much attached to the family, and seemingly very contented. The landlord was absent in Washington, but the landlady was at home and well able to entertain us. We found her in the fields directing and assisting the slaves in planting potatoes. She was a strong, muscular woman of great spirit, but with a gentle manner and tender feelings. With old Greek hospitality, before asking any questions she brought out the wine for our refreshment. She spread a fine table with spring chickens and cold meats and preserves, tea and coffee, and other things too numerous to mention. In the evening we went out on the veranda and sang, and later I went into the parlor and assisted a young daughter of the family in her music lesson. On retiring, the hostess gave us the best chamber in the house, with two large feather beds, so high that we had to run and jump to get into them. I sank into mine about two feet, — at least, my centre of gravity sank that distance, while my feet and head were raised high in air. This situation might have been quite endurable in winter, but on a warm summer night it was too hot and I could not get asleep till towards morning when the air was cooler. Captain Rice and Lieutenant Richards got snugly into bed, when they stirred up a nest of bees at the foot, and the way they jumped out of bed was laughable to see — at least, to the onlooker. They soon lighted a lamp and had a skirmish of about five minutes with the bees and succeeded in killing some and scattering the others. The rest of the night passed quietly. We had an early breakfast, and, receiving each of us a bunch of beautiful flowers from the children, and making them little presents in return, we started. The landlady would take nothing, though she kept five of us and our horses over night. We had two orderlies to accompany us.

We now directed our course towards Sugar Loaf Mountain, the highest elevation in Maryland. It had been used for a signal station by the armies of both sides. We found the upper air very refreshing, and enjoyed the beautiful view. Descending, we stopped for dinner at a house under the hill, and, as luck would have it, met there a very attractive Southern beauty. It was a long time before anything was said, as no one introduced us. At last I got up courage to ask her the name of a yellow rose that was in view on the piazza. This led to a talk, and the talk led to a conversation, and the conversation led to admiration, and admiration led to —. I must not confess the tender passion, lest I be thought too susceptible. But her beautiful eyes, her pearly teeth, her soft rich voice, her captivating smile — well, fate compelled us to take up our journey, and with lingering glances I left the Southern beauty in her home under the hill.

We started away at three o'clock towards Poolesville and reached Muddy Branch at 6.30, having had a very pleasant trip of about fifty miles.

The next morning I bade good-bye to our First Battalion and started at nine o'clock for Washington. The ride was very beautiful. Between the canal and the river there is a strip of land varying from fifty to five hundred feet in width and covered generally with a rich growth of trees that furnished refreshing shade. I made the twenty-three miles in a little less than three hours, and after resting my horse and having him rubbed down and fed, and after dining and visiting the Sanitary Commission, I started again at four o'clock and had got along about half-way to our camp at Vienna when I met one of our men who informed me that Vienna had been evacuated and nothing was left there. This was a great surprise to me. Hitherto I have always happened to be in camp when we have been ordered to move, and have generally succeeded in getting all my things away. This time a good many of my things were left behind, and it will take a long time to get what of my things was moved into order. I am writing now sitting on a box with my writing case on the top of my trunk. We are now at Falls Church, four or five miles nearer Washington than before, and we guard its whole front. It is a very pretty camping-ground. I have slept on the floor the last two nights here, and though I have found no soft side to the boards, they are better than that feather bed in the mansion by the Potomac.

June 8, '64. At 3 p.m. started for The Wilderness with five hundred men and a train of fifty ambulances to bring off some of the wounded who still survive.

June 19, '64. In my home church to-day. Rev. Nathaniel Hall preaches a sermon commemorative of brother Walter, who was killed at Cold Harbor. I wish I could be present, for I know that the flow of sympathy from our Pastor's full heart would be a balm to my wounded spirit. I hope that father will not allow this bereavement to trouble him overmuch.

June 20, '64. I have been to Washington to express money home for the men. I met Gen. Frank Bartlett, perhaps the youngest general in the service — only twenty-three. He graduated from Harvard two years after I did.

June 24, '64. I have received many tender expressions of sympathy in my brother's death at Cold Harbor from my friends among the officers here and from Mrs. Lowell, though hers was not given in words, but in looks and a warm pressure of the hand. She could not express it.

This afternoon, I had just come in from a ride of twelve miles and had taken my supper when word came that Mosby had captured forty of our New York Cavalry and had left three wounded men on the field at Centreville, fourteen miles from here. Major Forbes was ordered to go for them with one hundred troopers and two ambulances. The Doctor and I went with him. We started at nine o'clock and rode till 2 a.m., when we halted to rest the horses. At 3.30 we started again, and soon found the wounded men. Two were mortally wounded, the other seriously. The Doctor gave them some whiskey to stimulate their sluggish vitality, and some morphine to ease their pain and make them sleep. I got them into the ambulances, and we started back at about 5 a.m. As I rode behind the ambulances to be ready for any help to the wounded and the dust was very stifling and the sun very wilting, I became much fatigued; but, getting to camp at 10 a.m., I sponged myself all over and felt all right again.

June 26, '64. Sunday. On account of the heat I held my service at undress parade in the early evening — 6.45 o'clock.

July 3, '64. Sunday. I addressed the regiment at undress parade on the auspicious omens of success in our struggle for liberty and union.

July 4, '64. The regiment celebrated Independence Day with various sports — foot-racing, jumping of horses, and so forth. At 8 p.m. I started out on a scout with Major Forbes and one hundred and fifty men to watch the gaps of the Blue Ridge. [The story of the fate of this expedition is told in the body of this book, pages 93-144.]

September 2, '64. I had live minutes' notice to leave Charleston Prison. I did not haggle about the shortness of the notice, as it was to take me again under the Stars and Stripes.

September 11, '64. Sunday. Beaufort, S.C. I rode out into the country thirteen miles on horseback to see Will Gannett and his work for the freedmen. I addressed his plantation negroes at their praise-meeting.

September 13, '64. Hilton Head. At 11 a.m. I took the steamer Fulton for New York. Had a splendid day. Stayed on deck all the time.

September 16, '64. Arrived at The Narrows at 5 a.m. In the course of the day I called on Ned Wetmore and Horace Howland and Jim Fay — college friends. Took the night train to Boston and arrived home at 6.30 A.M., September 17th. Joyful welcome and glad return. In the course of the day I went to see Mr. John M. Forbes and Mr. William Amory to report on the condition of their sons — my messmates in prison.

Sunday, September 17, '64. Brother Richard loaned me a pair of black trousers and I went with the family to the old home church on Meeting House Hill.

September 18, '64. Dined with Mr. and Mrs. William Amory at Longwood, Brookline, and told them of my efforts to get their sick son — my messmate — released from the Charleston Prison, and encouraged them to believe that they would have him at home in a few weeks.

September 23, '64. By invitation of Mrs. John M. Forbes of Milton I took the lo a.m. train with her for New Bedford and then her husband's yacht Azalea for their summer home on the island Naushon.

Sunday, September 25, '64. All of us — Mrs. Forbes and her ten other guests besides myself — went to the west end of the island to spend the day. With thirty-two horses in the stable, all trained to the saddle, there was no lack of facilities for riding, and there were boats by the shore for rowing; and for delightful aspects of animal life there were herds of deer roaming freely in the woods.

September 26, '64. Besides taking two baths in the sea and two walks in the woods, I wrote to-day about twenty letters for the prisoners at Charleston, S.C, and sent them to their nearest relatives.

September 27, '64. Misses Annie and Jeannie Watson from Milton and Miss Katie Putnam from Boston came down to Naushon to-day and made the island still more attractive to a convalescing chaplain. I had intended to go home to-day, but decided to stop. This afternoon I met on the shore the marine artist Swain Gifford, who comes here frequently to sketch. You would think he had bidden good-bye to his senses to see him attitudinizing towards the sea, sometimes wrong side up to get impressions of the water from various angles of vision.

September 28, '64. Had a delightful ride horseback to-day with Miss Annie Watson.

September 30, '64. Mrs. Forbes and I had some very confidential conversations to-day, such as I never before had with any one but my sisters. She wanted to unburden her oppressed soul, and I was very willing with such a lovely lady to reveal mine. Every day here the ladies gather and work for the soldiers, knitting warm socks or gloves for the coming winter, or binding the silky softness of the long hairs of the milkweed into cushions of various shapes to relieve the bed-sores of the patients in the hospital. It has been a great pleasure to me to distribute these things among my men.

October 1, '64. Misses Putnam, Cabot, and Tyson, and Mrs. Swain, and Artist Swain Gifford and I bade farewell to Naushon. Had a splendid sail till the wind blew up a choppy sea and the ladies became inclined to seasickness. So, to distract their attention from themselves and the choppy sea, I started them to sing with me "Rally round the Flag," and as they shouted the "Battle Cry of Freedom" the sea lost its power over them and all was well.

Sunday, October 2, '64. Heard my minister, Rev. Nathaniel Hall, at the home church, and walked with him to his home after service. He invited me to address his people next Sunday. Took tea with Rev. James Walker, D.D., ex-President of Harvard.

October 4, '64. Went up to Milton and got a little thoroughbred Morgan mare — Annette — which Mr. John M. Forbes asked me to accept for service in the field.

October 6, '64. After dinner I went down to Newburyport and spent the night with Jacob Stone, father of Capt. Goodwin Stone, who was mortally wounded by a shot intended for me in the chase by Mosby, July 6th.

October 9, '64. From the pulpit of my childhood's church I told the story of my capture and imprisonment.

October 10, '64. Dined with Ned Amory at his home in Longwood. His father made me a present of one hundred dollars and gave me a letter of credit on London for twenty-five pounds sterling to be used in case I was captured again. I had it sewed within the lining of my coat-collar, where it would not be likely to be found by my captors.

October 12, '64. Called on Mrs. Lowell, mother of my Colonel.

October 13, '64. Father and I took my horse — Nettie — to the cars for New York in the morning, and in the afternoon I bade a tearful farewell to my home. Joy through tears. Took the five-o'clock Fall River boat-train for New York.

October 14, '64. I put my horse in charge of the Camden & Amboy Transportation Company for Washington, then called at the office of Francis G. Shaw, — father of my honored classmate Robert Gould Shaw, the hero of Fort Wagner, and of my beloved colaborer in camp and hospital, Josephine Shaw Lowell, wife of my Colonel, Charles Russell Lowell. Then I took the II a.m. boat for Staten Island to the home of Mr. and Mrs. Francis G. Shaw, where their daughter Josephine was eagerly and anxiously awaiting the time of her deliverance of her first child, and wished me to bear messages to her husband, who was fighting with Sheridan in the Shenandoah Valley. I had a very delightful four hours with mother and daughter and then took the boat back to New York with a thousand loving messages for my Colonel. But, sad to tell, they never reached him, as, only five days after, he received his fatal wounds at Cedar Creek. At that time I was in Washington calling upon his sister, Miss Anna Lowell, at the hospital, where I found many of the wounded of my own regiment. After returning to New York from my visit to Mrs. Lowell at Staten Island I spent a very pleasant evening with two Cambridge friends, Miss Watson and Miss Hobart.

October 15, '64. After spending the night at the Brevoort House and after making a friendly call on Ned Wetmore, I met another classmate, William Eliot Furness, by appointment, and he accompanied me on the neon train to Philadelphia and made me his guest at his father's house. After dinner, Dr. William H. Furness, who lives next door, sent in word that he would like to see me in his study. I had for a long time admired him for his courage in the championship of human freedom and had wished to be introduced to him. He at once invited me to speak in his pulpit on the morrow, though he told me he had his sermon all prepared. I was surprised at the invitation, being so little known to him. I objected on the grounds that I wanted to hear him and that I had no black clothes. He would not listen to either objection, and said he had a Quaker parish, and it made no difference to them what I wore. I at last consented to make a simple address from the platform in front of his pulpit and he offered to conduct all the other services. After the hymn he introduced me as Chaplain of the Second Massachusetts Cavalry and a brother in the ministry who had given himself early to the war for freedom and union, and had suffered captivity. He then came down from the pulpit and sat in the front pew where I had been sitting with Mrs. Furness. Then I told to his people the simple but moving story of my captivity in Southern prisons, and had from the beginning the tearful sympathy of the audience. There was one person in the audience who I knew was interested, for he looked as if he would jump over the railing of the gallery where he had been — much to my surprise — singing in the quartette-choir. There was another reason — as he told me after the service — for his greater surprise in seeing me. He had seen an item in the paper about the death of Tom Fox and Henry Hall, and my name had been linked with theirs as neighbors and schoolmates in Dorchester and classmates in Harvard, and he thought that I had been killed like them in battle. This choir singer was another classmate of mine, who had sung first bass with me in the college chapel choir and the Harvard Glee Club. He was Joseph Shippen, younger brother of Rev. Rush R. Shippen, and I knew he spoke sincerely when he said to me, "My face was one wreath of smiles and tears all the time you spoke." And Dr. Furness was so much moved that, as we walked home after church, he urged me to make up my mind to come and be his colleague. I also had an invitation to come to Germantown and build up a parish. Of course I could not give any encouragement to either invitation, as I must not desert the cause of my country for any personal advantage. I spent the evening with Dr. Furness and his son Horace and then took a night sleeper for Washington.

October 20, '64. After three days in Washington spent in gathering together my effects which had been stored during my imprisonment, and taking what I might need for service in the field, and after getting passes to the front for my horse and myself, I started at 8.30 p.m. by train to Martinsburg.

October 21, '64. I had to wait in Martinsburg all day for my horse to arrive. I spent a good part of the day reading Mrs. Hemans' poems. Indeed I read more of them to-day than in all my life before, and found that I liked her more than ever. Poor Nettie did not get in till 7 P.M., having had no feed since yesterday noon.

October 22, '64. Breakfasted at 7.30 and then saddled up and started at 8.30 for Winchester without rations or forage. Nettie did not like the feeling of the saddle-bags and the packed saddle and jumped a good deal. In her cavorting she jumped a brook four feet wide like a deer, but I retained my seat with perfect ease and at last subdued her. We went along with a wagon train a mile and a half long guarded by a brigade of infantry and a squadron of cavalry. The day's journey was twenty-two miles, and we went very slowly and with many halts. At three o'clock I was glad to get some bread and milk in a house by the way, and, as luck would have it, I found a small bag of oats by the side of the road and so satisfied Nettie's needs. It was a very cold day and hailed a while, but I arrived safely at 8 p.m. and put up at Virginia Hotel.

Winchester, October 23, '64. No trains going to the front to-day (Sunday), so I visited the cavalry hospital to see if I could find any of my men. I did find six or eight wounded or sick. They seemed delighted to see me, and were much interested to have me tell something of my prison experience. I divided ten dollars among them, and got from the Sanitary Commission a blanket for one of them who was both sick and wounded. I found also two officers. Captain Kuhls and Lieutenant Crocker, both wounded in the late fight in which Colonel Lowell was killed. Poor Mrs. Lowell! I parted from her last week and she said she would meet me next winter in camp. Poor Mrs. Lowell! That is all lean say. Words cannot express her bereavement. I wrote to her to-day.

October 24, '64. Started from Winchester at 7.30. Reached camp near Middletown at one o'clock, a ride of fourteen miles from Winchester by the road over which Sheridan galloped five days ago and saved the day at Cedar Creek. What a glorious victory was that! It was due, under him, to the valor of the Sixth Corps and the Cavalry. I am now camping on the field of the Battle of Cedar Creek. It was near this spot where Colonel Lowell received his mortal wounds. Lieutenant Colonel Crowninshield succeeds Colonel Lowell in command of the brigade, and I reported to Captain McKendry, commanding my regiment. It makes a very different appearance from that it had less than four months ago at Falls Church, near Washington, when I left it July 4th for the scout with Major Forbes which ended in our captivity. Poor fellow! he is still a prisoner of war. I sleep to-night with Dr. Oscar C. De Wolfe, whose place I took in the light at Aldie. He is now Brigade Surgeon. The band gave me a beautiful welcome back in a delightful serenade, among other pieces playing "Home Again" very touchingly.

October 25, '64. Breakfasted with Captain McKendry, Adjutant Kinne, and Dr. Johnson, who now, with me, are the only field and staff officers, and of the line officers only four are now on duty with the regiment. What a change from last summer, when we had twenty or thirty with us! In the fight at Cedar Creek we lost two officers and five men killed and three officers and twenty-one men wounded. We have only two wall-tents for the field and staff. I am to sleep to-night with Dr. Johnson. I spent most of the day talking with the men. They seemed very glad to see me, and shook my hand heartily with their rough grasp. They said they had been thinking of me a great deal. I wish I could do more for them. Towards evening the mail came in, and I attended to the distribution of the letters and papers and packages.

October 26, '64. It is not difficult here to live the simple life, — indeed there is nothing else to do. Just now the army is having a week's rest after the decisive battle of Cedar Creek, and we expect that the fall campaign is about over.

I have nothing here but what I brought along on my horse. It is quite cold and I have to sleep in my overcoat. My bed is first the ground, then a thin layer of straw, then my india-rubber blanket, then a shelter tent of cotton duck for the under sheet and a second shelter tent for the upper sheet, then a horse-blanket and a government woolen blanket for warmer coverings. I take off everything but my under flannels and socks, and put on my army overcoat and lie down and am quite comfortable. We eat our meals from tin plates on top of a box, and we sit about the box on pails upside down or any block or other support we can find. For food we have nothing but beef, hardbread, and coffee regularly; at times potatoes, bacon, and flour griddlecakes.

October 27, '64. Last night it rained hard and the wind blew the tent over so much that water collected on it and dripped through so that I was lying in quite a pool of water before I was wakened by it. I called to the sentry to straighten out the tent, and then I pulled out the cotton duck sheets which held the uninvited puddles of water, and lay down again in a dry bed. My Morgan mare — Nettie — does not like these exposures in the rain and cold, and is restless and pulls up her stake nearly every night. Last night she lamed herself in the effort.

Sunday, October 30, '64. I visited E Company, which just now is doing provost guard duty. Dined with Dr. De Wolfe. At five o'clock we had undress parade, and I spoke to the men on the lessons of my captivity.

October 31, '64. Wrote letters for some of the soldiers who had neither paper nor pens. Called on Colonel Crowninshield at brigade headquarters. Rode with Dr. Johnson to Strasburg and back, to see the fields that were fought over a few days ago.

November 1, '64. Captain McKendry, who is commanding the regiment, invited me to ride with him to the north fork of the Shenandoah, for observation.

November 2, '64. Orders came at 9 p.m. to be ready to move in the morning.

November 3, '64. Our brigade broke camp at 6 a.m. It rained all day, but my india-rubber poncho protected me well and we reached Winchester at 3 p.m. We encamped for the night on the outskirts of the town. Our official name is "Cavalry Reserve Brigade," commanded by my classmate Col. Caspar Crowninshield, and our march of sixteen miles to-day was in column of fours. First was an advance guard of fifty troopers, two or three hundred yards in front. Then came the baggage train of fifty-eight wagons in two lines side by side, that they might not be too extended for safe defence. By the side of the wagon train, marching along through the fields, was the brigade led by Colonel Crowninshield, followed immediately by the color-bearer and the provost guard; then the band, which played as we went through the towns. My regiment was the last in the column and made a rear guard for the train. Arriving near Winchester, the Colonel's inspector picked out a place on which to camp for the night. He chose a central place for the headquarters and disposed the regiments at convenient distances around it. Our place having been assigned, the regiment is arranged in four squadrons, one behind the other, and then the men dismount, unsaddle their horses and drive stakes by which to tie them. Then they pitch their tents, feed their horses and get their own supper. The field and staff officers are assigned a place in front of the regiment, and our headquarters wagon comes up and throws out two tents and our blankets and two or three camp chairs, and then the pioneers pitch our tents, drive stakes for our horses, and cut and bring wood for a fire, about which we gather. The pioneers are a corporal and five men. Their duty in battle is to pull down fences or build bridges for the advance. As soon as the tents were up, our servants made our beds and then began to cook our suppers. Our headquarters mess — consisting of Captain McKendry, commanding the regiment, and Adjutant Kinne and myself — had for supper the usual pork, hardbread, and coffee, which we carry with us, and, as extras, we bought white bread in Winchester and also some flour from which our servants made griddle-cakes. The two doctors — Johnson and his assistant — mess by themselves. We spent the evening sitting about the fire, though it still rained. Most of our evenings in the field are thus passed, as we have no candles and no desks nor tables to sit at in our tents. We all went to bed about 9 p.m.

November 4, '64. The bugle waked us at 4.30. We had all slept well, though it poured in torrents all night; the morning was dark as pitch, and it rained hard while we were at breakfast. But soldiers cannot wait for good weather, and at 6.30 the bugler sounded the order to break camp. Then the tents were taken down, the horses saddled, and the tents and blankets of the men were strapped to the saddles. The officers' tents and blankets were put into the wagon with the chairs. Then the bugle sounded forward and we started. The skies cleared soon after dawn, and we had a pleasant journey of twenty-seven miles and encamped again within three or four miles of Harpers Ferry, and had nice beds of straw and splendid fires of rails. Our brigade burned that night all the rails that could be gathered within a quarter of a mile, and the fences were five feet high and untouched when we came. No wonder the farmers dislike our visits; but this is war, and we are in a section of the country that is infested with guerrillas and has often been used as a path for the Confederates to the threatening of Baltimore and Washington.

November 5, '64. A large mail reached us last evening and I was very busy distributing it till we broke camp at 11 A.M. and moved to the outskirts of Charlestown and encamped within view of the spot where John Brown was hung. As we marched through the town the band played lively patriotic airs, but the stores were shut, the public buildings mostly in ruins, and the streets deserted. From the hill near by, which was the scene of the execution, can be seen the hills of a free State — of Maryland redeemed. John Brown's body lies a-mouldering in the grave, but his soul is marching on. We are here to be near the construction corps, which is building a railroad, for the Government, from Harpers Ferry to Winchester, and to act as a guard to protect the workmen from the raids of guerrillas. It is a bitter cold day and some snow has fallen. We have no rails here for our fires, as the army has been here quite lately and used them all, so we use green wood from the forest. Just as we were about to dismount, a sow and a litter of eight fat pigs came grunting down towards us. Alas! Poor pigs! A charge was made upon them with drawn sabres and not one was left to tell the tale, but many a soldier dined to-day on fresh pork. Before night, my servant got from a stack half a mile away a bundle of straw for my bed and made it luxurious.

Sunday, November 6, '64. It is milder to-day, and we had an undress parade at 5 p.m., at which I had a short service and spoke to the men from the text, "Here we have no continuing city." The aptness of the text to our present service brought a smile to the faces of the hearers.

November 7, '64. I rode out with Colonel Crowninshield to see the work of the construction corps. They get along now about a mile a day, but will soon go faster, and we expect to have to move to-morrow or next day to keep up with them.

November 8, '64. This is Presidential election day, and I sent home the vote of the regiment — Lincoln, 238; McClellan, 111. I received to-day a lot of papers and distributed them among the officers and men. I give the men about half a dozen sheets of paper with envelopes every day we are in camp. They write in pencil their letters and I address and frank them in ink. The men have no money now, and if they had it they could buy no paper here.

November 10, '64. We moved two or three miles today to keep up with the construction corps.

November 11, '64. I breakfasted with Mr. and Mrs. George Washington, who live near our camp. He is great-great-grandnephew of the Father of his Country. Mrs. Washington is a fine lady and a generous provider, as witness her table loaded with honey, apple butter, cider, hoecakes, corn cakes, apples, and coffee.

November 13, '64. Moved camp to Summit Point.

November 17, '64. Moved camp to Opequan Creek.

November 18, '64. Captain Holman of our regiment is now on Sheridan's Staff, adding another to the long list of our fellow-officers who have been honored by high promotion. Lieutenant Baldwin, who used to be a member of our camp quartette, was wounded two months ago and put into a house near by, and has lain in one position for nine weeks. He has received every possible attention from the tenants of the house and the neighbors, ^ but had seen no Union man. Imagine his joy when we camped here. I have taken him to-day the late papers. He cannot be moved yet, but in two or three weeks expects to be taken to his home in Newton, Mass. I received to-day six letters of anxious inquiry about the fate of certain men of our regiment. One of them was killed when I was taken prisoner. Another was killed two months ago near here. Sad news that I must send!

November 19, '64. I received to-day from Sammy Groom inkstand and pens. It is very kind of him to remember his old playmate and neighbor and to be so interested in the soldiers.

Thursday, November 24, '64. I offered prayer to-day at dress parade on the occasion of the annual New England Thanksgiving.

Sunday, November 27, '64. Had a full service at dress parade this morning. We are encamped now near Stephensons station.

November 30, '64. After I had gone to bed last night, orders came to be ready to move at daylight this morning. I got up at four o'clock, and before five minutes had passed, an emergency order came to be ready to move Immediately. So I flew round and ate a little breakfast and filled one of my saddle-bags with hardtack and started with the brigade at five o'clock. My servant carried the forage for both horses. We went through Berryville to Snickers Gap. When we forded the Shenandoah River, Nettie was almost swept away by the force of the stream. She is so small that I had to double my legs up to keep myself out of the water. Descending the eastern slope of the Blue Ridge, we could see why we came out as the smoke of a hundred barns and haystacks rose in Loudon County valley before us, the destructive work of the other two brigades of our division who had started one day before us. Our part in the work of destruction I have described in the body of this book.

December 3, '64. Returned to our camp near Winchester. I am delighted to find that Nettie seems equal to any work I am likely to require of her. She carried me the last four days with my saddle heavily packed, the first day fifty miles, the second day thirty miles, the third day twenty-five miles, and to-day fifteen miles, and came In fresher than when she started. She surprises every one by her endurance. I did not attempt to assist in carrying over the ford of the Shenandoah any of the livestock we gathered together in Loudon County. I remembered the difficulty I had in keeping myself out of the water when we crossed on the way out. It was a great work to get the droves of cattle, sheep, and hogs across the river, which was about forty rods wide. The hogs and the sheep absolutely refused to swim. So the hogs had to be killed, that they might give no comfort to the enemy, and each cavalryman took a sheep over on his horse.

Sunday, December 11, '64. No service to-day. The snow is six inches deep, and we have no shelter. It is very cold in this bleak valley. To give a little protection to Nettie from the wind I have had tall branches of pine stuck into the ground about her.

December 16, '64. It has been hard enough to live out of doors till the middle of December. A great part of each day in camp I could do nothing but stand before a log fire and turn round as upon a spit, to keep both front and back warm. It is too cold to read or write. I did read a little of Tennyson, but all laughed at me as crazy for doing it. The Bible and Tennyson are the only books I have. Just now I am in a log house that Colonel Crowninshield will occupy when he returns from his leave of absence to visit his home. Then I shall have a log house with Major McKendry, I have just received a letter from Mrs. John M. Forbes, saying that twenty-five more mittens are on the way. I have already distributed fifty-eight pairs. They save a good deal of suffering.

December 28, '64. Thank Heaven! I am back again safe. Have just returned from a ten days' raid towards Gordonsville. The hardships and suffering of a cavalry raid in winter can hardly be imagined. Cold hands and feet that cannot be warmed, sleeping on the snow, riding in the piercing wind from sunrise to sunset, breakfast at 5.30 and supper at 8 — no other meal, fording deep and rapid streams, my horse giving out on the third day, sights of suffering in others, men dismounted walking till their boots wore out and opened, exposing bleeding feet, — such things have made the last ten days full of weariness and suffering. It rained three days, snowed one, and the rest were dreadful cold. It doesn't seem as if I could get warm in a week.

January 6, '65. A large box of good things from home came to-day, and I thought I could not make a better use of it than to divide it among many. So, having with the help of Adjutant Kinne spread out its contents upon a large table in tin plates, I had "officers' call" sounded by the bugler right after "tattoo," and all came who were in camp — fifteen of them — and feasted till "taps," 8-8.30 o'clock. The bright faces, the good cheer, the warm thanks to the folks at home, cannot be described. I think the mince-pie received the highest praise, though the wreath-cake was the most admired, as both beauty and symmetry were displayed in its form. The cheese was also a highly appreciated luxury. The thin crisp cookies disappeared marvellously. I enjoyed so much the eagerness with which the things were eaten that I tasted of nothing but the mince-pie and the guava jelly. The only thing that remained was one box of guava jelly and this I am keeping for the Captain, who is on picket to-night.

January 9, '65. My Morgan mare is still very lame. I have not ridden her for a month. She has had to stand so much in the mud that comes here with every melting that the sores on the lower parts of her legs will not heal. Poor creature! I do not see how she can live through the winter. My man is working on the stable for her and London every day, and Is meaning to corduroy the floor with logs. Just now they are both standing in four inches of mud and do not lie down even at night.

For myself I think I have got over the bad effects of that freezing raid to Gordonsville, though now the cold makes me shiver quicker than it used to. I find great protection at night in a knit woollen cap that has been sent from home, and in the last few days I have distributed a dozen of them among the officers, who wear them in their quarters as an ornament almost as much as for protection. To-day two captains came in and asked if I had any of those knit caps left. I had just two, and they took them thankfully. One more came tonight, and I gave it to Ned Amory — my messmate in prison. He has just returned. Major Forbes — my other messmate — has not yet returned, as the formalities of exchange have not been completed. I hope he will be back soon. I rode to Winchester to-day and met two of General Sheridan's staff — Captain Holman, who used to be a line officer with us; and Assistant Medical Inspector John Romans, H. C. 1858, with whom I used to sing in the Chapel choir and College Glee Club at Harvard.

February 1, '65. Sheridan to-day held a grand review of all the cavalry in the Valley. It looks as if he meant to take us into action as soon as the season will permit. All the other officers when passing the General saluted him by dropping the sabre after lifting it to the chin. I, having no arms, lifted my cap, and old Phil — bless his soul! — returned the salute and lifted his cap to me.

Camp Russell, Virginia, February 10, '65. The days do not seem to lengthen very fast, so two meals a day satisfy us. I am in Headquarters mess with Colonel Crowninshield, Major McKendry, Adjutant Burlingham, and Quartermaster Pinkham. We have breakfast at 8, and dinner at 3. No supper. I get up about 7.30. I do not indulge in the luxury of a bath except in comfortable weather, and that happens at this season about once in two weeks. I have to thaw out the water nearly every morning before I can wash my face and hands. My poor hands are sorely chapped, and I cannot keep them looking clean. My servant comes in and makes a wood fire on the hearth and blacks my boots before I get up. My toilet and a few calisthenic exercises fill the time till breakfast, at which we do not linger long in this cold season, as the mess-tent has no fireplace. After breakfast I attend to the mail and send it off. Then I sit down to read or write till dinner, but am interrupted every few minutes by applicants for paper and envelopes, or mittens, or books, or information. After dinner, if the weather is anyways pleasant, I take a ride on my Confederate mare, Loudon, who is a fine animal with a dainty step as if dancing to music. It is a great pleasure riding her. I rode out to-day, though the snow is very deep, to see if I could find any stone fit to build a chimney for my new house. I saw some in an old cellar a mile out, but mostly hidden under the snow. As soon as it is possible I shall send out for some of them. My Morgan mare seems better of her lameness. To-day, while tethered, I saw her kick up her heels like a rabbit when he springs. "Retreat" is sounded at sunset and then we have music by the band. It is a great treat to us. After that, I read till the mail comes at seven o'clock, when I assort and distribute it. If I get letters myself, I generally answer them the same night. If I have no writing to do, I read till ten o'clock, and, after warming my feet, climb into my bed. I say *climb,* for it needs some gymnastics, as my bed is higher up than my shoulder. It is a bunk right over Major McKendry's.

This week I have been rejoicing in the declared determination of Congress to establish universal freedom. Now let them give us *men* to carry it out. The sword must still be our savior. The Rebels will fight to the bitter end.

February 12, '65. I received last night an atlas from home. It is just what was wanted here. Men go on furlough to all States from Maine to Iowa, and many have asked me for a map to find the best way. Then too we have not seen the field of Sherman's operations. Today is Sunday, my usual distribution day, and I have for each company some copies of the *Transcript, Journal, Advertiser, Post,* and *Christian Register* from Boston, and the *Evening Post, Army and Navy Journal,* and *Christian Inquirer* from New York, and also *Littell's Living Age* and the *Atlantic Monthly.* I gave also a pair of knit mittens to the first sergeant of each company, to be given to any man who needed and deserved them. The money that has been sent to me has gone as fast as it has come. No one else has any money here, and I run the mess. The paymaster is daily expected, but it is ten months since we have seen him. We also are suffering many other privations — our effects, clothes, boots, blankets, and so forth, stored in Washington and but just beginning to come to us, without enough wagons to draw wood for our fires, our horses suffering for lack of shelter, with no hay but once a week, with few blankets, water and wood nearly two miles away, and yet this is the severest winter ever known in these parts. But nearly everybody is cheerful and expecting better things soon. I long for fruit very much. We have nothing but onions to keep us from scurvy. Major McKendry brought lately some apples from home and gave me two and I ate them as a starving man would.

February 21, '65. We are ordered to be in readiness to move. This is only the second day that I have been in my new home. When a month ago my friend Rev. Henry Wilder Foote of King's Chapel sent me a big box of books that he had gathered among his parishioners [see Note 4.] I had no good place to put them, as I was tenting with Major McKendry. So I had a new house built for me, with walls of heavy logs and floor of split logs, the space enclosed being about sixteen feet by eight feet, the fireplace of stone in the middle of one side, my bed in the end, my writing-table opposite the fireplace, and shelves for books along the same side. Now I fear the shelves will be useless, but the books I will try to get to some hospital, as Foote suggested. Since "taps" I have been writing to him my thanks for the splendid collection. I have had at least fifty callers to-day, and everybody got a book to his liking. They are mostly in fine editions, and have been a great acquisition to us.

February 26, '65.

Camp Russell, Virginia.

My dear Brother Richard, — This is probably my last home letter from the Shenandoah Valley. Reveille will sound at three o'clock to-morrow morning and we must up and away. I received yesterday the two dollars you enclosed, and am much obliged for the promptness with which you sent it. It came when I was actually in debt, and so was doubly acceptable. I have now over $250.00 loaned out in the regiment, and in my pocket only $2.50 with which to start early to-morrow with Sheridan on a raid of unknown direction and length. You may think this is poor economy in me, but I think it satisfies the rules of a higher economy. At least *I* am satisfied. We *hear* that the Paymaster has started from Washington, but we *know* he hasn't reached here, and we do not see any chance of his catching up with us. Nobody has ever yet caught up with Sheridan after he started on a raid. It must be very hard on the families of the soldiers in this regiment, as most of my men have not received a cent of pay for ten months. They however keep wonderfully cheerful, though they often speak of it as hard.

I doubt whether we ever return here. Still I have no idea where we are going. Being a Yankee, I take the liberty of guessing that we are to join Grant, and I surely hope so.

To-day I have been very busy packing. I have put my regimental library into two large boxes and nailed them up and directed them to the Sanitary Commission, but I do not know as they ever can be got there. We are two miles out of Winchester, and all baggage and stores are going to Harpers Ferry. The agents of the Commission must have their hands full to get their own stuff to the rear, and will scarcely be able to send out here for the books. Still I am going to try it, and have sent an orderly to Winchester to see if it is possible. If the books fall into Rebel hands, they will not aid their cause. The spirit of every page of them is against disloyalty, and would be worse than a spy or a traitor in Rebel camps. Of course we take along with us only what is absolutely essential, not one wagon except for ammunition. It is very early to open the campaign, but Grant knows no winter quarters. The mud here is half a foot deep and will try the horses severely. I did not quite see how I could get along. Loudon could not carry me and my blankets and forage, and Nettie is still lame. What should I do with her? I could not turn her out to starve. Yet I know of no one who could take her to the rear. And what should I do for a pack-horse. Nothing is impossible to him that believeth, so I gave myself no anxiety, but kept my eyes open for any opportunity. One soon offered itself. Colonel Crowninshield, I discovered, has more horses than he can take care of when we move. So I proposed to him to buy one, or to take one along and keep it for him. (Please excuse a parenthesis. This moment my boxes of books have gone. I am so pleased! I feared they would be lost. The orderly I sent carried a note from me to the Agent of the Sanitary Commission in Winchester asking him to send, if possible, a team for the books. The orderly just arrived back escorting a team of the Commission, and bringing a note from the Agent saying that books were always acceptable, especially the kind that I had. Now, after employing happily our leisure for two months, they will go elsewhere on the same errand of mercy to cheer and exalt the soldier. Wilder Foote will be especially pleased when he hears this.) Now to return and take up the dropped thread of my story. The Colonel preferred that I should take and use one of his horses for the present, and indeed was glad of the chance to have her taken care of. She is a dun-colored mare, as stout as a buffalo and almost as wild. The Colonel advises me not to ride her in a fight, as then she is perfectly unmanageable. I shall be careful about it, but I think I can master her by kindness and will. I believe with Richard Wade — in Winthrop's story of "John Brent" — that all that is needed is for the horse and rider to feel that they have the same will. If a horse is obstinate I try to make him believe that my will lies in the same path with his, feeling sure that soon his will follow in mine. The Dunn, as I call her, has a tremendous neck, very masculine indeed. She disdains the curb and insists on tossing her head scornfully — in which perhaps she is feminine. But I shall make as if I did not notice her, and she will soon leave it off. The only way to meet haughtiness is with silent neglect. The Dunn is not handsome, though she is very spirited. Her best quality for my purpose is her toughness and strength. I shall pack sixty pounds of forage on her the first day, and ride Loudon with only my overcoat and poncho. My servant will go with me, and my horses will be better provided for than in any former expedition. I am also in luck in having found a man who is going to the rear and will take Nettie in charge. He is Hiram Mellen of our Quartermasters' Department.

Here I must stop off short. It is 10 p.m. and I must write to Mrs. John M. Forbes to acknowledge the receipt of fifty more pairs of cavalry mittens for my men. It will please me greatly to be able to tell her how nicely I have provided for the mare that came from her husband's stables. Dr. Emerson of Concord will also be pleased, as he used to ride her. Please tell Sister Mary that I was delighted with the book she sent me — "John Brent." I never tire of reading of the chivalric virtues. Indeed I have tried to emulate the true Knights of Chivalry, though I have added Duty to the knightly virtues, giving it the precedence before Honor. Love and Duty claim my highest devotion, and for them I will battle to the end.

My love to all the family,

Charles.

April 6, 1918. After this last letter of February 26, '65, I could not keep a diary till the end of the war. I wrote home a few letters in pencil, but it is almost impossible to decipher them now. Some years ago, however, I wrote out all the movements of the cavalry till the end of the war and they will be found in the body of this book. The whole book has been a labor of love scattered over many years, under the impelling feeling that, having passed through so many and so various experiences in the course of my service in the last two years of the Civil War, I ought to set them down plainly and truly, so that, when the history of the Civil War shall be written, my individual testimony may help in forming a true judgment. And I have also felt that while the chords of the human heart thrill to the touch of courage and devotion, the story of the Civil War will find eager listeners and stimulate responsive heroisms.

www.ingramcontent.com/pod-product-compliance
Lightning Source LLC
Chambersburg PA
CBHW032112090426
42743CB00007B/325